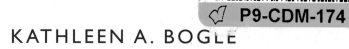

KATHLEEN A. BOGLE

HOOKING UP

Sex, Dating, and Relationships on Campus

New York University Press • *New York and London*

NEW YORK UNIVERSITY PRESS
New York and London
www.nyupress.org

Library of Congress Cataloging-in-Publication Data
Bogle, Kathleen A.
Hooking up : sex, dating, and relationships on campus / Kathleen A. Bogle.
p. cm.
Includes bibliographical references and index.
ISBN-13: 978-0-8147-9968-0 (cloth : alk. paper)
ISBN-10: 0-8147-9968-X (cloth : alk. paper)
ISBN-13: 978-0-8147-9969-7 (pbk. : alk. paper)
ISBN-10: 0-8147-9969-8 (pbk. : alk. paper)
1. College students—Sexual behavior—United States. 2. Dating (Social customs)—
United States. 3. Universities and colleges—Social aspects—United States. I. Title.
HQ35.2.B65 2007
306.73084'20973—dc22   2007029765

New York University Press books are printed on acid-free paper,
and their binding materials are chosen for strength and durability.

Manufactured in the United States of America
c 10 9 8 7 6 5 4 3 2 1
p 10 9 8 7 6

Contents

Acknowledgments

There are many people who helped make *Hooking Up* possible. I am so grateful to all of them because I know this book would never have happened without them.

I want to begin by thanking my mentor and friend, Joel Best, for believing in me and this project and for his invaluable feedback during every phase. The best thing that ever happened to me career-wise was being assigned as Joel's teaching assistant during my second year of graduate school at University of Delaware. It was Joel who encouraged me to do this study on hooking up. Before I interviewed a single person or wrote a single page, Joel told me to "picture the book on the shelf." Here it is and it would not have happened without him.

I was fortunate to have many other influential teachers during graduate school whom I would like to thank, especially Ronet Bachman, Anne Bowler, Cynthia Robbins, and Gerry Turkel. Thanks also to Kathleen Tierney for teaching me how to conduct qualitative research. I also want to acknowledge Margaret Andersen, Susan Miller, and Rob Palkovitz, whose insights and comments helped to shape this study.

I would never have started on the path of becoming a sociologist if it wasn't for the mentors I had as an undergraduate at Saint Joseph's University. I especially want to thank Raquel Kennedy-Bergen for inspiring me to choose this profession and helping me during so many stages along the way. I am also thankful to Dan Curran and Claire Renzetti, who were instrumental in getting me started in graduate school. I was fortunate to return to my alma mater and teach there on a visiting basis for a few years while I expanded my original study and transformed it into a book. During that time, I was lucky enough to work with George Dowdall, the best colleague anyone could ever have. I am grateful to George for his advice and guidance on this project and beyond.

I am very thankful to NYU Press for believing in this book. I particularly want to thank Ilene Kalish for making this opportunity possible and Salwa Jabado for helping to see it through to the end. This book benefited immensely from the comments of all the reviewers for NYU. A special thanks to Laura Carpenter for her thoughtful feedback during the revision process.

Thanks to all my friends for seeing me through the long journey of writing this book, especially Kerri Barthel, Cecilia Burke, Kim Delaney, Jacki Hallinan, Katie Jones, Bob Mascioli, and Victor Perez. I am particularly thankful to Kara Power, who was very helpful during the final stages of writing and revising. I am also grateful for the encouragement of my friends and colleagues Kenny Herbst, Eli Finkel, Piotr Habdas, and Andrew McElrone.

I am appreciative of the many students, friends, and strangers who have spoken to me over the years about their experiences with dating and hooking up; their words helped inform my work. I owe a special debt to the people who agreed to be interviewed for this project; they generously contributed their time and shared the personal stories that made *Hooking Up* possible.

Finally, this book would never have happened without the support of my family. Thanks to Aunt Ru for all the prayers and well-wishes. Thanks to my parents for cheering me on all these years. Thanks to my brother-in-law, Bill Benedict, for all the dinners and for putting up with all the clutter. Thanks to my niece, Gracie, for being the bright spot of every day. And finally, I would like to thank my sister, Jeannie, who knows the material in this book as well as I do. She has read through chapters, helped me figure out how to organize things, and in general helped me make this book much better. If this book is successful, it is because of her.

Introduction

The journalist Tom Wolfe, a keen observer of American culture, offered this musing on junior high, high school, and college students:

> Only yesterday boys and girls spoke of embracing and kissing (necking) as getting to first base. Second base was deep kissing, plus groping and fondling this and that. Third base was oral sex. Home plate was going all the way. That was yesterday. Here in the year 2000 we can forget about necking. Today's boys and girls have never heard of anything that dainty. Today's first base is deep kissing, now known as tonsil hockey, plus groping and fondling this and that. Second base is oral sex. Third base is going all the way. Home plate is learning each other's names.[1]

Clearly, times have changed. Most images that we see today of college students are in a sex-charged atmosphere like MTV's *Spring Break*, where bikini contests, bump and grind dance contests, and "beach sports" with barely clothed contestants are common scenes. Comparing today's "co-eds gone wild" with our idea of college students of yesteryear, it is perhaps easy to jump to the conclusion that our young people are in moral decline. But it is too simplistic to characterize the change in moral terms. Wolfe's "bases" point to something much more than an increase in sexual activity among today's youth. I would argue that today there is something fundamentally different about *how* young men and women become sexually intimate and form relationships with one another. For American youth, particularly college students, "dating" and mating has become a whole new ball game.

Dating, which permeated college campuses from the 1920s through the mid-1960s, is no longer the means to *beginning* an intimate relationship.[2] College students rarely date in the traditional sense of the term. Do they have sexual encounters? Yes. Are they interested in finding boyfriends and girlfriends? Many are, yes. But unlike previous generations, college students today are not forming relationships via dating.

I want to suggest that two factors have been especially important in the demise of traditional dating on college campuses.[3] First, young people are postponing marriage. Age at first marriage is at an all-time high; the typical groom is 27; the typical bride is 25.[4] Although today's men and women may be delaying marriage, they are often sexually active from adolescence; the average age of first intercourse is 17.[5] Second, a growing proportion of young people nationwide are spending the early years of their adult life on college campuses. From 1970 to 2000, enrollment in undergraduate institutions rose by 78 percent.[6] Thus, college has become an increasingly important setting for early sexual experiences. So, if college students are not dating, just what are they doing?

In 2001, a national study on college women's sexual attitudes and behaviors revealed that instead of dating, many students were "hooking up."[7] The study defined a hookup as "when a girl and a guy get together for a physical encounter and don't necessarily expect anything further."[8] The results of this study sparked a media firestorm over the idea that hooking up had replaced dating on college campuses.[9]

Media reports often portray an extreme version of hooking up. It is not so much that the reports are false as much as they don't represent the whole truth. A typical story line comes from Karen Heller of the *Philadelphia Inquirer*, who reported that "the latest lie teenagers tell themselves is about having 'friends with benefits,' the ability to have sex, to 'hook up,' without the attendant drudgery of relationships. This means that kids expose private parts, exchange bodily fluids, risk pregnancy and STDs, but don't have to plan Saturday dates." This piece leaves readers with the impression that anyone who has hooked up has engaged in sexual intercourse or some other form of "risky" sex. However, hooking up covers a wide range of activities and many college students use the term to refer to "just kissing."

In other cases, media references go beyond portraying the extreme to actually giving a misleading definition of hooking up. It's been defined as "oral sex," "a one-night stand," or "engaging in a lot of promiscuous sex." These definitions are narrow at best, and often fuel public concern that today's youth are engaging in behavior that is a danger to their physical and emotional well-being. Even given that the ambiguous nature of the term "hooking up" makes it difficult to figure out what is really going on, it is still irresponsible, though not surprising, for journalists to add to the confusion by presenting only the most risqué stories in order to sell papers.

Further, hooking up has been connected to an array of social problems, such as binge drinking, drug abuse, and sexually transmitted diseases. In addition, feminist scholars have been concerned about the link between hooking up and sexual assault, while conservatives have linked hooking up to being raised by divorced parents.[10] Some of the concern over the link between hooking up and other problems is legitimate, but these potential connections do not justify denouncing the hookup system on those grounds alone.

Much of what has been said about hooking up falls on one end of the spectrum or the other. The mass media takes on a moralistic tone, suggesting that young people are engaging in immoral behavior that will ultimately lead to their doom, whereas recently released books like *The Happy Hook-Up: A Single Girl's Guide to Casual Sex* authored by women of the hooking-up generation make light of the hookup scene.[11] Neither of these opposing perspectives provides the most useful way to analyze the current culture, nor do they add clarity to the discussion.

MY HISTORY WITH HOOKING UP

My introduction to hooking up came firsthand. During my own college career in the early 1990s, hooking up seemed to be at the center of the social scene. I recall spending a lot of time talking to friends, who were attending colleges up and down the East Coast, about whom they hooked up with, whom they wanted to hook up with, or who they "heard" had hooked up with whom. Although many of these conversations were just for fun, there was also a more serious side to these discussions. Students I knew often struggled with various aspects of hooking up; for example, "how far" a hookup should go, how to act with your hookup partner the next day, and how to turn a hookup into a relationship. Although most of my close friends were female, I saw male friends struggle with hooking up as well. From my standpoint, it appeared that hooking up, for better or worse, was an entrenched part of the college experience.

Fast-forward to 2000. As a graduate student in sociology, specializing in gender, I was having a conversation with one of the members of the sociology department whose two sons were about to embark on college life. I found myself trying to explain the phenomenon of hooking up to someone who came of age during the dating era. When I was finished going on and on about how different relationships are in college nowadays, he replied to all my ramblings by saying: "Why don't you do a study of that?" From that conversation, this book began.

I started by looking at the phenomenon of hooking up through a sociological lens. I wondered when hooking up started; after all, it didn't used to be that way, right? I wondered if my observations of how hooking up worked held true for others. I wondered why the "rules" (or lack thereof) that governed the hookup system on campus seemed no longer to apply once I graduated. In other words, I wanted to take my personal observations of the college hookup scene and place them in a larger context.[12] As a first step, I reviewed the existing scholarship and was stunned to find no studies on hooking up prior to 2000.[13] Virtually all of the past research on college students and relationships referred only to dating.[14] Much of the research during this period focuses on heterosexual dating couples once they are already in a relationship. Relatively few studies examine how college students establish themselves as a couple in the first place. Those that do assume that students are dating in the traditional sense and then proceed to ask questions based on that assumption.

A few sexual behavior researchers over the past few decades did acknowledge changes on the American college campus. These studies often look at college students' attitudes and behaviors regarding premarital sex, "casual" sex, or "risky" sex.[15] Results indicate that college students have become more liberal over time in terms of both their attitudes on sex and their sexual behavior. Although this literature documents change, it does not address one of the most important differences in sexual behavior on college campuses. That is, the way that college students get together to engage in sexual activity—the how and the why, as opposed to only the what.

As my research continued, a handful of studies on hooking up emerged. The first was led by a team of psychologists at the College of New Jersey, revealing that 78 percent of undergraduate students at a large college in the northeastern United States had engaged in a hookup.[16] They defined a hookup as "a sexual encounter, usually lasting only one night, between two people who are strangers or brief acquaintances. Some physical interaction is typical but may or may not include sexual intercourse."[17] Ultimately, the researchers concluded that "some students were hooking up on a weekly basis."[18]

The results of a second study, conducted by the Institute for American Values, indicate that hooking up is a nationwide phenomenon that has largely replaced traditional dating on college campuses. This study examined the sexual attitudes and behaviors of college women across the country and found that hooking up was a common activity that dominates male-female interaction on campus. The key findings included that 91 percent of college women believed hookups occurred "very often" or "fairly often" on their campus, and 40 percent had personally engaged in a hookup encounter since coming to college. The researchers concluded that "hooking up, a distinctive sex-without-commitment interaction between college men and women, is widespread on campuses and profoundly influences campus culture."[19]

A BETTER UNDERSTANDING

This book builds on the previous studies, but is distinct in many ways.[20] I wanted to look at how relationships form or how people get together both during college and after. By interviewing college students, I gained the knowledge of experiences and observations they shared in their own words, which I believe is ultimately the best way to understand their relationships. I did not assume that the students were hooking up or dating; instead, I asked them to talk about how men and women initiate sexual encounters and romantic relationships.[21] Given that the meaning of "hooking up" is often debated, I thought it important to let those involved in the hookup culture explain what it means to them.

When I talked to college students and recent graduates about sex and relationships, I wanted to capture the experiences and observations of both men and women. Including men in the study fills a void left by the national data on hooking up.[22] I interviewed a total of 76 people from 2001 to 2006, 34 men and 42 women.[23] I spoke to 51 undergraduate college students of all grade levels (ages 18–23) and 25 alumni (ages 23–30); this enabled me to consider whether there are differences in how men and women interact in college compared to after. I asked the alumni many questions about their college years; therefore, data on the college experience were generated for all interviewees. Nearly all of the people

I interviewed were white (95 percent). The lack of diversity is partially due to the lack of diversity on the campuses I studied and partially by design. I decided not to oversample minorities because research suggests that how college men and women interact varies by race.[24] There is also a lack of diversity in terms of sexual preference, with 96 percent of those I interviewed identifying themselves as heterosexual.[25] Although the number of people I interviewed from diverse backgrounds was small, I learned a number of things about how these students initiate sexual and romantic relationships (see chapter 4). Hopefully, these preliminary findings will stimulate future research in this area.

I conducted interviews with students and alumni from two different types of universities to ensure that the findings were not limited to one type of campus or geographic area. The universities are in different states; one is a large state university on the East Coast, the other is a smaller faith-based (Roman Catholic) university in the Northeast. There are many similarities between the two institutions. Most students on both campuses are white and middle or upper-middle class. Both universities are considered primarily residential, with the majority of students living on campus or in nearby apartments or houses with fellow students. Despite these similarities there are also key differences. One university is public, the other is private. The state university has more than three times the number of full-time undergraduates as the private university. There are also significant differences in terms of campus culture and policies for students living in residences; for example, the faith-based university has a rule against having sexual intercourse in university-owned resident facilities.

I began by asking the people I interviewed some background questions, and then I posed many questions about their experiences and observations of how men and women meet, get together, and form relationships. Although most people I spoke with were similar in terms of race and class, I tried to interview a diverse group of students in terms of gender, grade level, and major. I also made a conscious effort to interview different "types" of students. For example, I interviewed some students who were in fraternities/sororities and very much a part of the stereotypical, alcohol-centered college social life, as well as some students who neither drank alcohol nor attended parties. For the alumni portion of the study, I interviewed people from many different professions. Additionally, I have spoken to hundreds of college students about these issues as well as many twenty-something singles.

These conversations have taken place everywhere from bars to living rooms and from classrooms to dormitories.

Like most studies, my findings do not necessarily speak to the experiences of all college students or recent graduates. Nor can I say what percentage of college students (or young alumni) are hooking up, or how often they do it. What my study can show is what hooking up means, how it works on the college campuses I studied, and how it changes after college.

SPEAKING OF HOOKING UP

"Hooking up" is not a new term. Although media references did not begin until around the turn of the twenty-first century, there is evidence that the term "hooking up"—and presumably the practice—was being used by college students across the country since at least the mid-1980s.[26] But "hooking up" is a slang term and slang by definition is an informal and nonstandard language subject to arbitrary change, so it is not surprising that there is some confusion and disagreement over the meaning of the term. In fact, the young people I spoke with use many slang terms to describe their intimate interactions. By examining the phrases they use in context, from "hooking up" to "friends with benefits" to "booty call," I discovered not only what they mean in general, but also that they mean different things to different people, particularly men compared to women.

My challenge as a researcher is being able to find the right language to explain what I uncovered about these relationships. This has been a particular challenge with regard to hooking up. Can hooking up be characterized as a "phenomenon" or is it a "system"? Perhaps a more sociological way of talking about it would be to refer to it as a culture (i.e., the hookup culture on campus). Rather than choosing among them, throughout the chapters that follow I use these terms interchangeably to describe what hooking up is and how it differs from traditional dating. Ultimately, I found that one of the most useful ways of comparing today's hooking-up culture with the dating era is to look at each as a "script."

Sociologists believe that how a person behaves in a social setting can resemble an actor following a script.[27] In other words, the cultural norms that we live by can dictate how people act in a given situation. In their classic sociological analysis, John H. Gagnon and William Simon argue that sexual behavior is socially learned.[28] Contrary to biologists and psychologists, who often discuss sexuality in terms of "drives" and "urges," Gagnon and Simon believe that individuals internalize what they call "sexual scripts" in order to interact with the opposite sex.[29] For instance, in the United States, sexual scripts suggest that sexual interaction begins with kissing, then sexual touching, and ultimately culminates in sexual intercourse (i.e., the "bases").[30] What is called "scripting theory" not only sheds light on the content and progression of sexual interaction, but also on the appropriate scenarios defined by society for sexual behavior to ensue. Thus, cultural norms can dictate a "script" for when, where, why, and how sexually intimate interaction can occur. Without these scripts, sexual behavior can lose context and meaning.[31]

These sexual scripts are different for men and women and, some sociologists argue, largely determine the roles men and women play during sexual interaction.[32] Traditionally, men take on the role of aggressor while women take on the role of gatekeeper. Men initiate sexual interaction; women decide if men will "get any" sexual contact and, if so, how much women will "put out." There are also culturally prescribed roles that both men and women play in seeking potential sexual partners.[33] The roles that men and women play are shaped by cultural influences in the context of both a specific social setting, such as the college campus, as well as a specific historical time period.[34]

In the next chapter, I will detail how from the 1920s through the mid-1960s the traditional sexual script dictated that dating was the means for men and women to become sexually intimate. The dating script permeated all social classes, including middle- and upper-class men and women attending college.[35] However, in the second half of the twentieth century, a series of changes in the culture, as well as in the environment of the college campus, created the possibility for a new sexual script to emerge. These changes set the stage for the new hookup scene to emerge and flourish, particularly on college campuses.

PLAN OF THE BOOK

A basic sociological concept is that individuals are affected by their social world. The people who are coming of age during the hookup era are not only drawing on their own moral compass to guide their intimate behavior; they are also profoundly influenced by their social setting (e.g., the college campus), their peers, and the times. In other words, college students and young alumni are not merely acting in isolation; society is providing a script for them to follow. Preliminary studies indicate that hooking up is the dominant script on campuses today, but this does not mean that *everyone* is following this script in the same way, or even at all. What it does mean is that there is a way of getting together that exists at the *center* of college life. Although those in the margins are many, they still recognize the dominant script and are affected by it.

In the chapters that follow, I will explore how one's environment affects how young singles begin sexual and romantic relationships both in college and after. The best place to start understanding the way men and women get together today is by looking at how they got together in the past. In chapter 2, I will look at the rise and fall of dating in the early twentieth century through the mid-1960s and the ensuing rise of the hookup.

With this foundation in place, I will let the words of the men and women I talked with illuminate their intimate lives. In chapter 3, I describe the hookup scene on campus, showing how it happens, with whom, and under what circumstances. I also explore the sexual norms of hooking up, highlighting how they differ from the dating era. In chapter 4, I will discuss the features of the modern college campus that made it conducive to the emergence of a hookup culture. I also consider how other factors, such as fraternity / sorority membership and alcohol use, affect participation in hooking up. In chapter 5, I examine how college students are influenced by their peers. Specifically, I will consider how students' perception of what others are doing sexually affects their own behavior. In chapter 6, I focus on how participation in the hookup culture is different for men and women. I also examine how the traditional sexual double standard applies to the hookup culture.

In chapter 7, I turn to a discussion of life after college. I present alumni accounts of how the singles' scene changes once students leave campus. I explain why men and women favor traditional dating once they are situated in a new environment. In chapter 8, I conclude by comparing and contrasting the traditional dating script with the modern hookup script.

As you begin reading this book, try to put aside what you have heard in the media about hooking up. Before deciding whether you believe hooking up is something to be concerned about or celebrated, let's first look at what it is and how it came to be. In my own analysis, I found some aspects of hooking up to be less troubling than is often assumed, and other aspects very troubling. In the end, the script in any given period should not be analyzed for the purpose of deeming it "good" or "bad," but to understand the role it plays in our lives. I know that what I present here will not be the last word on hooking up, but I hope it will make a significant contribution to the growing scholarship in this area.

I have spent the last six years immersed in all things related to hooking up and dating. By talking with college students and "twenty-something" college graduates, I have come to understand how private matters are part of something bigger. That is, our personal stories of sexual encounters and relationships are inextricably linked to the social context in which we find ourselves. Although the accounts of the men and women who talked with me cannot capture the experiences of all college students and young alumni, I hope that by listening to them the reader will take away a deeper understanding of how modern relationships begin in college and beyond.

2

From Dating to Hooking Up

In olden days a glimpse of stocking was looked on as something shocking
Now heaven knows anything goes . . .
The world has gone mad today and good's bad today
And black's white today and day's night today
When most guys today that women prize today
Are just silly gigolos.

The lyrics of this Cole Porter song titled "Anything Goes" are telling. They speak of a lax in society's propriety and values; the irony is that the song dates back to the 1930s. Messages like this one convey a sentiment that rings true in any time period: change is scary. As society tries to come to terms with the changing mores of today's youth, there is a tendency to characterize the change as frightening. In one magazine editor's opinion, adolescent morality may be "tumbling toward Shanghai on a sailor's holiday."[1] The implication is that the ways of the past were superior.

Many media pundits have called for a return to a more traditional style of courtship. Again, the gist is that the old way is the better way. I agree that it is helpful to examine today's hookup culture in light of the dating era. However, we should take a closer look at what young people were *actually doing* in the past before we long for a return to it.

Uncovering how young people became sexually intimate in the past is a difficult task given that information on the intimate aspects of life did not exist prior to the twentieth century.[2] What we do know about earlier Western societies is that the process for most young middle- and upper-class people to find potential mates was heavily monitored by parents, their families, and their communities.[3] This close supervision ensured two things. First, there was a limit to how much sexual interaction would be permitted, with most of society forbidding intercourse until marriage or at least until the family had approved an engagement.[4] Both the community at large and the family had a vested interest in ensuring that a child was not born out of wedlock.[5]

Second, familial supervision was deemed necessary in order to ensure that the mate chosen was suitable (in terms of social class, etc.) and had potential as a marriage partner.[6] The mate selection process was heavily supervised by parents and other adults in part because practical considerations were of the utmost importance in finding a mate. For example, men were not considered eligible for marriage until they demonstrated that they could financially support a wife and family.[7] However, in post–Industrial Revolution Western societies, romantic feelings were given greater importance. Over time, romantic feelings began largely to outweigh material considerations in the search for a potential partner.[8] Romantic feelings are greatly affected by sexual attraction; therefore, sexual attraction became an increasingly important aspect of intimate partnering throughout the nineteenth and twentieth centuries.[9]

Over the past hundred years, there have been three distinct scripts guiding young men and women's intimate lives, each emerging during a period of transition. I will examine each one, but let's begin by turning back the clock to the beginning of the twentieth century to see how young people at that time got together and ultimately formed relationships.

THE CALLING ERA

According to social historian Beth Bailey, for the first decade of the twentieth century "respectable" young men would "call" on respectable young women at their home. The object of the call was to spend time with the woman of interest as well as her family, especially her mother.[10] Many rigid guidelines were followed during the "calling" era. Young women and their mothers controlled the practice of calling. That is, they and only they could invite a young man to come to their home for a calling visit. Such a visit typically consisted of spending time in the woman's parlor with her and her family. During the visit, the young woman might play the piano to entertain her guest. The young man and woman might be given some degree of privacy for part of the visit, particularly if the mother knew her daughter really "liked" the young man.[11]

A perfect illustration of the calling script can be found in the Christmas classic, *It's a Wonderful Life*. In the film, the female lead, Mary Hatch (played by Donna Reed) has had a crush on George Bailey (played by Jimmy Stewart) since childhood. One scene depicts an evening when George calls on Mary at home, where she lives with her mother. George wears a suit for the occasion, and Mary receives her visitor wearing a pretty dress. When George arrives, Mary invites him to sit with her in the parlor so they can listen to records. Since Mary's mother does not approve of George as a suitor for her daughter, she repeatedly tries to interrupt the visit by spying on them from the top of the staircase in her bathrobe. Mary's mother demands to know: "What are you two doing down there?" Mary, irritated by her mother's persistent meddling, teases her by responding: "He's making violent love to me, Mother!" Her joke shocks not only her mother, but her gentleman caller, too.

As entrenched as the calling system was among middle- and upper-class circles, this script did not work for the lower or working classes. Most members of the lower class lacked the facilities to entertain young men in their homes. Thus, lower-class youth ultimately stopped trying to aspire to the middle- and upper-class system of calling. Instead, they began going out somewhere together, which became known as going on a "date." The term "date" can be traced to the late nineteenth century, when it was first used as a slang term by some in the lower class.[12] It referred to occasions on which a man obtained sexual favors from a lower-class woman.[13] Later, the term spread beyond this narrow, illicit meaning and the more modern use of the word took hold.

THE DATING ERA—"RATING AND DATING"

The phenomenon of dating did not remain exclusively in the lower class for long. Dating emerged next among rebellious upper-class youth who began going out, away from the watchful eyes of parents. A date might consist of a woman dining out alone with a man or going to the theater.[14] Regardless of the precise location of the date, it required that a man and a woman "went somewhere" outside the home in order to enjoy each other's company.[15] Dating was not a matter of upper-class rebellion only, but also grew out of changes in society. Women at this time in history were becoming increasingly a part of the public sphere, with growing numbers attending college, taking jobs, and in general becoming more a part of the public world that was still largely considered the province of men. With this increased access to the public sphere, dating began to supplant calling as a way for young people who were interested in each other to spend time together. In addition to women's newfound freedom from parental and community supervision, the advent of the automobile was a major factor in creating and maintaining this new arrangement.[16] Young men's access to cars made the idea of taking a woman "out on the town" increasingly possible.

From its inception in the first decade of the twentieth century, dating spread throughout U.S. culture until about the mid-1920s, when it became a "universal custom in America."[17] In other words, by the 1920s dating was the dominant script for how young people would become sexually intimate and form relationships. Willard Waller's classic sociological study on dating first revealed many of the norms of dating on the college campus. Waller examined the dating customs of college students at Penn State University in the 1920s and 1930s.[18] To begin, Waller defined dating by distinguishing it from courtship. Courtship involves people of the opposite sex getting to know each other en route to marriage. Dating, on the other hand, is not true courtship because the intent is not to marry.[19] Thus, Waller characterized dating as a sort of "dalliance relationship." These relationships were particularly prevalent in college because students (especially men) wanted to delay marriage until they graduated and were settled into their postcollege careers. Given that those who dated did not intend to marry, Waller argued that dating was dominated by "thrill seeking." Men were often seeking some form of sexual gratification. Women, on the other hand, were often looking to have money spent on them, including expensive gifts.

It is important to note the environment in which all of this took place. Waller's study was conducted at Penn State, a large school, where most students lived on campus; half of the male students lived in fraternities, and most came from a middle- or upper-middle-class background. Although women started attending college in greater numbers during this period, there was still a six-to-one male-to-female ratio on campus at the time. Dating consisted of going to college dances, the movies, or to fraternity houses for Victrola dances and "necking." A whole host of norms accompanied the phenomenon of dating. For instance, dating was almost exclusively carried on by fraternity men. Freshman men were not allowed (by tradition) to date coeds, and women from outside the university were "imported" for some of the bigger occasions on campus.

Waller argued that dating on this campus took place under what he referred to as "the rating and dating complex."[20] Both men and women did not want to date someone who did not "rank." Competition for dates was fierce, and the "Class A" men on the rating scale wanted to be sure only to be seen with "Class A" women, and vice versa. Students went to great lengths to rate high on the dating scale. For men, rating high depended on belonging to a top fraternity, and having good clothes, dancing skill, a good pick-up "line," access to a car, and money to spend on dates. For women, rating high depended on getting a reputation for being a sought-after date.[21] To ensure that they appeared to be a hot commodity, women avoided being seen too often with the same boy (so they did not scare off other potential dates).[22] To remain in high standing, women consistently had to date Class A men only. Women also avoided drinking in groups or frequenting the beer parlors. Women's prestige on campus would decline once they were no longer a fresh face on campus, due to indiscretions, or if they were too readily available for dates.[23]

Peers were heavily involved in monitoring who was dating whom. In fact, some women did not date at all because the dates they could "get" were ridiculed by their peers. Waller noted that the involvement of peers combined with the system for dating on campus created antagonisms between the sexes. He attributed part of the reason for these antagonisms to the unbalanced sex ratio, which left many men shut out from the dating pool altogether. Additionally, Waller noted that this system was particularly difficult for those who rated low on the dating desirability scale. In other words, those who did not "rate" were often left behind.

Waller acknowledged that, in some cases, dating led to true courtship and ultimately to marriage. However, the system of dating made this outcome unlikely. Instead, Waller argued that dating often became exploitative.[24] Men exploited women for sexual favors, and women exploited men by "gold digging." Waller believed that exploitation occurs only when one party is masking his or her true intentions. Thus, if both parties realized the relationship was not "going anywhere," then the relationship was not exploitative. However, in most cases, one party was more interested in the continuation of the relationship than the other. This created a scenario where one person could get what he or she wanted from the other by promising to keep the relationship going. Waller concluded that with heterosexual dating relationships, we may surmise that the party with the least interest in continuing the relationship has the most control.

Dating in the 1920s and 1930s was largely a competitive enterprise. In fact, dating was secondary to "rating" or popularity. One dated in order to rate among one's peers.[25] To achieve the goal of "rating," one would date as many members of the opposite sex as possible as long as those individuals were believed to enhance one's popularity rather than detract from it. At this point in history, it was seen as scarcely better to date one person than to date none at all.[26] In other words, most young people looked down on exclusive dating relationships before one was ready to get engaged and marry.

One's popularity as a date was not determined mostly by intrinsic qualities of the individual. Instead, popularity, which was largely defined by the peer culture, determined who "made the cut" in terms of being a worthwhile date. At some schools, rating was not merely determined informally by word of mouth. Rather, in some cases, lists would be floated around college campuses to help determine one's dating value. For instance, some women at the University of Michigan rated the "BMOCs" (i.e., Big Men on Campus) according to their campus dating stock. "Those qualifying were rated either A—smooth; B—OK; C—pass in a crowd; D —semi-goon; or E—spook."[27] This list was used as a guide for women on campus to determine whether they should accept a date or not. Whether or not such lists were taken seriously by college women, the fact that these lists were created provides evidence of how much peers were involved in rating and monitoring each other's dating partners.

THE DATING ERA—"GOING STEADY"

Despite the prominence of the norms discussed above throughout the 1920s and 1930s, they did not last. Dating continued; however, the onset and aftermath of World War II in the 1940s led to a new version of the dating script.[28] During this time, men literally became a scarce resource. Millions of men were now in the armed forces and went overseas during the war and, unfortunately, thousands of men never made it back home alive. Awareness of this scarcity of eligible men changed the tone of the dating scene. Popularity in terms of getting the greatest number of high-ranking dates possible went out with the war. In its place came an increasing focus on exclusive dating or "going steady" with one person. College girls who reveled in the number of dates they went on with a variety of partners in the 1920s and 1930s were replaced by college girls hoping to be "pinned" to one fraternity man or hoping to be engaged soon to their soldier fighting overseas.[29] Dating took on a more serious tone for men during this era as well. Men who wanted to be "big men on campus" during the rating and dating era now longed to settle down.[30]

The end of World War II ushered in a period of economic prosperity in the United States, which also had an effect on dating. Employment opportunities and a booming economy gave young men the financial stability to afford to marry sooner than they could in the previous era.[31] It is well documented that in the years after the end of World War II, the median age of marriage dropped, the number of children per family grew, and, in general, a heightened focus on a harmonious domestic life took hold.[32]

Like the previous rating and dating script, the going-steady era carried its own set of conventions. "Steadies" often gave each other something to wear to indicate to onlookers that they were "taken." Such symbols were the youths' answer to a wedding ring. For example, a young man might give his steady girlfriend his class ring to wear or the letter sweater he received from his participation in athletics. Local conventions varied on this point, with some steadies exchanging rings, the girl wearing the boy's ID bracelet, or even both steadies donning matching "steady jackets."[33] One might wonder whether such conventions were followed in order to make it easy for those who were unattached to know who was "off limits," or whether this practice was a way to indicate who had the status of a steady dating relationship—or perhaps both.

In addition to symbols of steady relationships, other conventions were widely practiced. Specifically, young men were expected to take their steady girlfriends on a certain number of dates per week. This practice manifested itself with somewhat different local norms in terms of the exact number.[34] However, as in the rating and dating era, steady dating was not expected to lead directly to marriage. There could be many steadies along the way before a mate was chosen.[35]

The going-steady era has been immortalized in films like *Grease*, which portrays students in the senior year of high school in the 1950s. Many elements of the going-steady script are brought to life here, such as young women wearing their steady's ring or letterman's sweater, and having Saturday night dates at a dance, malt shop, or drive-in movie. The film also depicts the sexual norms of the time period with the "good girl" lead character, Sandy, fighting off advances from her boyfriend, Danny.

CALLING VERSUS DATING

In addition to the changing norms for how young men and women got together and formed relationships between the calling and dating eras, there were corresponding changes in power, peer influence, and degrees of sexual intimacy. During the calling era, young women (and their mothers) controlled the invitation to "call." With dating, it was exclusively the man's right to ask a woman out on a date in order to enjoy the pleasure of her company for an evening. This represents a fundamental shift in power: men were now in control. This shift was likely due to the monetary aspect of dating.[36] Men were expected to pay for themselves and their date. At this time, it was assumed that women either earned less money than men or had no money of their own at all. Thus, it was the man's responsibility to treat the woman to dinner, the theater, or some other form of entertainment. But with this ability to pay came power. Men had the power to ask women out. Women, of course, had the power to decline an invitation, but could not initiate a date without risking their reputation as respectable young women. Additionally, men had the power to decide when and where the date would take place. Since he was paying, he had to decide what he felt like doing for the date, what he could afford, and how much the woman was "worth" in terms of spending.[37]

Power was not the only thing that changed with the dating era; peers became increasingly important as well. With calling, the family had had the greatest influence over the choice of a gentleman caller. Dating, on the other hand, moved into the public sphere, at least partially away from the watchful eyes of parents. This was particularly the case on the college campus, where parents were even farther removed from the process. In the absence of parents, peers began to exert greater influence over one's choice of a dating partner. Furthermore, since dating had largely become somewhat of a popularity contest, it became important to follow the dominant script of the times (e.g., going steady) in order to be part of the "in" crowd.

As intimate relationships moved away from parental supervision, increasing sexual intimacy entered the equation. During the dating era, particularly when couples went steady, relationships lasted long enough for the couple to become increasingly close. With this closeness came increased opportunity for sex. However, it was not only steadies who engaged in sexual behavior; there had been sexual interaction among those in the rating and dating era also.[38] Although no nationally representative samples that documented the sexual behavior of American youth were available, smaller-scale studies and an onslaught of publications (both scholarly and mainstream media) dealt with sexual behavior. These sources indicate that "necking" and "petting" were the norm among youth.[39] Precise definitions of these practices do not exist, but necking was generally believed to include "stimulation" from the "neck up" with the "main areas of sexual stimulation remaining covered by clothing."[40] With necking, the neck, lips, and ears are "utilized extensively as sexual objects."[41] Petting involved greater sexual intimacy and included "literally every caress known to married couples but does not include complete sexual intercourse."[42]

Both necking and petting likely occurred even before the dating system took hold in the 1920s.[43] Evidence of this can be found in the love letters of courtship partners in the eighteenth and nineteenth centuries.[44] However, the importance of these sexual acts lies not so much in the acts themselves, but in their increasing visibility and acceptance among an emerging youth culture.[45] As the twentieth century progressed, necking and petting on dates, especially with steadies, became a hallmark of the youth dating experience. Thus, the dating script, particularly during the 1940s and 1950s, dictated a greater degree of sexual intimacy than the calling era had allowed.

Regarding premarital sexual intercourse, evidence suggests this happened during the dating era, but it was not the norm.[46] In a particularly ingenious quantitative study, conducted in 1984, sociologist Martin Whyte surveyed women in the greater Detroit metropolitan area about their dating, mating, and marriage experiences. The study focused on women between the ages of 18 and 75 who indicated that they were currently or had previously been married. The women were placed into three major categories: prewar brides, marrying in the years 1925–1944; baby boom brides, marrying in 1945–1964; and those who first wed during the years 1965–1984. These data give us the clearest sense of how much change has taken place since dating began. Despite some continuity across time periods, Whyte documented what he refers to as an "intimacy revolution" among those in the most recent cohort.[47] "Among the prewar brides, only 24% had already lost their virginity (prior to marriage), according to our rough estimate. For the baby boom era brides this figure increases to 51% and in the post-1965 cases to 72%."[48] Whyte favors the term "intimacy revolution" to "sexual revolution" because, while the majority of women in the latest cohort had premarital sex, this act was often taking place in the context of a steady relationship and in many cases was happening with one's eventual spouse. Although there was a significant increase in women having sexual intercourse before meeting their eventual husband, or "pre-premarital sex," in all three cohorts the majority of women had premarital sex with their eventual husband only.[49] Only 3 percent of prewar brides and 17 percent of baby boom brides had sex with someone other than their eventual husband. This percentage rose to 33 percent among brides in the most recent (post-1965) generation.[50]

As these data show, dating and moderate levels of sexual intimacy, especially necking and petting, were an increasingly common part of the youth experience from the early part of the century through at least the mid-1960s. As the twentieth century progressed, greater sexual intimacy emerged, but for those in the mainstream this sexual intimacy was generally restricted to intimate relationships where a likely outcome was marriage. However, the custom of dating in order to get to know someone of the opposite sex en route to potential sexual intimacy has not remained the norm among American youth. In the latter part of the twentieth century, a shift was underway, particularly on college campuses, which allowed a new script to emerge.

THE EMERGENCE OF THE HOOKING-UP ERA

Despite the dominance of dating from the 1920s, eventually changes in society led to yet another shift in the script. In the mid-1960s, changes in the way young people were getting together had begun to occur.[51] This shift away from traditional dating was particularly apparent on college campuses.[52] College students began socializing in groups, rather than pair dating, and "partying" with large numbers of friends and classmates. Parties represented more than just a social outing; they became the setting for potential sexual encounters. At parties, students generally consumed alcohol while trying to meet new people with whom they could potentially become sexually intimate or to initiate encounters with classmates they already knew.[53] In addition to the sexual possibilities, parties were a place to find a potential romantic partner and begin a new relationship. Is it possible that the mid-1960s marks the end of formal dating and the emergence of hooking up on the college campus? I believe that a number of sociohistorical trends, both cultural and demographic, that coincide with this time period suggest that this is the case.

The 1960s are widely known as a time of great change throughout our society, particularly among youth. The advent and increased availability of the birth control pill coupled with a liberalization of attitudes toward sexuality led to changes in what was socially acceptable to do sexually. In fact, intercourse became thought of as a sign of intimacy and physical pleasure rather than merely a means of reproduction.[54] With these reproductive and attitudinal changes came changes in sexual behavior. Precisely how dramatic the change in sexual behavior was is the subject of much debate. However, most scholars agree that there was a discernible change in sexual behavior. In other words, sexual intercourse prior to marriage was no longer taboo but was becoming the norm for both women and men.[55] Along with the increase in sexual intercourse prior to marriage came an increase in other avenues of sexual expression for heterosexuals. Sexual acts that had previously been reserved for marriage (and after intercourse had taken place) were integrated into earlier "bases" of the sexual script.[56] Specifically, oral sex became an increasingly common element of the sexual script throughout the second half of the twentieth century, particularly among well-educated whites.[57] Thus, the sexual possibilities for unmarried heterosexuals were expanding.

A second source of cultural change that could be relevant to the emergence of the hookup culture is the women's movement. Feminism has fundamentally affected the roles available to men and women in many aspects of life, including the areas of relationships and family.[58] In addition to the variety of roles and choices available to men and women in adult life, there are also more choices available to boys and girls throughout their childhood and young adulthood. This seems particularly true in the area of sexuality. Feminists have promoted the idea that women should be free to be sexual both in and out of marriage and that not only "bad" girls like sex.[59] Furthermore, feminists have challenged the idea that only men can pursue women. Thus, the interjection of feminist ideals into our culture has changed the way men and women interact and relate to one another. Some of these changes in the "rules" for how men and women should behave have likely contributed to the hookup script emerging on the college campus. In other words, gender politics affect sexual politics.[60]

Fueled by changes occurring throughout the culture, American youth by the mid-1960s had "come increasingly to value the expression of personal choice" rather than "conforming to adult expectations."[61] One manifestation of this rise in individualism was college students rebelling against the in loco parentis system. Throughout the twentieth century, most colleges and universities had many rules designed to control sexual behavior. For example, there were separate dormitories, strict curfews (particularly for women), visitation was heavily monitored, and overnight stays in one's room by someone of the opposite sex was forbidden.[62] College administrators were deemed responsible for their students' behavior, particularly toward the opposite sex, and their task became increasingly challenging as more single-sex institutions became coeducational.[63] Ultimately, students prevailed in the battle with administrators over privacy and sexual freedom. Student-conduct policies, such as those mentioned above, declined along with other changes sweeping the country in the 1960s and 1970s. Most college campuses today allow virtually unrestricted access to the opposite sex.[64] Furthermore, the idea that the university administration is responsible for their students' sexual behavior has changed. Instead of focusing on sexual behavior per se, universities have shifted their resources to warning students about sexual assault and sexually transmitted diseases.

In addition to the cultural changes underway during the 1960s, a number of demographic trends are relevant to understanding why hooking up emerged and formal dating declined on college campuses. First, there has been an increase in the median age at first marriage in the United States.[65] Currently, the median age for first marriage is approximately 25 for women and 27 for men. This contrasts with 1960, when the median age at first marriage was approximately 20 for women and 23 for men.[66] Thus, the number of people getting married during their college years or immediately after has sharply declined in the past 40 years.

Despite this delay in marriage, on average young men and women become sexually active by age 17.[67] These demographic realities are relevant to the sexual script on the college campus because now young co-eds are under less pressure to find a spouse during their college years, yet they are sexually active. Therefore, they have plenty of time to "play the field" before settling down with a lifelong mate.[68] This creates a situation where it is possible to spend one's college years in more casual relationships than may have been the case earlier in the twentieth century.

Another trend that is likely to be relevant to the emergence of the hookup era is the dramatic increase in women attending college. By 1972, three times as many women were attending college than there had been just twelve years earlier in 1960.[69] Today, women far outnumber men on many college campuses in the United States. In fact, currently there are approximately 80 men for every 100 women enrolled in college.[70] Compared to the dating era, men are now a scarce resource on campus. The imbalance in the sex ratio is likely to particularly affect campuses with a high residential population, where social interaction is primarily with fellow students. For college men in the hookup era, there seems to be power in *lack* of numbers. In other words, if there are not enough men to go around, the ones who are there have greater power to determine what suits their needs when it comes to interacting with the opposite sex. Therefore, women may have had to adapt to a script that is particularly beneficial to some college men.

These interrelated changes, in the culture and demographics of 1960s society, paved the way for a change in the dating script. Although no one can pinpoint a moment in time when students stopped dating as the primary means of getting together with the opposite sex and started hooking up, there is evidence that the shift was likely well underway by the 1970s.[71] The next step is to take a more in-depth look at the hookup script. With the two major twentieth-century scripts, calling and dating, as a backdrop, I will next present the experiences of college students and young alumni today.

3

The Hookup

What does it mean to hook up? Consulting a dictionary won't help, since most dictionaries do not even include an entry on hooking up.[1] Even college students have trouble articulating a definition. My exchange with Tony, a senior at State University, demonstrates the uncertainty.

KB: Define hooking up.
Tony: Taking someone home and spending the night with them. I mean intercourse is probably like a big part of it, but I think if you take someone home and hook up, then that's hooking up.
KB: So, could hooking up mean just kissing?
Tony: Yeah.
KB: What does it usually mean?
Tony: Having sex.
KB: So most people you know when they say "hooking up" they are having sex with somebody?
Tony: Yeah (hesitantly) . . . it depends who the person is, like I can read my friends like really, really easily. Like if my one roommate says he "hooked up," that means he brought a girl home and this, that and the other thing. . . . But, like if other kids tell me they hooked up, you got to ask, not pry into their life, but it could mean a lot of things.
KB: What do you mean when you say it?
Tony: When I say "hooked up"? [I mean] that I took someone home.
KB: But, [you are] not necessarily explaining what happened?
Tony: Right, I don't like to kiss and tell [laughs].

Collectively, the college students and recent graduates with whom I spoke were able to convey the meaning of hooking up as well as the norms for following the hookup script. However, as individuals they were often unsure whether the specific way they used the term reflected how the student body in general used it. As Tony pointed out, the meaning of hooking up depends on whom you ask.

Despite the confusion over the term, college students at both of the universities I studied indicated that "hooking up" was widely used on campus to refer to intimate interaction.[2] Although my interviewees may have used the term somewhat differently, they consistently identified hooking up as the dominant way for men and women to get together and form potential relationships on campus. This does not mean that everyone on campus engages in hooking up; but students do consider it to be the primary means for initiating sexual and romantic relationships. Among those least likely to participate in hooking up are racial minorities, students who are *very* religious, and those who are already in exclusive, committed relationships (who therefore have no need to be looking for new partners). Most other students participated in hooking up, albeit to varying degrees.

DEFINING HOOKING UP

Some students, like Tony, feel that "hooking up" generally refers to "having sex"; however, many others indicated that when they say "hooking up" they are referring to something less than intercourse. To some it means "just kissing" or "making out." Others said hooking up involves "fooling around" beyond kissing, which includes sexual touching on or underneath clothing. Still others suggested that hooking up means "everything but" intercourse, which translated to include kissing, sexual touching, and oral sex. Most students acknowledged that different people use the term differently. In fact, many students were already familiar with the term "hooking up" from high school.[3] Their previous exposure to hooking up added to the confusion because the definition they used in high school did not always match their college classmates' use of the term. Thus, you cannot be sure precisely what someone means when he or she reports having "hooked up" unless you ask a follow-up question to see how much sexual activity took place. Nevertheless, some students feel they know their close friends well enough to know what they mean when they say it (i.e., their group has a shared meaning of the term). This is the case with Faith University senior, Trent.

KB: Define hooking up.
Trent: Kissing.
KB: So, if someone did more than kissing then it's not hooking up?
Trent: It is, but I don't know. Yeah, like hooking up in one sense is like you hook up with a girl and if you're hooking up with someone and it happens a few times, then I guess whatever happens, happens.
KB: Could hooking up mean sex?
Trent: Nah.
KB: So, it's different than sex?
Trent: Yeah.

In another conversation, Kyle, a senior at State University, offered the following:

KB: How would you define hooking up?
Kyle: Just kissing and maybe a little groping.
KB: Hooking up isn't sex?
Kyle: No. I know a lot of other people define it differently.
KB: So some people say it and it might mean sex?
Kyle: Yeah. None of my friends would. But I have heard it used that way.
KB: So if someone says they hooked up you don't know what they mean, you just know it is something sexual?
Kyle: Yeah. It involves that. But not sex, everything but sex.
KB: Oral sex could be hooking up?
Kyle: Yeah.

Lisa, a sophomore at State University, had this to say:

KB: Can you define hooking up?
Lisa: I don't know, anything from kissing to having sex.
KB: So, it could mean intercourse, it could mean to kiss someone?
Lisa: Well, usually if it's a good friend and we're talking about it, they'll tell me if they had sex, but if they say "hooking up" it could mean anything from, in my opinion, kissing to having sex.

Clearly, "hooking up" does not have a precise meaning; it can mean kissing, sexual intercourse, or any form of sexual interaction generally seen as falling in between those two extremes.

The ambiguous nature of the term should not be surprising. During the well-publicized scandal of 1997 between former president Bill Clinton and Monica Lewinsky, the public debated what it means to say "have sex" or "have sexual relations" after the president emphatically declaimed, "I did not have sex with that woman," only to have DNA tests confirm the presence of semen on her clothing. Still, Clinton and his supporters argued that his statement was truthful if one defines sex only as sexual intercourse. However, much of the American public scoffed at this narrow definition, favoring a broader definition of sex, which would encompass sexual touching and oral sex. What was interesting about this debate was how views on the subject broke down along generational lines. Researchers found that members of the younger generation were more likely to agree with Clinton's contention that oral sex did not really "count" as having sex with someone.[4] Perhaps then it is not surprising that the more recent term, "hooking up," does not have a universally agreed upon meaning, either.[5]

Several students I spoke to alluded to the confusion over what hooking up meant. This may stem from regional variation in usage or even more localized variation between high schools. As Kim, a sophomore from Faith University, put it:

KB: You mentioned hooking up a minute ago. How would you define that?

Kim: [Laughs] That's kind of funny actually because at home, like in Virginia, hooking up is like more than kissing, but not all the way. And so I would come here and I would hear people, like my friends, say: "I hooked up with this guy and this guy." And I was just thinking: "These people are crazy that they would do that with that many people!" But then I just found out this year that here hooking up [sometimes means] just kissing or making out with a guy at a party.

Even more confusion was generated when college students were discussing hooking up with someone from a different generation. For instance, some female students mentioned that problems arose when they called home to fill their mothers in on what was going on with "guys" at college. Gloria, a freshman at State University, told her mother that she had been hooking up and this revelation created some panic on the other end of the telephone.

KB: Do people you know [ever] use the term hooking up to refer to sex?

Gloria: I've never heard that. But my mom saw on the news that hooking up meant oral sex and I always tell my mom, "I hooked up with this guy and he was so nice." I tell her that all the time. And she called me after that news session [and said], "What does hooking up mean?" Because I was telling her I [hooked up with] . . . Billy and Joe and Rob. I was like: "No, just kissing." I guess I never heard it [used] for having sex.

KB: You said [previously hooking up referred to] fooling around?

Gloria: Right. Fooling around is not having sex, but [it can be] like oral sex.

Interestingly, Gloria's definition of what it means to have sex does not include having oral sex. Many of the students I spoke with noted the distinction between sex and oral sex. This provides further evidence that there may be generational differences in perceptions of what counts as sex.[6] Adding to the confusion are media references to hooking up that portray only the most risqué scenarios of hooking up, when in reality students use the term to encompass a much broader range of sexual behavior.

It is likely that there is another reason for the ambiguous nature of the term. When students say, "I hooked up," they leave the details of the encounter to the listener's imagination. Both men and women may have reasons to be intentionally vague. Men, who often want to feign more sexual experiences than they actually have, can say they hooked up and hope the listener infers *more* than actually happened sexually.[7] Women, on the other hand, who may want to protect their reputations, can say they hooked up and hope the listener infers *less* than what actually happened sexually.[8] When students speak to their close friends, they may know what the others mean when they say the term or they may feel close enough to ask a follow-up question on the subject. However, for those who are not friendly enough with the speaker to warrant knowing more intimate details, someone can simply say, "I hooked up," and leave it at that. This does not imply that interested parties will not resort to other means to find out what really happened. However, such parties will have to rely on secondhand accounts and rumors to satisfy their curiosity.

Clearly, "hooking up" is a vague term when it comes to finding out what happened sexually between two people. However, there are several other defining features of the script for hooking up, beyond the sexual aspects, which were largely understood by college students in my study across the board. College students recognize hooking up as the pathway to a potential romantic relationship, yet a hookup does not guarantee *any* commitment beyond when the encounter takes place. After hooking up, someone can opt to ask for the other's phone number or can try to make plans to meet somewhere in the future, but most students indicated that this is not the most common outcome. Instead, students said that the most likely outcome of any particular hookup encounter is "nothing," which means not hearing from the person again unless you coincidentally see him or her at another social event and decide to hook up again. Although most hookup encounters do not lead to an ongoing romantic relationship, the possibility is there. Many students, particularly women, often hoped that a hookup would evolve into some version of a relationship. Therefore, all hookup encounters cannot be characterized as "casual sex" or "one-night stands" when often one of the parties is hoping that it will lead to "something more," and, at least some of the time, it does.

HOW IT HAPPENS

Hooking up is an outgrowth of how college students socialize today. Instead of socializing in dating pairs as they did earlier in the twentieth century, college students tend to "hang out" socially in groups at dorms, parties, or bars.[9] Although the groups at the beginning of the evening may be single-sex, it does not stay that way for long. For example, a group of young women may prepare for an evening out (i.e., get dressed, put on makeup, etc.), and then go to a campus party together.[10] However, once they arrive, they find college men there and mixed-gender interactions begin. At the end of the night many individuals at the social event pair off with someone of the opposite sex to hook up. Kevin, a senior at Faith University said:

> KB: We were talking about the hookup scene and I'm trying to get a couple details about it. So would you hook up every weekend?
> Kevin: Not every weekend . . . it wasn't like the weekend was over if you didn't go out and hook up. I would go out to have fun and if I hooked up—bonus.
> KB: Bonus? [Laughing]
> Kevin: It was a nice way to close the night.

One of the most difficult things to get college students to explain is how hooking up happens.[11] For many, hooking up was such a normal and taken-for-granted part of their social lives that it was difficult to get them to step back and explain how such an event develops. When I asked students to explain how someone would end up hooking up with someone with whom they had no prior sexual interaction, they would often answer by saying "alcohol" or "I don't know, it just happens." For example, Jack, a sophomore at Faith University said:

> KB: Just take me through a typical scenario of how it [hooking up] works if you were trying to explain it to someone . . . who doesn't know how it works yet.
> Jack: I really can't explain it because to this day I don't understand it.

Despite their initial vague answers, when probed with follow-up questions students eventually explained how hooking up happens. The first step is identifying a hookup partner. The person one hooks up with may or may not be someone known prior to the night of the first hookup. In some cases, the two parties were friends first. In others, they were acquaintances and had "seen each other around" or taken a class together. Under these circumstances the man and woman may have spent some time flirting or showing sexual interest prior to the night of the hookup. In still other cases, the hookup was what many students referred to as "random" (i.e., there was no connection to the other person before the night of the first hookup). However, in cases where the two parties were total strangers, there was often a friend or acquaintance who was able to provide an introduction.[12] Lisa, a sophomore at State University, was one of the many students who agreed that hooking up could happen under any of the above circumstances and no one scenario loomed larger than the others.

KB: Would you say, typically with hooking up, that the people usually know each other or would you say that hooking up usually is someone you just met at a party?

Lisa: Umm, I guess it could go either way really. But, that's hard. I guess it would probably usually be someone they know. I mean, it does happen with someone you just met, but I think usually . . . it would be someone you're friends with or you met a few times in your class, you know what I mean, someone who you . . .

KB: Have some idea who they are?

Lisa: Yeah, yeah.

KB: Do students generally hook up with the same person repeatedly or would it be more one and done, once you've hooked up with someone that's it?

Lisa: I think it just depends on who the person is.

KB: Well, among your friends, which is more likely?

Lisa: Sometimes people have a crush on a guy so they'll just keep doing whatever [sexually] with that guy, but you know they won't ever end up with anything [relationship-wise]. The girl who just wants to randomly have sex, she just hooks up with whoever, whenever she feels like it [laughs]. But, it's not necessarily all one and done situations, you know what I mean? If they have feelings for that person or some sort of something, it will happen again. I guess if they hook up and then they're like: "Uh, I don't really like him at all," then that will be it [they won't hook up again].

Regardless of how the two parties know each other, there has to be some way to get from having never been sexual with someone to becoming sexually intimate. Two issues must be considered here. One is: How does someone select a potential hookup partner? The other is: Once a potential partner is identified, what needs to occur to facilitate the first sexually intimate encounter? With regard to the first issue, attraction is the central issue. Students across the board seemed to favor the idea that initial attraction is the trigger to a potential hookup that evening.[13]

On the college campus, a number of qualities make someone attractive to potential hookup partners. First are one's looks. A striking physical appearance seemed to be the most valued quality a woman could possess. Jack, a sophomore at Faith University, discussed how physical appearance affects how women interact with men in potential hookup situations.

> *Jack*: It all depends on who the girl is. Those girls that think they're so much better looking than everyone else, they're going to wait for the guy to come up to them, they're not going out of their way. I don't know, I guess they see it as a disgrace to themselves. And girls who know that they're good looking, but also know what they want, . . . they're going to go up and talk to you and they're going to be the ones who are worthwhile to talk to.
>
> *KB*: So, looks are a big factor for girls in who has status and who doesn't and it affects how they interact it seems?
>
> *Jack*: Well, talking amongst my friends, we decided that girls travel in three's: there's the hot one, there's the fat one, and there's the one that's just there. It's always true, without fail.

College women, such as Lee, a freshman at Faith University, also recognized the importance of men's physical appearance in choosing potential hookup partners.

> *Lee*: Looks have a lot to do with it in the whole hooking up thing. You see someone that is really good looking, you are going to hook up with [him] regardless of if [he has] anything nice to say, especially if you are drinking. I think that is the primary concern, even if [he is] an asshole . . . if [he is] good looking, a girl will still hook up with [him].

Another valued quality among men, at both campuses, was fraternity or athletic team membership. At State University, fraternity membership was a particularly valued attribute for males. Kyle, a senior at State, suggests that fraternity men have more opportunities for sexual encounters with women: "I think a lot of guys are sex driven and it just manifests itself more prominently in fraternity men because of their stature on campus." The idea of fraternity men being the "big men on campus" has a long history in the United States, dating as far back as the 1920s.[14] More recently, sociologists Patricia Yancey Martin and Robert Hummer examined the fraternity selection process at a large state university in the 1980s. They found that the pledging process ensured that the most "macho" men would become brothers. Men who were less athletic, less likely to drink alcohol, and less inclined to have a conquest mentality toward sex, were more likely to drop out during the pledging process (or perhaps never attempt to pledge in the first place).[15]

For women, neither sorority membership nor athletic team participation seemed important. Thus, for women, physical appearance plays a more central role in attracting the opposite sex than it does for men. Similarly, anthropologists Dorothy Holland and Margaret Eisenhart found, in their study of two southern universities in the early 1980s, that a woman's status on campus was determined almost exclusively by her perceived level of physical attractiveness among men. Men's status, on the other hand, derived from many different sources (e.g., fraternity membership, athletic status, academic major, intellectual ability). Therefore, college men were valued for many attributes, while women had to rely solely on their looks.

Once a desirable partner is identified, it is necessary to find out if the feeling is mutual. Ascertaining whether someone is interested in a sexual encounter is an important aspect of the hookup script. Students indicated that this is done indirectly, without actually asking whether the other person is interested in becoming sexually intimate. Rather, nonverbal cues indicate potential sexual interest.[16] In this regard, students said that eye contact was important, as was any form of paying particular attention to the person of interest. Special attention could be paid through having a one-on-one conversation with someone for a significant period of time or "hanging out" with a particular person for a considerable portion of the evening. On the other hand, lack of eye contact, looking around the room while someone was talking, or moving on to mingle with others were deemed obvious indicators of lack of interest in hooking up. Kevin, a senior at Faith University, believed he had a particular talent for assessing whether a girl was interested in hooking up.

Kevin: Like I always say, I know in the first 30 seconds whether or not I'm going to hook up with a girl. The first time I talk to [her].

  KB: You know?

Kevin: I know.

  KB: How do you know?

Kevin: I know just because I can sense it, the vibe, just them. The way they are, the way they talk, the way they engage in the conversation, are they into me or are they not into me? I can pick it up in 30 seconds. I can look at my friends and say: "Guys, this is no good" and we can move on to other girls.

  KB: You can tell [if a girl is interested] even for them?

Kevin: Yeah. I can say: "Tommy, this girl wants you. You stay, I am moving on." You know what I mean, I can tell in 30 seconds . . . pick up on the vibe of them. Are they eager to hang out? If they want to hang out . . . you are going to have a good time tonight, you are going to party with them and maybe you're going to hook up. But if they are hesitant and they are on guard about you then forget it, move on.

  KB: Define "on guard." What are they doing that lets you know that they don't like you?

Kevin: Umm. Not making eye contact. They're kind of still looking around while you are talking to them—they are not interested. They are absolutely positively not interested. They are . . . not asking you questions back if you are asking questions . . . 30 seconds you can tell.

Although not all students claimed Kevin's talent for quickly recognizing whether a hookup was possible, both men and women indicated that the stages leading to hooking up involved a series of nonverbal cues. The majority of students agreed with Kevin that eye contact and a certain "vibe" are key components of discerning interest in hooking up. Students also mentioned overall body language, "joking around," and "flirting" with someone in order to indicate interest in a potential hookup.[17]

Where to Go

Once it is determined that the right vibe is there, the two parties have to figure out where to hook up. Again, they must figure this out without actually verbalizing that they are planning to hook up. One of the factors that seemed to determine the location of the hookup was how much sexual interaction was going to take place. Many students, like Emily, a sophomore at Faith University, indicated that when they hooked up, they were "just kissing" or "making out" with someone. In some cases, they felt no need for this to take place in private, so they were willing to hook up right at the social event, whether it was a campus party or bar.

> KB: If you hook up with someone, what happens next? I mean do you sleep over with them that night or how does it work?
> Emily: I don't usually ever [sleep over].
> KB: Where does it [the hookup] happen?
> Emily: I would say at parties most often or maybe back at your dorm . . . later on if you're hanging out with them.

Since there is a taboo against getting more physical than kissing in front of other people, those interested in a greater degree of sexual intimacy would find a private room to hook up or would return to the dorm room or apartment of one of the partners. This does not mean that everyone who goes home with someone intends to do more than kiss, some students valued privacy for any level of sexual intimacy.

A second factor determining the location of a hookup was whether one of the students had a preference for sleeping overnight or not. Some students said they like to leave the hookup partner that night, thereby avoiding the awkwardness of waking up the next day next to someone. Some students I interviewed also mentioned wanting to avoid the "walk of shame," or walking home the day after a hookup in the same clothes they wore the night before. Style of dress varies significantly between the daytime and nighttime, so that it is obvious to onlookers if someone is still in their nighttime wear. Interestingly, women seemed more concerned with the walk of shame than their male counterparts. In addition to these considerations, some students indicated that they preferred not to sleep over with their hookup partner because they had trouble actually sleeping with someone in the same bed; so it was deemed better to part that night. Max, a sophomore at State University, referred to these problems associated with spending the night with a woman.

Max: Hopefully they didn't sleep over.

 KB: Oh, they don't stay over?

Max: If I have any say, I hope not.

 KB: So you hook up and you walk them home?

Max: Yeah, for me, yeah, hopefully.

 KB: And why do you say that?

Max: I'm like a "scoocher," I like totally want to sleep well, like, I want to scooch all around my bed.

 KB: So, you find it physically uncomfortable for them to stay over?

Max: Right. On top of the fact, then it's the whole, maybe it's a cop out, but I think it's easier when you're both kind of tipsy or whatever then the next morning to wake up and be like now we're both hung-over and you know like [groans] and then you have that awkward conversation, you know what I mean?

 KB: Right.

Max: So, I totally would want to avoid that and not have to go through that.

For those who do choose to spend the night after hooking up, there did not seem to be any convention with regard to whether the location was the man's or woman's dorm room or apartment. Students indicated that they made that choice based on situational factors. For instance, who lived closer to where the two met? Who had a better setup for someone staying over (e.g., his or her own bedroom)? In some cases, female students took into account where they would feel safe. Some men indicated that they were aware of this and therefore were willing to give up "home field advantage" in order to make the woman feel safer. Although decisions are made about where the hookup will take place, this can be accomplished without outright acknowledging that the plan is to hook up. Jack, a sophomore student at Faith University, illustrates how the two parties can figure out where the hookup will take place without verbalizing their full intentions: "You can just be having a conversation and suddenly she'll be like: 'I really haven't been to your house at all this year.' And then [she] comes back with you [to hook up]."

How Far to Go

Once the partners begin to engage in a hookup encounter, each person must decide how far to take things sexually. Obviously, an individual's own moral beliefs and sense of self factor into how one conducts one's sex life.[18] But these are not the only factors guiding what takes place during a hookup. Perception of what peers do sexually also affects the level of sexual interaction. What students believe is normal within the context of the hookup culture seems to greatly affect how they conduct their own sexual behavior.

Identifying the sexual norms is somewhat difficult given that hooking up encompasses such a wide range of sexual behavior. "Just kissing" may be the norm for a particular person or a particular group of friends on campus, while sexual intercourse is the norm for others. Despite this variation, there is one norm, specific to the hookup culture, which dictates how much sexual interaction is likely to happen. Some college students in my sample indicated that they would go farther sexually with someone during a hookup if they did *not* really like the person or did *not* think that there was any chance for a relationship with that person. On the face of it, this seems illogical. Why would students be more sexual with someone they did not really like or did not envision as a potential partner? Many college students realized that getting too sexual with a hookup partner early on is not a good way to begin a relationship. Students indicated that you should "take it slow" with someone you really liked and "get to know each other" for a while. Too much sexual interaction in the early stages of meeting someone was seen as ruining any chance you might otherwise have to pursue a relationship with that person. According to Max, a sophomore at State University:

Max: If I see a girl and I think we're just going to hook up, then it's probably like *we can do whatever* [sexually] and it's not a big deal and . . . I won't see her as dirty, but if it's a girl that I potentially want to have a relationship with and she does do all of that in the beginning, then I would kind of perceive her as dirty.

KB: If "she does do all of that," [meaning] sex, or even less than that?

Max: Well, even less than that. [Emphasis by interviewee]

As Max suggests, it is acceptable to do "whatever" with someone sexually who is "just a hookup." Although Max says he would not perceive a girl as "dirty" in that situation, the point seems to be that he does not care. If it is just a one-night stand, it does not seem to matter.

Some college women seem to have realized that men think less of them if they are too sexual during an initial hookup or in the early stages of a series of hookup encounters with the same person. Thus, women will sometimes alter how much they are willing to do sexually to fit the situation. If she likes a man and wants him to like her back, she is less likely to be very sexual with him. The concept of being less sexual with someone if you actually like him (or wanted him to like you) was echoed by several of the women. Marie, a senior at State University said:

Marie: [If] I know I kind of like this person, [then] maybe [I won't do] anything [sexually] because I want this person to respect me and maybe not just look at it as a hook up. Because I feel like when you sleep with somebody, then they tend to look at you as just a hookup.

  KB: If you like someone, you would be less sexual with [him]?

Marie: Hmm-hmm, yeah.

Jen, a junior at State University, echoed Marie's opinion.

The more that I like somebody the more I *don't* want to have sex with them. . . . And I can kind of tell when someone tries to have sex with [me] right off the bat or that night I just feel like it's not really showing respect. I feel like when you really like somebody they're not going to try [to have sex immediately] because they have respect for you. [Emphasis added]

Violet, a junior at State University, said she would recommend not hooking up with someone at all if you have genuine feelings for him.

Violet: I think you learn that if you hook up with somebody it is probably just a hookup and nothing is going to come of it. And if you have any invested feelings in someone, I wouldn't hook up with him at a party drunk. But if you are a freshman you go into it thinking: "I am going to have a good time, drink and talk to the person I want and when I am drunk I can really say what I want to say." . . . And I think that when you get further in school . . . you learn that things aren't always the way that you would think that they'd be.

> KB: So would you say that freshmen girls would think that a hook up might turn into something [relationship-wise] and girls that are sophomores, juniors and older would realize that that is not the case?
>
> *Violet*: Yes.

Importantly, Marie, Jen, and Violet were juniors or seniors at the time of their interviews. Thus, they had had many opportunities to learn how the hookup script works in college. It seems likely, as Violet suggests, that many young women are less aware of these norms, particularly during freshman year. Thus, less experienced college women may be sexual with someone with the hope that such behavior will lead to a relationship; they may not suspect that their sexual availability decreases their chances of having the man pursue a relationship. One quantitative study confirmed what the upper-class women I spoke with believed; that is, 49 percent of college students who engaged in sexual intercourse during a hookup encounter said they never saw the person again.[19] Indeed, members of the campus culture had to *learn over time* the rules of the hookup script.

WHAT HAPPENS NEXT

There are many potential outcomes of a hookup encounter. The college women I spoke with, particularly after freshman year, came to realize that you "have no idea what will come out of a hookup." In a sense, hooking up is a roll of the dice. According to both men and women, the most likely outcome is "nothing"—the hookup partners part ways either the evening of the hookup or the next morning. No romantic relationship is directly pursued by either party, and their relationship returns to whatever they were to each other prior to the hookup. As Emily, a sophomore at Faith University, put it:

> KB: Generally speaking, of the students you know, if someone hooks up with someone is it likely that they're going to hook up with them again or is it more often that it happens once and doesn't happen again?
>
> *Emily*: More often it happens once and doesn't happen again.
>
> KB: And why do you think it works that way?

Emily: I think that's the accepted way that it is and I think that people drink and then they hook up and maybe there's attraction there and then it's not there anymore or maybe it's awkward or maybe you hook up with someone you don't really
know and then you don't really take the time to get their
number. Like sometimes when I hook up with people like I
might not have any interest in them, but it just happens to
happen and you don't expect anymore from it.

The students I spoke with indicated that if the two parties were friends
before the hookup, they try to stay friends. If they were acquaintances
before, they are cordial or perhaps even friendly when they run into
each other again. Since a hallmark of the hookup script is that there are
no strings attached, there is no reason for there to be any tension between the two after hooking up. However, both men and women often
indicated that they did feel awkward or "weird" with a former partner
after the hookup.[20] Both parties involved in the hook up are not always
in agreement about what will happen next; in fact, it is often the case
that one party is more interested in furthering the relationship than the
other.[21]

Although "nothing" is the most likely outcome of a hookup, that
does not necessarily mean that the two people never hook up again. The
fact that nothing usually results from a hookup means that no special
relationship is formed between the two parties. The majority of students,
like Lee, a freshman at Faith University, indicated that hooking up repeatedly with the same person was fairly common, even if there was little to no contact outside of the late-night party or bar interaction.

Lee: I see a lot of girls [that] will have someone in mind [that they
want to hook up with that night]. Not talk to them all week,
go to a party, go home with them, not talk to them the whole
next week, go to the party, see them again, [and] go home
with them. That is their person to go home with at a party. I
see that a lot.

KB: A lot of times it doesn't just happen one time, it is with the
same person repeatedly?

Lee: Yeah, but with nothing in the middle.

KB: No phone calls, no e-mails, no contact during the week?

Lee: Correct.

KB: Weekends only?
Lee: Right. [Laughs]

Repeated hooking up does not automatically lead to any semblance of a relationship. Indeed, if there is no contact with the person during the week or at any time other than weekend nights, college students viewed it as nothing more than a "repeat hookup."

Another possible outcome of hooking up is a variation of hooking up repeatedly, known as "seeing each other." This refers to cases where one college student will repeatedly hook up with the same person and there will be some attempts to "hang out" or spend time with the person in between hookup encounters. In addition to the phrase "seeing each other," some interviewees referred to this as "talking," or less often as "dating."[22] The contact between hookup encounters could take a variety of forms, including phone calls, text messages, e-mails, or instant messages. In addition to talking to each other, students suggested that they might also make plans to meet somewhere. However, the two would not go out alone; they would meet in a group setting and "hang out" with a larger group of friends and classmates, as is the case for most college-student socializing.

The type of relationships falling under the labels of "seeing each other," "talking," "hanging out," or "dating" are still characterized by a low level of commitment, where hooking up with someone else is still a possibility. These relationships also tend to be short lived, lasting a few weeks or couple months before disintegrating. Many of the college women indicated that it is men who decide whether to continue seeing each other or whether a relationship will evolve.[23] Furthermore, college women often seemed at a loss to explain why the man they were "seeing" decided to end things, as did Jen, a junior at State University.

Jen: You'll hook up with them for a week or two weeks consecutively and then something weirdo happens [laughing].
KB: Like what?
Jen: Like you'll see them with [another] girl one night and you are just standing there. I've seen that happen to my friends. No one ever really . . . sits you down and says: "I don't think this is working out," [they don't handle it] in a mature way. [Laughing]

Marie, a senior at State University, added, "A lot of girls are fine in relationships and the guys just change, something clicks in the guy where they're like: 'I don't want to be with you anymore.'"

The least likely outcome of hooking up is that it leads to becoming a couple. In other words, two college students hook up and then decide after some period of time to be an exclusive couple or boyfriend / girlfriend. These relationships are referred to as "going out" or being "together" or "with" the other person. Exclusivity is one of the defining features of these relationships. Hooking up with someone outside of the relationship is considered "cheating" and will likely lead to a breakup of the relationship. During their freshman year, many college students, both male and female, tried to avoid becoming part of an exclusive relationship. Freshmen, and others recollecting their freshman experience, spoke of wanting to make a lot of friends during their first year and "see what's out there." Becoming a part of an exclusive couple was seen as being at odds with these goals. Liz, a freshman at Faith University, said, "I was one of those [people who thought] like: 'Oh this is college, you know, I'm just going to keep my options open,' blah, blah, blah."

However, as students progress through their college years, some increasingly begin looking for an exclusive relationship, and female students seem considerably more interested than males that hooking up would lead to a relationship or at least something more than a one-time encounter. However, the hookup script does not seem conducive to relationship formation.

Rebecca, a sophomore from State University, explained how women are often interested in more than just hooking up, sometimes trying to turn a hookup into a relationship. To this end, Rebecca said women fool themselves into believing they have a relationship when this is actually not the case. Rebecca referred to this phenomenon as having "fake boyfriends." She explains what this means in the excerpt below.

Rebecca: I think girls . . . go to parties where they think the same guy [they have hooked up with before] is going to be. I think they try to hook up with the same person. And guys they might [try to hook up with the same person], but I really . . . don't think so. I think [men's motto is]: the more [girls], the better.

KB: The more different girls, the better?

Rebecca: Yeah, they like to have their little tally kind of thing
[laughs]. But, I think most girls want to try to find [or] stick
with one guy so they can pretend they're dating them.

KB: What do you mean by that, "pretend they're dating"?

Rebecca: Well, I do it all the time, I haven't had a boyfriend yet, but
I had two fake boyfriends. [Laughing] Oh, they were great
relationships [sarcastic tone]. You can kind of think that
you're together because you think you're the only one in his
life and he seems to care about you, you know? . . . You can
kind of just make believe that [you're together], like whatever he says you can twist it around to make it seem like
something else. So like: "Yes, he loves me [sarcastic tone]!"
And all of your friends are telling you that he loves you and
that you are bound to be married, but you're never [truly] together. So, it's kind of that whole fake relationship thing.

KB: When do you figure out that you're not really together?

Rebecca: Umm, when there's another girl.

Although college students believed relationship formation to be the
least likely outcome of hooking up, the fact that it is a possibility may partially explain what keeps the hookup script intact. One can hope that a
hookup is going to lead to something more (i.e., some version of a relationship). Although college students generally realized that there are no
guarantees, promises, or "strings attached," the hope of a hookup leading to a relationship may loom large in the minds of some who decide to
take part in hooking up. This may particularly be the case when a college
student hooks up with someone she or he knows and "likes" in advance
of the hookup. Several women indicated that knowing the rules of hooking up, especially knowing that nothing might come of a hookup, was
something they learned over time. In other words, they were somewhat
naïve their freshman year, but learned over time, "the hard way," to have
low expectations. For example, a senior, Marie, at State University said:

Because I trusted guys so much . . . so when I . . . hooked up, and when
they weren't all like lovey-dovey and then I don't know, then I'd hook
up with somebody else and I just learned through experience that not
every guy is going to fall all over you and be like: "Now I want a girlfriend." You know what I mean? A lot of them just want to hook up
with you and then never talk to you again (laughing) . . . and they don't

care! And that definitely takes a long time to realize and even now you might know it, but you might . . . because of the fact that you might want a relationship, even knowing that might not stop you [from hooking up] because you think: "This time it might be different." And you also have to learn that guys say a lot of things that they don't mean. They say a lot of things that you want to hear and you might fall for it, so it's really hard to trust guys in starting a relationship.

WHAT EVER HAPPENED TO DATING?

The script for how college students become sexually intimate has dramatically changed from the dating script, which dominated campuses from the 1920s through the mid-1960s.[24] The college students I interviewed said that they do not date in the traditional sense of the term.[25] Additionally, the alumni I spoke with confirmed that they did not go out on formal dates during their college years. College students do not initiate romantic relationships by asking each other out to dinner or a movie with the hope that something sexual might happen at the end of the evening. Thus, the dominant cultural/sexual script for most of the twentieth century (i.e., asking someone out for a date as the first stage toward finding an intimate partner) is no longer being used by most college students. The following excerpts from my interviews with Emily (sophomore, Faith University), Joseph (senior, Faith University), Lisa (sophomore, State University) and Jen (junior, State University) illustrate the point that the current script on campus does not begin with dating. These comments were typical of both male and female students at State and Faith University.

KB: Do you know any students that date?
Emily: Like date?
KB: That go out on dates.
Emily: [Laughs] Umm, no. [Laughs] I would say like if you have a boyfriend, maybe you'll go out, but I don't know, I think that's so out, like a culture from like my parents time that would ask each other out and stuff like that.
KB: So, the people you know don't do that at all?
Emily: No.

• • •

KB: When you look around at your friends, do a lot of people go on dates?

Joseph: Once they're actually boyfriend and girlfriend, I see them going out. But I usually don't see anybody with the approach of saying: "Do you want to go out?"

KB: Would you say that students date?

Lisa: Hmmm . . . not really, I don't think they really do that much. I don't know anyone who, that's what is really weird too when you were asking about how people get together in college, they just don't really do that [date]. At least, I don't know anyone who goes on dates.

KB: Have you gone on a date since you've been at State?

Lisa: I mean with my boyfriend now, but not before.

KB: Not before?

Lisa: No, not at all. I mean, nobody ever asked me [on a date]. I had boys that I liked or whatever, but it was never like that, we would just hang out or go to a party or whatever. None of my girlfriends have ever been on dates either since we've been here [at school].

KB: What do you envision when you hear the term "date"? What do you picture that to look like?

Lisa: I don't know, going to a movie and dinner or something, something where it's just the two of you. It doesn't necessarily have to be that [movie and dinner], that's just the typical thing, but like something that just the two of you are doing by yourselves.

KB: Would you say that students at State University date?

Jen: No.

KB: What do you envision when I say date?

Jen: I think about somebody picking you up, bringing you flowers [laughing], taking you out to dinner and maybe a movie.

KB: And students here don't do that?

Jen: No.

KB: Has anyone asked you on a date since you've come to State?

Jen: No.

KB: And none of your friends here have [gone on dates]?

Jen: I mean they've been asked out on dates I guess but it's *after they've been hooking up with the person* . . . I haven't gone out on a date here [at State University]. [Emphasis added]

In Jen and Lisa's response to the question on whether students date, they refer to a key issue. College students recognize what the dating script is, but they do not follow it in the traditional sense because a date is no longer the mechanism by which college students find potential partners. It is rare for students to engage in behavior that resembles a traditional date (e.g., a pair going to dinner or a movie together) unless they are *already* in an exclusive relationship. As Jen implies, the pathway to becoming a couple, when a date might occur, begins with hooking up.

The terms "date" and "dating" are still used on college campuses today, but they are used far less frequently than during the dating era, and they often do not have the same meaning they once did. Today, the term "date" is used to refer to (a) going out alone with someone with whom you are already in a serious relationship, or (b) the person you take to a formal dance. However, neither of these scenarios is very common because going on dates is no longer the centerpiece of campus social life as it once was.[26] The term "dating" is used by some students interchangeably with "seeing each other," "talking," or "hanging out" to refer to hooking up on an ongoing basis with someone you have some form of contact with between hookup encounters. According to the men and women I spoke with, students in this type of relationship would rarely, if ever, go out to dinner or the movies or any other public place to spend time alone together. Thus, college students' use of the term "dating" does not reflect the traditional meaning of the term.

DATING VERSUS HOOKING UP

Hooking up and dating are fundamentally different. Each carries its own set of norms for behavior, and although there is some overlap, there are several critical distinctions. During the dating era, men initiated the invitations to go out on dates.[27] The script for a date followed many widely recognized conventions. The man was supposed to contact the woman to ask for a date in advance, giving her at least several days' notice; he was responsible for planning an activity for the date, such as going to dinner or a movie, as well as picking the woman up and driving (or walking) her home. Because the man was responsible for the initiation and planning of the date, he had to pay for any expenses.[28]

By contrast, hookup encounters generally occur at the culmination of a night of "hanging out" among a large group of friends and classmates at a campus party or local bar. Either the man or woman can initiate the interaction, but in either case the cues would be nonverbal. College students said that you can "just tell" when someone wants to hook up by his or her eye contact, body language, attentiveness, and so on. Neither the man nor the woman is responsible for the expenses incurred during the evening. In most cases, the only expense would be alcohol, and college students usually pay their own way or may buy "a round" of drinks for their friends.

Alcohol also seems to play a more central role in facilitating the hookup script than it did in the dating era.[29] In fact, alcohol is not only available at campus social events that culminate in hookup encounters, but it is often consumed by one or both parties involved in the hookup.[30] Many students, like Larry, a senior at Faith University believe that drinking alcohol lowers their inhibitions, thereby making a hookup possible: "Sometimes it's just something that happens, like you have something to drink and you just feel this sudden attraction for someone and they feel this attraction for you and it just happens and it ends after that." Without alcohol as a social lubricant, it is unlikely that college students would be able to signal interest in a hookup and deal with the potential for rejection inherent to this script. This "need for alcohol" may account for the increasing role that "partying" has played in the social lives of college students over the past several decades.[31] Thus, alcohol use and alcohol-centered events (e.g., campus parties) play a critical role in making hookup encounters possible.

Another difference between hooking up and dating is that the timing and meaning of sexual activity has changed. When the dating script dominated campus life, college men and women went on dates first and then, in some cases, became sexually intimate with each other. Through dating, couples could get to know each other better or build a relationship by spending time together as well as facilitate potential sexual interaction.[32] College men used to ask women to go on dates with the hope that something sexual, such as necking or petting, might happen at the end of the date. In the hooking-up era, this sexual norm is reversed. College students, following the hookup script, become sexual first and then *maybe* go on a date someday. In fact, going on a traditional style date is likely to happen only if the two partners progress to the point of deciding to become an exclusive couple (i.e., boyfriend / girl-friend), as reflected in Lee, Marie, and Jack's responses.

KB: Would you say that students go on dates? What do you see around you? What is the most common?

Lee: Most common is just hooking up. I don't really see people go out on dates that often, unless they are [already] in a relationship. [Freshman, Faith University]

Marie: Most people I know, just meet people by meeting them out at a bar and hooking up and then *from there* if somebody is interested, then they might see you out more [and something further might happen with them], I don't think anybody really goes on dates unless they are [already] in a serious relationship and they're boyfriend and girlfriend, then they might be like: "Oh, do you want to go out to dinner?" But, that's about it. [Emphasis by interviewee] [Senior, State University]

KB: Would you say that students date or they go on dates?

Jack: [Pauses] Some. Like the ones that have gotten into serious relationships, yes. They'll go out to dinner . . . but everyone else it's just: "I'll meet you at this party" or "I'll meet you at this bar." [Sophomore, Faith University]

Hooking up is the first step; going to dinner or a movie or any other typical one-on-one date happens much later or not at all for the majority, who never reach the point of a full-fledged relationship. Therefore, hooking up reverses the traditional "date first, sex later" formula that governed intimate relationships on college campuses from the 1920s through the mid-1960s.

Moreover, in the dating era, the sexual norms dictated that the degree of sexual intimacy would increase between partners over time. Or, as a couple became increasingly committed, sex would escalate.[33] The hooking-up script does not require a correlation between sexual intimacy and relationship commitment. A hookup can include anything from kissing to sexual intercourse between partners, even on the first encounter. In fact, many students indicated that they were more likely to "go farther" during a hookup encounter if they did not have strong feelings for their partner or when they believed turning the hookup into a relationship was unlikely.

Dating is no longer the centerpiece of college social life. Instead of dating, college students today socialize with large groups of friends and classmates and pair off to hook up. Hooking up is its own script, with its own norms for how to meet, get together, become sexually intimate, and manage the potential formation of relationships. Although students are aware of these norms, many of them also feel that they had to learn them over time. Discovering that a relationship is not a probable outcome of a hookup encounter was difficult for some (usually women) who wanted "something more," but they felt powerless to get what they want. Those unhappy with the hookup script had to come to terms that it was the "only game in town," at least on campus.

4

The Hookup Scene

The college campus is not the only place where people hook up, but there is something unique about campus life that makes the hookup culture flourish there.[1] In my conversation with Jen, a junior at State University, she talked about the difference between living at home during summer break and being on campus. She touched on many different aspects of college life that make it more conducive to hooking up than dating.

KB: So what's different about home that would make you go out on a date there and not here [at school]?

Jen: [Guys at home] don't have this incredible access to girls like these guys have . . . and there are very beautiful girls here [at State U.], and they have a whole bunch of them in a concentrated area with their apartments and massive amounts of alcohol involved. That's just great opportunity for them [guys at school].

KB: For *them*?

Jen: Yeah definitely. I guess whatever way you look at it; it's a great opportunity [to hook up] if that's what you want. [At home] you like have to meet the parents. And it's not like if I go out and I meet somebody at home that I am interested in, when I'm at a bar or wherever we meet, it's not like I'm going to see him the next night at the same place, or in a week on campus, I might not see him again. So he'll take your number. And if they want to get to know you it's not like they can come over to your parents' house and sleep over . . . they actually have to make that effort to take you out on a date. So that's probably the difference.

KB: And you have gone on formal dates at home [during summer break]?

Jen: Yes.

Jen's explanation of why campus is an easy place to hook up underscores a key point: environment has a major impact on how we conduct our sexual and romantic lives. Environment can refer to many different things, such as geographic location (e.g., the northeastern United States) or neighborhood (e.g., a student's immediate social setting).[2] Although these aspects of environment have an effect on college students, it is the college campus that makes the hookup system thrive.

SEX ON CAMPUS

Hooking up is a means for experiencing casual sexual encounters, but it is also a means for beginning romantic relationships. Many of the college women with whom I spoke were interested in hookup encounters evolving into relationships; men, in general, were less interested in pursuing committed relationships. Regardless of what individual college men and women want, many recognized that, for better or worse, their college years are a time for less serious romantic relationships. Since hooking up is a no-strings-attached approach to sex and relationships, it facilitates "keeping things casual." This outlook on relationships is fueled, in part, by the way students define what it means to be in college in general.[3] Many college students referred to college as being a time to "party" or a time to "let loose." As freshmen, they enter college with the notion that a large part of their college experience should center on having fun. Although college administrators might like to believe that college is about academics, for many students the social aspect of college is equally important, if not more so. Several students, particularly men, spoke of picturing college life to be like the film *Animal House*, which portrays an alcohol- and party-centered lifestyle. Certainly, not all students feel this way. I interviewed many devoted students who put classes first and anything else second. However, even those who do not buy into the idea that "college equals partying" cannot help but be affected by the number of students who live by that sentiment.[4]

If many students define college as a time to have fun and "party," it is not likely that these same students will want to pursue only committed, exclusive relationships, which are believed to interfere with the goal of having fun. As Lee, a freshman at State University, put it: "I had a boyfriend senior year [in high school] and he goes here also. We decided before we got here that we were going to break up and see other people just to do the whole college thing or whatever."

Similarly, Max, a sophomore at State University, discussed how some of his female friends who are currently in relationships often say that experiencing college life is more important than being faithful to a boyfriend. "Then even here [at school] some of the girls are like: 'Yeah I have a boyfriend, *but then again I'm a sophomore in college.'* . . . So, I think the word 'couple' here is vague in the sense that you know in high school what you thought would be cheating . . . may not be [considered] cheating here [at school]. I don't know, it's difficult; it's a touchy subject" [emphasis by interviewee].

Tony, a senior at State University, also talked about the merits of keeping relationships casual during college before entering the "real world" changes things.

> *KB*: Would you say that if somebody hooks up that they tend to hook up with the same person repeatedly or is it generally different people?
>
> *Tony*: For me, it's generally a month or so.
>
> *KB*: You hook up with the same person for a month?
>
> *Tony*: Yeah, and then like I don't know, I find like little like flaws. I don't want to sound like an asshole, but you find little like things that you're not too attracted to and it kind of fades away a little bit. And it might, maybe the girl finds little things too [that she doesn't like about him]. It kind of fades away and then someone else comes along. I think being a senior right now is a big part of it. I think a lot of the seniors right now just like to have someone to hook up with on a steady basis because they know they're going to be graduating soon and once they graduate like that's it, no more college life, so you might as well do it up while you can.
>
> *KB*: Why do you think it will be different after college?
>
> *Tony*: Because you know, real life, real jobs, I've got to wake up every morning at 9 o'clock and do the whole corporate thing. Umm, I think it's a lot easier right now.

In addition to students defining their college years as a time to party, they may also be keeping relationships casual because they are in no hurry to get married. Although there may be some students, particularly women, hoping to meet their future spouse in college, there are many others who are in "no rush" to find their future spouse.[5] Most students I interviewed were not preoccupied with thoughts of marriage, yet almost all of them planned to marry by their mid- to late twenties or early thirties.[6] Therefore, most students believed there would be plenty of time after graduation to find their future spouse.

Despite both male and female college students expressing their wishes to marry several years after graduation, men and women's different timetables for marriage may affect the dynamic between them on campus. In general, women indicated that they were interested in marrying sooner than men: age 29 was their absolute deadline for getting married.[7] Men, on the other hand, did not refer to a deadline for marrying. It seemed that many men wanted to get married *"no sooner* than [age X]," while several women were hoping to get married *"no later* than [age Y]." Violet, a junior at State University, was one of a handful of female students who indicated that marriage was on her mind.

> KB: Do you think about marriage at all?
>
> *Violet:* [Laughing and animated] I was looking at a bride book today while I was at work this morning and I was like: "I can't wait to get married! I just have to have a boyfriend first." It's a mess. But I like all that stuff.
>
> KB: When do you picture yourself getting married?
>
> *Violet:* I'd like to get married after I get a job. But I do need a boyfriend [first]. I have always thought about getting married at age 25. I don't know why but that specific age I always think about. When I get married I want to be 25.

Not surprisingly, none of the college men I spoke to spent time thinking about their future wedding day.

> KB: Do you think that either guys or girls are looking for someone that they're going to end up marrying while they're in school?
>
> *Joseph:* I don't. The way it is now it's like people don't even think about that stuff until they're older now. . . . I know guys who have been dating their girlfriends now for two years. If you mention marriage then they get all like: "What?" [Laughs]

It seems likely that because some women are interested in marrying younger (than most men want to), they are more interested in finding a potential spouse during their college years.[8] Given that the hookup culture is not particularly conducive to relationship formation, this may put men and women's agendas for relationships at odds.

The trend toward marrying later may be fueling the hookup culture on campus. If students do not intend to marry until at least three years after graduation, there is no significant pressure to find their future spouse during their college years. This is particularly the case for the college men, who suggested they did not plan to marry until their late twenties or early thirties. This translates to 5 to 10 years after college to look for a potential spouse. Thus, one's college years can be spent in less serious relationships than those that occupied previous generations. The current hookup script offers a casual alternative to more serious, potentially marriage-bound relationships.

College men and women delaying marriage is part of a larger trend of young people delaying many of the traditional role transitions characteristic of becoming an adult (e.g., parenthood, home ownership, full-time employment, etc.). Due to the postponement of these role transitions, along with changing conceptions of what "becoming an adult" means, researchers have found that over the second half of the twentieth century, 18–22-year-olds have become less likely to think of themselves as adults.[9] Psychologist Jeffrey Jensen Arnett found that traditional college-age youth and beyond (18–25) is a distinct period in the life course. Arnett refers to this life stage, which is after adolescence, but before full-fledged adulthood as "emerging adulthood." Emerging adults are free from some of the parental supervision that adolescents have, but do not have the work and family responsibilities of adults. This freedom allows for experimentation in many areas of life, including relationships.[10]

There may be another factor to consider, which may help to explain why college life lends itself to casual relationships. On many campuses nationwide, there are more women than men. On both campuses included in this study, close to 60 percent of the students are female. In addition, college women often perceive that there are too many "beautiful girls" on campus competing for too few eligible men.[11] This gives women the impression that college men have plenty of women from whom to choose, while college women are stuck competing for a scarce resource. Since most students on both campuses tend to revolve their social lives around university life, they have few opportunities to meet nonstudents.[12] Therefore, for college women, it seems that there are not enough men to go around.

For college men, there may actually be power in lack of numbers. Given the real or perceived sense that there is a shortage of men, there is great incentive for women to "hold on" to one man; however, there is very little incentive for college men to be in an exclusive relationship. This situation puts men and women's goals at odds.[13] Some of the students I interviewed, particularly at State University, like Marie, a senior at State, were keenly aware of the male/female ratio on campus and how this favored men's interests.

> *KB*: So, [from what you are saying] it seems like the guys decide [when it is a relationship or not]?
>
> *Marie*: I feel like they do, I definitely feel like they do because most of the girls I know are looking for *something*, you know someone, even if it's not serious, someone that is there to hang out with and talk to, [girls want] a feeling of being close to someone and I don't know if it's even guys don't want that, it's just they don't care if they have that, it's like: "Whatever." It could be any other girl any night and you know that's fine with them. [Emphasis by interviewee]

Jen, a junior at State University, had this to say:

> *Jen*: I think this school has a lot of pretty girls in it and I do think that's a factor [in understanding male/female interaction on campus]. Because I've been to visit other schools where it's not like that and the guy ratio is stronger. It's different.
>
> *KB*: So there are less guys here is that what you mean by guy ratio?
>
> *Jen*: Hmm-mm. Yeah . . . I just think there are so many pretty girls and that's really not, I don't think too common . . . because there are too many options for these guys. You know? They're not anything that special and they are probably getting to hang out with and having such beautiful girls be so into them . . . I think that it's just great for [men on campus]. They come here and it's just like wherever they turn there's [another girl] and the girls are willing, too.

KB: Willing to what?

Jen: Just hook up with them, you know . . . if the situation was reversed and this school . . . overwhelmingly had awesome looking guys and you know the girls were kind of just all right . . . it would just be in the reverse, I think.

The benefits of having more women than men on campus did not escape several of the male students either. Kyle, a senior at State University, mentions what happens when male friends, particularly friends from the Naval Academy, come to campus for a visit and see how many girls are available. "I don't think every school is like State. . . . I have two friends that go to the Naval Academy. They love coming here; it is like Christmas for them. They are like 'I can't believe [it]. This is great! *I would pay to go to school for this*' because [school] is free for them" [emphasis by interviewee].

Men from Faith University also recognized that the male / female ratio on campus worked to their advantage. Kevin, a senior at Faith, suggests that there is no point wasting a lot of time on one girl: "My attitude is that there are so many girls out there it does not even matter [which one you go after for a hookup]. You can't go psycho over girls, there are just too many of them out there."

Both men and women recognized that men could use the sex ratio on campus to their advantage. While men enjoyed the benefits of the surplus of attractive women on campus, the women expressed displeasure over the opportunity men have to easily find new hookup partners or keep relationships with existing partners casual.

COLLEGE LIFE MAKES HOOKING UP EASY

The hookup system is sustained on campuses because aspects of college life make it simple. One factor that makes hooking up easy is the admissions process. Generally, the college one attends reflects one's social class. At the two universities included in this study, the students are primarily drawn from middle- and upper-middle-class households. There are very few students at either university who would be classified as children of working-class or poor parents. In addition to social class, students at these universities have other important similarities: the overwhelming majority of students on both campuses are white; and, at

Faith University, most students are Catholic and many attended private or parochial high schools. Thus, students at both universities are surrounded by people like themselves. It is well documented that individuals tend to match for potential romantic relationships with people that are similar to themselves in terms of race, age, religion, and social class.[14] This fundamental, although often taken-for-granted fact of life on campus creates an environment where hooking up is more likely. Students can choose hookup partners from a sea of eligible classmates.

Despite the obvious similarities among the student body, on college campuses containing thousands of people, most are strangers to one another. However, students do not *seem* like strangers to each other because they have so much in common—at least they have enough in common to be at the same college in the first place. Students also do not feel like strangers because many of them share friends; so when socializing, a friend is generally there to vouch for any person of interest. The point is that this atmosphere of trust and familiarity makes hooking up easier. Without such an air of familiarity, the hookup system would likely break down.

Another aspect of life on campus that contributes to the hookup culture is the proximity of college men and women to one another. Students living on campus reside in dorms and houses filled with fellow students. Even those who live off-campus are often in apartments or houses near many other students.[15] There are very few restrictions currently on college campuses to keep men and women from having access to one another to engage in hooking up. When asked whether there were any campus policies in place that made it difficult to bring someone home for a hookup, most students suggested that this was no problem whatsoever. However, Jack, a sophomore, mentioned that Faith University does have a policy forbidding sexual intercourse in campus housing.

KB: Do you think the fact that [Faith University] is Catholic makes any difference regarding [sexual interaction on campus]?

Jack: The only thing I could say about that is the "no penetration" rule in the dorms, that's the only thing I can see that would make any other school different.

KB: What's the "no penetration" rule? I never heard of that.

Jack: Apparently you're not allowed to have sex on campus; if you do you're thrown out of school.

KB: Is that right? Has that ever happened to anyone? How would anyone know if you did [have sex] or not?

Jack: An RA walking down the hall hears a girl moaning in her room or hears the bed banging against the wall or your next door neighbor calls security, anything.

KB: Is that something people are worried about, that they are going to get caught? Do people not have sex in the dorms because of that?

Jack: No, they definitely do, they are just a little more careful. It's not announced as much. If you live off campus, it's like: "Who did you bring home last night, I heard the wall shaking?" It's just kind of understood, on campus is definitely tougher.

Thus, there are no campus policies, at least none that were strictly enforced, that keep college students from having easy "late night" access to one another.

Since many residence halls and off-campus housing are within walking distance of a bar, party, or other social event that college students attend, students can go to one another's residence to hook up without violating the taboo of getting in a car with a stranger. Students also generally travel in groups; therefore, a friend is never far away. If a college woman wants to get away from a college man who is trying to hook up with her, she can often rely on her friends to help her out of a difficult situation. Many of the college women I interviewed spoke of "safety in numbers" and "keeping an eye on one another" to help avoid potentially dangerous situations with men. In some cases, a specific woman would be asked to stay sober for the evening to make sure "nothing bad happened" to any of her friends who were drinking alcohol. Living in close proximity to fellow classmates often makes students, especially women, feel safe engaging in a hookup.

A final issue, which makes college campuses an environment conducive to hooking up, is the attention college students pay to what the others are doing. No doubt many college students, particularly during freshman year, are very anxious to be a part of the social scene on campus. Not many people are comfortable being an outcast, nor do they want to be labeled as different than everybody else. Therefore, one of the reasons college students follow the hookup script is likely to be their desire to fit in. The students I interviewed also said that discussing what other students were doing sexually was a common pastime. Thus, who hooked up with whom as well as how far the hookup went sexually is often a topic of conversation among college friends. As Kyle put it: "When I am around my friends I say: 'Did you do it?' They say: 'Yeah I had sex.' . . . We are pretty candid with each other so they will clarify [what happened sexually], unless she is ugly or something. Then they won't tell you, because they are going to get their balls busted."

The pervasiveness of the hookup culture on campus may stem from the lack of privacy and the gossipy nature of life in college. Students are aware of what their classmates do to socialize, form relationships and engage in sexual encounters; and many may go along with hooking up because that's the thing to do.

WHO IS HOOKING UP?

The hookup culture transcends gender, grade level, and institution. Both men and women on the college campuses I studied took part in the hookup system. Additionally, hooking up was not limited to any particular grade level, although a few students suggested that it was more prevalent freshman year. The hookup script was also not confined to one particular campus; in fact, it was pervasive on both campuses I studied.

The universities I studied had some important differences: one is a large state-sponsored university with a diverse population; the other is a smaller faith-based institution where the student body is largely Catholic. Fraternities and sororities exist on both campuses. However, Greek life was more central to the experience of students at State University. Despite the differences, hooking up is very much a part of the social landscape on both campuses. Any differences in norms for the hookup scene seemed to be related more to the size of the institution than its religious affiliation or lack thereof. In my interviews with students at Faith University, I asked whether they thought the religious affiliation of the school had any affect on hooking up on campus. Most students insisted it was completely irrelevant. Lynn, a sophomore, had the following to say:

KB: Do you think Faith University is different in any way because of being a Catholic school?
Lynn: No.

KB: So, Faith would be the same as state schools or wherever?

Lynn: With like hooking up, yeah . . . the Catholic school part does-n't really have [anything] to do with hooking up. Hooking up I think is across the board, it would happen at any col-lege.

Trent, a senior, and I had a similar exchange:

KB: Do you think male-female interaction would be the same no matter what school you went to?

Trent: Yeah.

KB: So, if you went to [a larger state school] or anywhere it would be the same?

Trent: Yeah, the same thing just a different size.

KB: Do you think there's anything different about this school be-cause it's a Catholic school? Does that matter?

Trent: Not really.

KB: So, Catholic or public or state or whatever, the same thing?

Trent: Yeah.

When I asked students on both campuses if they thought the way men and women interact would be the same at other colleges or if there was something unique about their campus, most indicated that they ex-pected it would be the same. Many students mentioned that they had visited other schools to spend time with friends and found hooking up to be common among students there, too. The only difference men-tioned was that some large colleges were deemed "party schools." These schools have a reputation for heavy alcohol consumption and a party atmosphere, with many alcohol-centered social events happening each week. Colleges with this reputation tend to have not only a large student population, but also an active Greek life. Some students sug-gested that this atmosphere might make the hookup scene more anony-mous. In other words, students can hook up and never cross paths again. At smaller institutions this outcome is not a possibility. Max, a sophomore at State University, mentions the anonymity of hooking up at a large school, "You can totally hook up with a girl here and never see her again."

Similarly, Larry, a senior at Faith University, believed there are more anonymous "one and done" type of hookups at the larger state schools, based on his experiences visiting friends at such institutions. "I think [large state schools] would be more random hookups. There would not be as much opportunity at [large state schools] for a long-term relationship. There are just so many people and you don't get to know someone as close as [here at Faith University]."

Although hooking up was commonplace among the student body at both Faith and State universities, there were certain circumstances that affected one's degree of involvement in the hookup scene, including clique and alcohol use. A student's circle of friends, or clique, was a good predictor of how entrenched he or she was in hooking up. The students I talked with who belonged to popular groups on campus, such as fraternities / sororities and athletic teams, were more likely to be heavily involved in hooking up. Fraternity men in particular believed that finding hookup partners was very easy.[16] They suggested a typical number of different hookup partners would be twenty to twenty-five during a semester when they were unattached (i.e., not in an exclusive relationship). Kyle, a senior at State University, mentions how his fraternity brothers can have sex whenever they want to, while this may not be the case for nonfraternity men on campus. "The majority of students probably don't have sex as much as they would like to. My friends have sex, they can and they do when they want to, most nights."

The ease with which fraternity men find hookup partners is not surprising given their notorious involvement with hosting alcohol-driven parties on campus.[17] Greek members are typically at the center of social life on campus; therefore, they are frequently in situations conducive to hooking up.[18]

For students in non-Greek friendship circles, involvement in hooking up was varied. Many students flock to fraternity parties, or other events featuring alcohol, even though they do not actually belong to a fraternity or sorority. These students seemed to have no difficulty finding a hookup partner for the evening. This point is illustrated by Trent, a senior at Faith University. Despite not belonging to a fraternity or thinking of himself as "anything special" looks-wise, Trent reports having great success finding women interested in hooking up.

Trent: If you want to hook up with someone at this school you can any night of the week . . . it just depends if you want to.

KB: Is that regardless of what you look like and what you have going on?

Trent: Like it all depends really on the person. Like I can honestly say I can pretty much hook up with a girl pretty much every night of the week if I wanted to.

Importantly, not all men and women find following the script for hooking up as easy as Trent describes it. Unlike fraternity men, non-Greek students believed a single person would hook up with anywhere from three to ten different people per semester.

KB: Do you know how many people you've hooked up with since you came to [Faith U. two years ago]?
Emily: Umm, maybe like, not necessarily [all] people that go here, maybe like fifteen, maybe like a little more than that.
KB: OK. About fifteen since the beginning of freshman year?
Emily: Yeah, probably.
KB: What do you think would be typical in that regard? In a semester, what would be typical for the people that you know? How many people would someone hook up with in a semester at [Faith]?
Emily: Umm, I would say, like three to five. [Sophomore, Faith University]

Some students found hooking up to be more difficult to accomplish on a regular basis. Ed, a senior at State University, was one of the men who said that his circle of friends found it difficult at times to find hookup partners.

KB: Would you say that hooking up is something that is happening every weekend amongst the group of people you know?
Ed: No, no. We make fun of each other for that, for having it [hooking up] not happen. And that doesn't help the situation.
KB: Because you want it to happen, but you don't always end up with someone?
Ed: Right.

In general, students who struggled with finding hookup partners seemed less involved with social events, particularly events that involved alcohol.

It is important to understand why alcohol plays such a major role in the hookup script. Typically, hookups are initiated during alcohol-centered socializing. According to the college students I spoke to, alcohol makes initiating sexual encounters easier by setting a tone of "kicking back," "letting loose," or "partying."

KB: Say you weren't in a relationship, how would you get together with girls?

Larry: Probably like you're hanging out with a group of male friends, let's say you go to a bar and you're going to meet people obviously from [Faith U]. Around here, the bars are packed with [Faith] people. . . . You know you basically meet them at bars, you're drinking, you're dancing, at different parties you get to see them around campus, so you get to feel people out and things like that . . . maybe I've seen them on campus that day and I say: "What are you doing tonight? Maybe I'll see you [at the bar]" and then the scene changes a lot. Well, the scene changes a lot in that respect if you see someone on campus and you know you'll be talking, let's say male/female, I'll be talking to a girl and you'll be talking about school and stuff like that and then you drop a line and say: "I'll see you at [the local bar] tonight" and you go [there] and they come up and give you a big hug and kiss and the conversation just gets into everything, like crazy things, it really changes from when you're on campus to an outside social experience, it really does change, I feel it really does. [Senior, Faith University]

At bars and parties, college students may be in an environment where they can meet potential hookup partners, but the alcohol helps facilitate the interaction between potentially interested parties. Without alcohol as a social lubricant, the series of nonverbal cues (e.g., eye contact, body language, etc.) used to determine if a potential partner is interested in a hookup could be rather nerve racking. College students also firmly believed that alcohol lowers their inhibitions and makes them want to hook up. Violet, a junior at State University, offered, "When I drink I get like in the mood to hook up and I just want to go and meet as many different people as I can. And I think that is the way that I react when I drink and I am more likely to hook up . . . when I am drinking."

Many other students I spoke with echoed similar sentiments. They suggested that alcohol not only makes them want to hook up, but also leads to (a) hooking with people they otherwise would reject (due to their "beer goggles"), and/or (b) going farther sexually during a hookup.[19] Lynn, a sophomore at State University, discussed a hookup encounter under the influence of alcohol with someone in whom she was not really interested.

KB: How does something get to the point of hooking up . . . how does that interaction happen?

Lynn: Umm, [pauses], well, I'm just trying to think of my experience. Well, one of the nights we had a toga party, it's like an initiation party and everyone gets really drunk and . . . everyone hooked up with everyone else [laughs] and it was just like all crazy and . . . I don't even remember what happened because I was pretty drunk, but I ended up kissing one of the other swimmer guys, that was all that happened. But, later I was like: "Ewww, why did I do that?" But, I don't really remember exactly how it got to that point.

In this particular case, the hook up consisted of "just kissing" and Lynn did not seem particularly upset by it. However, in many cases, heavy alcohol use and subsequent sexual activity can be a dangerous combination. In many states, intoxication is deemed inconsistent with the ability to give meaningful consent to sexual activity.[20] Moreover, in many states, sexual activity while the victim is intoxicated meets the legal definition of rape.[21]

Since students believed that alcohol is a common component to hooking up, students who did not drink alcohol, or at least did not feel comfortable drinking in a party atmosphere, had more difficulty following the hookup script than the more party-focused cliques.

WHO IS NOT HOOKING UP?

With few exceptions, the hookup culture seemed to permeate most groups on campus. However, I did interview several people who did not partake in the hookup scene. Some of these students were already in exclusive relationships. Usually, their relationship began with a hookup or it had carried over from their high school days. Since they were not looking for new partners, they had no need to engage in hooking up. For other students, finding a relationship at college was important because they were not interested in socializing the way that mainstream college students do. One student I interviewed, Robert, considered himself very different from most of the students at Faith University in terms of his interests, outlook on life, and day-to-day activities. He was very involved in student government on campus and an active member of the Boy Scouts. Robert met a woman he was romantically interested in during the first week of his freshman year. He pursued the woman by giving her his Boy Scouts "business card." Although she rejected him at first, he was later able to befriend her and their friendship evolved into an exclusive relationship, which involved going out on dates regularly.

> KB: Did you want a girlfriend because you weren't comfortable with [the hooking-up] system? Or did it just so happen that you found a girlfriend?
>
> Robert: Actually I abhor the whole idea of [hooking up]. I don't think you actually allow yourself to get to know the other person [that way]. . . . So I didn't really think of it as a manly thing to see how many girls [I] could get. I was never outrightly denied by a girl until [my current girlfriend] came along. [She] totally denied me the first time I ever met her. . . . But I really didn't like the idea of trying to get as many girls as [I] could [via hooking up]. Since I was traveling so much [with the Boy Scouts], I almost told her: "I will be traveling a lot and if this will be hard tell me now because I don't want to string you along." So I wasn't looking for a girlfriend [per se], but I wasn't looking to hook up with people [either].

Although Robert acknowledged that the hookup system was typical for men and women on Faith's campus, he was not interested in doing that himself and felt that his lack of interest in hooking up, in favor of a more traditional style of dating, made him "abnormal."

Another student I spoke to, Hannah, a junior at State University, abstained from hooking up due to her religious beliefs. Hannah believed her Christian faith was a central part of who she is and what she does; religion was not just another demographic category, something in the back of her mind. Rather, she possessed a very active faith; it was a central part of her identity and her daily activities. Hannah rejected the dominant hookup culture on campus because she believed hooking up was immoral. "The people I hang out with aren't really those kind of people who just have a one-night thing. I think of hooking up as a one-night kind of thing and myself and people I know don't do that."

Hannah was not a part of the alcohol-centered, party lifestyle; instead, she socialized within a close-knit group of friends who were also very religious.

Hannah: I don't really feel comfortable spending time with people who don't think in a similar fashion to me.
   KB: Do you consider yourself part of the mainstream of State University in terms of what students do socially?
Hannah: No.
   KB: What do you think of as mainstream and how are you different from that?
Hannah: Mainstream [means] the weekend starts on Thursday, you know, you go out drinking and partying, that kind of thing.
   KB: That's what you feel most students do?
Hannah: A lot do that and it kind of overshadows those of us who have a mellow weekend.

Hannah and her friends were interested in finding serious relationships. Although she found a relationship with someone who shared her religious beliefs, she said that many of her friends had difficulty finding "mature" relationships on campus. It may be that some students, like Robert and Hannah, seek exclusive relationships to avoid the hookup scene on campus.

Although most of the participants in this study were white, I did interview a few minority students.[22] These men and women recognized that hooking up was very common on campus; however, they did not engage in this practice. Lannette, an African American sophomore at Faith University, knew what hooking up meant, but did not do it herself.

   KB: Is [hooking up] a term you use or is that a term you just more heard?
Lannette: Um, I don't really use the term "hooked up" so it's more what I hear. Like if someone said: "Yeah I hooked up with

him," I understand what they're talking about. But, me personally, I wouldn't say [it].

KB: Are you involved in . . . the hookup scene at all?

Lannette: No, cause I mean . . . I'm not really the type that just goes
around and hooks up with random people. That's just not
my . . . you know, that's not who I am. . . . Even if I'm interested in a boy, I won't just hook up with [him] randomly. . . .
Like, I want to get to know him first and all that. That's just
not my thing; so I'm not really in that whole category, just
hookups.

Instead of hooking up, she indicated that she generally met men
through friends or local "hangouts" at home. Once she met someone of
interest, she would start "talking" to him. During the process of getting
to know each other, the two may go out on something resembling a traditional date or they may "just chill" together at someone's home. Lannette, and other minority students I spoke with, used the term "talking"
somewhat differently from their white counterparts.

KB: What about the . . . word, I think you mentioned it—"talking." If someone says "we're talking" what does that mean?

Lannette: It means like, I guess, um, when you're interested in someone, I guess you want to, if you don't already know them
you know you want to get to know them so you know you're
I guess "talking" to get to know the person. Um, you're not
necessarily with them or . . . so you might think: "Okay it's
possible that we would become . . . a boyfriend or girlfriend,
but you know maybe not." So it's like kind of like a beginning stage of a possible relationship. Um, talking to someone
is pretty much just getting to know them. . . . If you already
do know them, like if . . . you're friends for a while and you
start talking—it's more like: "Okay I realize that I might
want to be with you." So you spend more time with them
and you kind of limit talking to other guys or girls.

For the minority students I spoke to, particularly African Americans,
"talking" preceded being "with" someone as an exclusive couple.

Lannette also indicated that her minority friends on campus do not
participate in the hookup scene on campus. Their decision to abstain

was not necessarily a moral one, but perhaps more of a practical decision. The people I spoke with said many minority students are not interested in sexual encounters and relationships with white students (and vice versa). Therefore, on campuses that are overwhelmingly white, minority students often socialize among themselves on campus and keep close ties with friends from home.[23]

In addition to speaking to a handful of minority students, I also talked to a few gay and lesbian students.[24] These students said they were not involved with the dominant hookup culture on campus. These students often struggled to reveal their sexual identity to fellow classmates and, therefore, had difficulty finding other gay and lesbian students for potential sexual and romantic relationships.

> *KB*: So for meeting someone . . . of the same sex or socially interacting, how does all of that work for you? How does it work if you're not . . . heterosexual . . . [at Faith University]?
> *Timothy*: You're like: "Is he [gay] or is that just wishful thinking?" [Laughing] I wish I had glasses I could like put on and people would appear; it's like my glasses would be blue if they see people who are blue that means they're gay. [Freshman, Faith University]

Unlike heterosexual students who had a system in place to find partners, homosexual students were more or less on their own in their quest to find potential partners. As Timothy added, "It's harder to meet anyone, other than like to go to a bar that you know specifically everyone's gay or most people are because there are straight people, a few, that go to gay clubs and stuff. But um, you don't know on campus [who is gay]." Jonathan, a sophomore at Faith University, offered the following: "No one at the gay bar is going to smack you on the head because you're like: 'Hey you want to dance?' and they're like: 'No I'm straight, I'm sorry.' Nobody's going to freak out at you at the gay bar because you asked them to dance because *you're at a gay bar.* But on campus . . . you couldn't just be like: 'Hey do you want [to get] a drink?' or something" [emphasis by interviewee].

Gay students would like to be able to meet other gay or lesbian students and initiate relationships on campus; however, the lack of options for doing so leads them to look for off-campus alternatives for socializing and forming potential relationships. Having to go outside the arguably safer confines of the campus perhaps puts these students at greater risk; on the other hand, as Jonathan points out, there is a level of acceptance and security that they can find in "gay safe" or "queer positive" spaces that often are difficult to find on the college campus.[25]

Students who do not participate in the hookup culture on campus are on the margins of the social scene and they know it. For some, the hookup scene is not a viable option due to their minority status or sexual orientation. For others, avoiding hooking up is a choice. Some students do not like the hookup scene and others find that they do not possess the social skills needed to navigate the hookup script. One student, who considered herself extremely religious, was very opposed to the hookup scene. Rebecca, a sophomore at State University, preferred to develop friendships with men that she hoped would evolve into relationships. When she was not successful finding a boyfriend her way, she reluctantly engaged in hooking up a few times. However, she was disappointed that these encounters did not lead to a relationship, either. "Because I hooked up [with him] before we went to spring break and then I decided that *he needs to be a man* and start the relationship, you know [I would tell myself], I'm not going to do anything [to start the relationship] and umm, after I stopped talking to him that's when I heard that he was hooking up with other girls" (emphasis by interviewee). Rebecca's frustration with the fact that hookup partners often do not initiate a relationship is consistent with many women on campus.[26]

Simon, a junior at State University, also had problems with the hookup system. In Simon's case, he was interested in finding a relationship, but did not want to do so via the hookup script. He felt that his personality did not lend itself to initiating sexual or romantic encounters with strangers.

KB: Is [State U.] a place where you can find relationships easy? Or is it hard here?

Simon: I think it's easy; I am just not very good at it.

KB: What do you think is the reason you are not good at it?

Simon: I think it's easy because there are so many people here and the overwhelming ratio of females to males; isn't there?

KB: 60 percent [female], 40 percent [male].

Simon: Yeah. But I am just not very good at going, especially with just like going up to somebody completely new that I know nothing about. I am a very shy person generally. [Laughs]

Simon did not like the alcohol-driven party scene that he felt most students were involved in on campus. Therefore, he tried to rely on close friends to introduce him to women, but did not have much luck finding a relationship this way, either. Due to his struggles, Simon admitted that he once resorted to calling a former high school girlfriend to come over to his place for a hookup encounter. To his surprise, she agreed.

Even students who were heavily involved in the hookup culture on campus recognized that various factors, including personality and attractiveness, dictate someone's success with this script. The shy "Simons" and the reserved "Rebeccas" of campus do not travel in the same social circles as the "popular crowd." Kevin, a senior at Faith University and an outgoing athlete who frequently hooked up, discussed students who are not as successful in the hookup scene.

Kevin: On the other side there are guys that probably aren't very good at hooking up, probably don't do it a lot. . . . They are not comfortable in themselves to initiate hooking up. We are in a bar and nobody looks different, everybody is wearing the same Banana Republic clothes, the same Gap [clothes] . . . it's hard to differentiate anybody so it's you; you are selling you. . . . [Some guys] are not good deal closers in this setting because they don't have the game. I don't want to say the word "game" again because you probably don't like that word, but they don't have enough game to close the deal.

KB: I'm fine with the word game, but I still want you to explain a little more what game is.

Kevin: The ability to talk. The ability to interact and communicate with the opposite sex. That's your game. Your game would be like your angle. How you talk, how you communicate, how you express yourself. Some guys will come up and tell you their whole life story or some guys will treat you like shit in order to get you to like them more, which happens. It sounds crazy, it sounds like the most asinine thing in the world, but it happens. That's their game; that's their angle. Trying to get to know you, hook up with you, whatever their objective is. Because I could meet a girl . . . and all I want to do is get to know her. That's my game. Ask her questions about herself, where she's from . . . ask her if she knows people I know, maybe that will lead to stories. If I'm interested in her I'm almost pumping her for information and vice versa goes for her. If she starts pumping you for information, she's interested in you too.

There may be individuals who abstain from hooking up; however, there is no obvious alternative for them if they are interested in sexual interaction with the opposite sex on campus. Although some students were able to find a relationship without hooking up, most students see hooking up as the "only game in town." Due to the lack of alternatives, most students either adapt to the hookup scene or get left out. Thus, whether one is an active participant, a moderate participant, or someone who abstains altogether, no student is untouched by the pervasive hookup culture on campus.

5

The Campus as a Sexual Arena

On the cover of *Glamour* magazine's February 2006 issue is 21-year-old pop singer / actress and "America's Next Sweetheart," Mandy Moore. Among the cover stories in this issue is a feature entitled "Are you normal about sex? Intimate details on what *everyone's* doing." Popular-culture sources, like this one, are one of the ways by which young people get information about sex and relationships. Like most men and women, college students want to know what is "normal," because understanding the norms for their peer group helps them to navigate their own sexual lives.[1] College students' perceptions of what their peers are doing sexually are shaped, in part, by the messages they receive through pop culture, but perhaps even more so by peer culture. College students do not have to pick up a magazine or turn on the television to find out what their contemporaries are up to—they can just look around campus. This makes the college campus a sexual arena.

Some of the students I interviewed, like Adrienne, a senior at Faith University, keenly felt a sense of watching and being watched and talking and being talked about in the campus sexual arena.

Adrienne: Yeah, definitely [I have] a complex about looks around here [on campus]. There's a saying that [Faith University] gives out more eating disorders than diplomas. . . . when I came here for open house, I was like: "Oh [this is a] laid-back kind of campus." The girls are like dressing in Gap or Old Navy or something like that. And then I came here [to start freshman year] and I was like: "Oh my God it's like all the girls are dressed up, done up, all the time." [I] never felt like you could wear sweatpants to class. The girls were "on" like 24/7 and it made me very self-conscious.

KB: Why do you think the girls are dressed like that and why are they "on" all the time?

Adrienne: I think a lot of it is like fashion. There is like very wealthy [students here]. I feel like that's what they spend their money on is like clothes. Everybody here, not everybody, a lot of people here have really nice clothes from all the designers and stuff like that. So they know how to dress if they . . . come from that kind of circle. So I think they dress for that. But I do think on the weekends they dress like revealing for the guys. So I think they do, like hope to attract guys when they're doing that.

Another senior at Faith University, Robert, added this exchange:

Robert: I think a lot of women dress comfortably for *them* but for *guys* [they see it as] very provocative. If you look now on this campus, [you will see] very short, shorts and tight shirts. You can see cleavage and I think guys kind of accept that and they also will just sit out there and look. They'll be like: "She's an 8. She's a 5, or a 10+." Guys still rate girls when they walk by. Guys like to look at girls and their body structure.

   KB: Would girls be thought of as "sleazy" or "slutty" if they were dressing in a provocative way or is that just [seen as] normal?

Robert: I think it is just normal, as long as it's not see-through. [Emphasis by interviewee]

Adrienne and Robert describe somewhat of a fishbowl existence for students on campus, particularly women. Students were aware that they were on display for other students, especially members of the opposite sex; but watching one another extended far beyond observations on style of dress. Students were also monitoring one another's sexual relationships. Outside of campus, sexual encounters are largely a private matter; but during college, men and women are highly aware of what their peers are doing sexually. Much of the hookup script, from the initial signaling of interest to pairing off with someone, is enacted publicly. At parties students watch one another, the next day they gossip about each other, and while socializing with close friends, they ask about their sexual and romantic relationships. Gloria, a freshman at State University, had firsthand experience of this: "[A few acquaintances and I] were talking the other day out [in front of the dorm] having a cigarette . . . they were like: 'Who do you think is [a virgin]?'" Kevin, a senior at Faith University, elaborates:

> [When you are at a party with friends], they will see you putting work in. Like if I'm at the bar with my friends and me and you meet and I'm talking to you all night, then I disappear with you, I don't say: "Hey, I'm leaving," we just disappear. The next morning I come home, they will know that. [And then they'll say:] "Did you go home with that girl you were talking to? Oh shit!" They'll know that they saw me putting the work in. Talking, hitting on, that's what it is. So if you are not out with them and you walk in [the next day], they are not going to do that, but you may say: "I hooked up last night." In college, every morning it was like ten of us sitting around watching TV on three different couches. So if someone did walk in, say it was Tyler, [we would] say: "Tyler, we saw you working on that girl last night." He'd be like: "Yeah, I'm coming home right now." We call it the walk of shame, which is the walk across campus after you hooked up in the same clothes you went out in the night before.

On the campuses I studied, this fascination with one another's "personal" life was central to the college experience.[2] Thus, sexual behavior, far from being a private matter, is happening under the watchful eyes and curious ears of all who inhabit the college campus.

PERCEPTION OF OTHERS

College students' preoccupation with the sexual behavior of their classmates is not all for idle gossip. By studying how other men and women behave, college students learn the norms for their peer group, which in turn affects their own choices. It is important to find out how students view their classmates' behavior because students define their own sexual behavior relative to others, particularly other students of the same sex. College men I spoke with perceive other men in the hookup culture as being very preoccupied with sex. When I asked if they believed the stereotype that men's actions are sex driven, almost all of the men agreed with the stereotype. In fact, several men suggested that college men cannot avoid being preoccupied by sex because it is "natural" for men to be this way. Kyle, a senior at State University, agreed:

> *KB*: There is a stereotype that college guys, especially fraternity guys are very sex driven, that that is what they are looking for. Would you agree with that?
>
> *Kyle*: You are in a big house, a lot of beer, you have a lot of friends and have parties, and if that results in [sex, so be it] . . . I think all guys like to have a lot of sex [not just fraternity men]. It's just testosterone.

My exchange with Trent, a senior from Faith University, further amplifies this attitude:

> *KB*: Do you think either guys or girls typically have more [hookup] partners?
>
> *Trent*: Oh, guys without a doubt.
>
> *KB*: And why do you think that is?
>
> *Trent*: Guys, *it's just the way we are.* I really don't know . . . the guy will go for it more than a girl would, like he'll go out and try to hook up, where a girl will just see what happens, you know what I mean. That's at least my experience. [Emphasis added]

Although the men generally thought that all college men, including themselves, were preoccupied with sex, they suggested that it was *other* men who had really low standards or would be willing to "sleep with anyone." Or as Kevin, a senior at Faith University, put it, "A few of my friends . . . don't care what the girl looks like, they just want to get laid." Another senior at Faith University, Trent, said, "I'm not like my one friend; he'll hook up with anyone just to hook up with her. You know, he'll sleep with anyone just to sleep with them, he doesn't care." Jack, a sophomore at Faith University, offers a similar view.

> *KB*: So, it depends on the girl [whether she will have sex or not]? What about guys, does it depend on the guy or is the guy up for whatever the girl is up for?
>
> *Jack*: There have been cases where I turned [sex] down, but most of my roommates . . . they generally are up for anything.

Consistent with other college men I spoke with, Kevin, Trent, and Jack defined their own sexual behavior relative to what they believed others were doing in the sexual arena. These men were very active members in the hookup scene, yet they viewed their sexual behavior as "not that bad" compared to what some of their friends do. Inevitably, it was other men who engaged in truly promiscuous behavior, not the person I interviewed.

While many men favored the idea that college men are looking for sex, the women I interviewed believed that college women were looking for relationships. As Adrienne, a senior at Faith University, put it, "It always seems like the girls want to . . . come back for more contact [after a hookup] and the guys are like one night, that's it." Lynn, a sophomore at Faith University, agrees:

> *KB*: What about girls, what do you find girls are looking for in terms of guys, are they looking for sex, too, are they looking for hooking up, are they looking for relationships?
> *Lynn*: If the girl likes the guy, I think she might be interested in finding out if she wants to pursue a relationship. I kind of think guys have this theory that either you hook up or you get married. Like if I was to tell [a guy] I liked him then he would get like so scared and freaked out because [men think]: "Oh my God that means we have to be in a relationship" and it doesn't mean that. I think most girls are looking to try and pursue a relationship, but aren't just going to go up to a guy and be like: "Oh, want to be my boyfriend?" you know what I mean? I think that girls do look for relationships more than guys would.
> *KB*: From what you just described . . . when you said looking for a possible relationship, you might be interested in *something* happening, but don't expect it overnight to be a really close committed relationship. Is that what you mean?
> *Lynn*: Exactly. [Emphasis added]

Liz, a freshman at Faith University, offered the following:

> *KB*: Do you find either guys or girls are looking for relationships?
> *Liz*: Girls are; guys are not.
> *KB*: Why do you think girls are?

Liz: Why wouldn't you want a boyfriend because it's kind of like you're living with them. You know what I'm saying? Like, if you have a boyfriend at home it's different because like you live at home [with your] mom and dad you know. You can't be out until [whatever time] you want. You can't do whatever you want. And here you can and I mean you're the one who sets your own rules. But, if you have a boyfriend like oh how nice would it be if I could just like, oh I just want someone to watch a movie with right now. Or like, I just want to like go out to dinner with him. Or I just want to stay in and like hang out with him, and you can do that. Oh like, I'm going to sleep there tonight or he's going to sleep here tonight. And like you can do that here and you can't do that at home. And girls realize that I think more so than guys and that's what they want. Like: "Uh, if I just had a boyfriend it would be so much better right now because like there's nothing to do and I can just hang out with him." You know? And um, that's how we look at it.

KB: And why don't guys feel the same way?

Liz: Well, maybe because they don't like doing that kind of stuff as much as girls do. I mean some guys do I guess but for the most part I'm sure they'd rather go out and get drunk than sit at home with some chick you know and watch TV. And that's like all I want to do [laughs].

Many women echoed these sentiments. That is, they think college women are looking for something beyond a hookup, although they do not expect "instant relationships," either. Rather, they perceived college women as wanting to find someone with whom they could at least potentially have a relationship. Some, on the other hand, believed college women wanted a greater level of commitment by seeking a relationship with "marriage potential."[3]

Despite their belief that college women were looking for relationships, the women I interviewed suggested they knew some women who would "randomly" have sex outside the context of a relationship. Just as the college men believed that *other* men were engaged in more promiscuous sexual behavior than themselves, the college women believed *other* women were the promiscuous ones. Lisa and Lee, two sophomores at State University, are examples of this mentality.

KB: Would you say that most students are having sex or are most
     stopping short of that?

Lisa: [laughs] A few of my . . . girlfriends . . . just randomly have
       sex with people [laughs], but I don't do that.

Lee: One of my girlfriends is not [in a relationship] and she is
      very promiscuous. For her it's just—if it feels good, do it.
      That mentality.

KB: You said this one friend is promiscuous. What fits your def-
     inition of promiscuous?

Lee: Sleeping with a number of guys without having a relation-
      ship. I mean she is friends with them, she knows them, it's
      not like they are random guys. But they are not her
      boyfriend, they don't have any ties.

Similarly, Diane, a sophomore at Faith and a very active member of the
hookup culture, explained that when she has a hookup encounter, it
only involves kissing. However, she believed others take a hookup
much farther sexually.

Diane: Like I won't go home with a guy and like sleep with him that
        night. [But other] girls do that.

KB: Okay, what do you think other people do typically?

Diane: Typically either they go out, get drunk, hook up with a guy,
        go back, either have sex with him or give him like head. So
        like, I don't do that either. Like my roommate does that. And
        like a lot of people do [but unlike them] I'm just like in
        charge.

In addition to looking to their same-sex counterparts on campus, college students are also interested in what the opposite sex wants. I
asked both men and women what they believed about each other. According to the men, college women want three things. At a minimum,
women want something more than just a hookup or casual sex. Second, some women want exclusive relationships; and, third, at least
some women want to find a potential marriage partner. Ed and Kyle,
both seniors at State, addressed the differences in what men and
women want.

KB: What do you think guys or girls are looking for. . . . Are they looking for relationships, are they looking for sex? What do you think they're looking for?

Ed: I would say that guys are mostly looking for sex. And some of the girls are looking for sex, but more girls than guys are looking for relationships, but not necessarily a permanent relationship just something that's more than just a couple hookups or casual sex.

KB: Are men and women both on the same page or are they looking for different things?

Kyle: I would say that sometimes the girls are looking for different things. One of my close friends just was going out for six months and the girl said she wanted it to move to the next level and get engaged and it scared him off. On average, more of the girls want more than just the "one and done" thing. . . . Probably [girls want] to "go out" [i.e., become a couple].

Later in the interview, Kyle discusses whether he thinks men and women are looking for potential marriage partners during college.

KB: Do you think both guys and girls are looking for [marriage]?

Kyle: I think girls more so than guys. I know girls who come to college, and major in painting or sewing or something, to find guys, to find people to go out. They take majors that, not that you need to make a ton of money, but you are going to have a difficult time in today's job market finding a job that is going to make any living.

KB: So you think they are here spouse shopping?

Kyle: Not the majority, but I do know girls that do that.

Kevin, a senior at Faith University, offered a similar view:

KB: [You said earlier that] guys are looking for sex all the time. What are girls looking for?

Kevin: A husband.

KB: Even when they are [in college]?

Kevin: Hmm-hmm.

These men seemed to believe college women today are not much different than their 1950s-era counterparts. It was during this time that people began to suggest that women attended college in order to get their "MRS" degree. This idea was not completely unfounded considering two-thirds of women who attended college in the 1950s dropped out before finishing their degree, usually to marry.[4]

Just as the college men I spoke to believed that some women are looking for sex, but most are looking for relationships, the college women believed that some men are looking for relationships, but that most are looking for sex. Some took this a step farther, believing that men were very focused on sex with multiple partners, even when they were already hooking up repeatedly with one particular woman.

> *KB*: Do you have any sense of what people are looking for out of [a hookup]? Do you think people are looking for relationships or the physical . . . aspects?
>
> *Gloria*: I think guys definitely look for the hottest girl and want to "get ass" from that girl and want to say they got it from that girl. [Freshman, State University]

> *KB*: If someone is not in a relationship, how many times might someone hook up in a semester, like how many different people in a semester?
>
> *Marie*: Guys, God, they'll hook up with anybody [laughing], it really just doesn't matter. I've seen guys with a different girl every week, they don't care. I've seen guys cheat on their girlfriends and not care. Girls definitely care more. And I think if girls, even if they're not in a relationship with somebody, but they have hooked up with somebody a couple times, they tend to not hook up with someone else just because they like this person. I think guys will hook up with every other [available] person [even] if they are [primarily] hooking up with one person [laughing]. [Senior, State University]

> *KB*: Would you say that guys or girls typically have more [sex] partners or are they about the same?
>
> *Jen*: Guys. Umm, guys do.
>
> *KB*: Why do you think that is?
>
> *Jen*: Because they want to.

KB: And girls don't want to?

Jen: They don't feel the need to as much as guys do. Because [in theory] a girl could have just as many partners as a guy, but there has to be a reason why guys have more [sexual partners] and it's because they go after it more.

KB: So would you say that guys are more sex driven, and looking for that more?

Jen: Yeah I think that [guys] have a better ability to separate sex and feelings. [For] girls, it usually means a little bit more. It is harder to make that distinction so [girls] might be more hesitant to sleep with somebody than guys would. [Junior, State University]

Both men and women I interviewed believed that men have more sexual partners than women.[5] For college women, this led to concern that men would engage in sexual intercourse without any genuine feelings for the other person. Given this concern, Jen offered advice to incoming freshman women to avoid being hurt by men who are only interested in sex: "I would basically [advise]: 'Keep your eyes open to people and make sure you're not stupid about the guys that you like. You should make [sure] that they can't pull a fast one on you. You know how [some] guys think that they are going to have sex with you one night and never call . . . so you just have to be aware.'" Women's perception of men as being focused on sex without feeling applied particularly to fraternity members. According to several of the college women I spoke with, fraternity men are "all alike" and they tend to "use" women for sexual purposes without any interest beyond that.[6] Lisa, a sophomore at State University, had this to say about fraternity men:

I don't like the frat guys, at least a lot of them and I just think they're all cocky and they think the world of themselves and they're not really that cool [laughs]. To me, they're all little spiked hair look-alike guys . . . there's still, I think there's still a lot of sexism that goes on and . . . there's still things that need to be better. . . . I've seen girls kiss each other just because they want to get attention, not because they're lesbians or whatever. And the frat guys encourage them to do stuff like that. So, stuff like that, I just think is so stupid and I mean, it's partly the girls' fault for wanting that kind of attention and doing whatever they can to get boys' attention. But, it's also the guys' fault for encouraging it and, you know, trying to get girls to do stuff like that.

In addition to Lisa, several other women believed fraternity men embodied the persona of the sex-driven college male. Moreover, these women believed that fraternity men mistreated women in order to maximize their sexual conquests.[7]

Overall, students' perceptions on the motives of their peers were correct. In general, men are more likely to pursue women for sex and women are more likely to pursue men for relationships.[8] Both men and women did acknowledge that some women engage in hooking up for sex, while some men want girlfriends. Thus, there are differences within gender (as well as across gender) in how students interact. However, I found that the disparity between the motivations of men and women was a significant theme that profoundly affects the interaction between the sexes on campus.

DISTORTED PERCEPTIONS

Despite students' interest in the sexual activities of their classmates, their perception of what is going on behind closed doors is often inaccurate.[9] Although the initial stages of the hookup script occur out in the open at campus parties or bars, much of the sexual activity between hookup partners happens in private. Therefore, figuring out what others are doing sexually is often left to guesswork. One misperception that students have is that virginity is rare.[10] Students believed the hookup scene was pervasive on campus, so they felt it was unlikely that many of their fellow classmates could maintain their virginity. Interestingly, even those students who were virgins believed the overwhelming majority of students on campus were not virgins. When asked whether there might be a lot of virgins on campus, Adrienne, a senior from Faith University, said, "No. I don't think so . . . like freshman year in college I was like, I just felt like I was like the only virgin."

Students also suggested that even if someone was still a virgin when they came to college, they would not remain that way for long.[11] Several students indicated that they did not know even one person they believed to be a virgin.

KB: Do you think virginity is common [on campus]?

Marie: Not anymore. Not in college, maybe freshman college girls, there were plenty of girls I knew that were virgins as freshmen that definitely were not [virgins anymore] by the end of their freshman year.

KB: Do you know anyone that is [a virgin] now . . . male or female?

Marie: Nope. [Senior, State University]

Jack, a sophomore at State University, relayed the following:

KB: What about virginity, do you think that's something that's common on campus?

Jack: Gone by next year.

KB: [Laughs]. So, freshmen might come in that way, but they don't stay that way?

Jack: Not very long.

KB: So, do you know anyone that still is [a virgin] now that you're a sophomore?

Jack: [Pauses]. Hmm, no. Yeah, I actually do know one [girl that is a virgin].

Although college students did not think there were many virgins on campus, some of them did view virginity positively.[12] A couple students, who were sexually active, even suggested that they wished they were still virgins (or at least they wished they had "lost" their virginity to someone else or under different circumstances). I asked Emily, a sophomore at Faith University, how virginity was viewed.

Emily: I think it's positive, like to be a virgin is a positive thing, like I think virginity is something that is important and sacred and shouldn't just be given away.

KB: If you feel comfortable answering, have you had sex before?

Emily: Yes.

KB: In high school?

Emily: No, in college. . . . This is bad, but it was a really bad decision and I was drunk and [there are] a lot of issues I have around it . . . it's not so much that I care that I'm not a virgin, it's just that I care that I have to say that it was *with him*, so [there are] a lot of issues, but it was a bad decision. [Emphasis by interviewee]

Other students seemed neutral on the subject; that is, they did not express a strong opinion one way or another about virginity. These students described the decision to have sexual intercourse as an individual or personal decision.

> KB: Is virginity ever something that is talked about on campus? Do you know anyone who is a virgin or is that something they keep private?
>
> Violet: In my group of friends, they talk about everything. My one best friend from high school is not having sex until she is married. And she had no problem telling anybody that, it is not a big thing for her.
>
> KB: Is that something that people view positively or negatively?
>
> Violet: I don't view it any way. I have friends who have sex and who don't. It's all a personal preference. [Junior, State University]

Although some students, like Violet, implied that there are no negative consequences for being a virgin or for being sexually active, the majority of people I interviewed indicated otherwise. For women, a host of concerns accompany the decision to become sexually active. Men, on the other hand, reported a risk of being stigmatized if they decided to remain a virgin.[13] Several male students mentioned that a man who was known to be a virgin would be mercilessly teased by his male friends. Kevin, a senior at Faith University, recounted an interesting story in this regard.

> KB: [Is] there anyone that [is] known as a virgin, either male or female?
>
> Kevin: Oh yeah, but none at my school. (Laughs) This is a great story for you actually. My friend Don went away to school [in a different state] and he was a fraternity brother and I used to go visit him . . . and his buddy Mike [is] a good looking guy . . . he's a music major . . . he does not seem gay, [he is] very [muscular]. . . . And one Thanksgiving, [Don and Mike came up for a visit to a local bar and] Don looks at Mike and says: "Hey, your wallet's open, show him your V-card."

> And I was like: "What's your V-card?" And [Mike says]: "Here you go" [and hands the card to me]. So, [Mike's friends] had the card made for him, it was a V-card, a virgin card, and whatever girl he first has sex with, he's got to give her the V-card and she has to keep it. And I'm like: "Oh, my God, you told these guys [that you're a virgin]?" . . . He's very confident, he doesn't care, he laughs about it. So, I look at him and I'm like: "So, you're not a deal closer, huh?" And he's like: "Nope." And that's his problem . . . a lot of girls like him, they flirt with him, but he can't close the deal.

Despite perceptions, virginity is not a rarity. A national study on college women, conducted in 2001, found a 39 percent virginity rate. This study also found that the virginity rate was still 31 percent among college women in their senior year.[14] Other national data on both college men and women indicates that the virginity rate is approximately 25 percent.[15] Regardless of the precise number, there are more virgins on campus than most students believe.

The way students I spoke with viewed virginity (and the loss of it) was consistent with sociologist Laura Carpenter's findings on the meanings men and women assign to virginity loss. Specifically, in her book *Virginity Lost,* Carpenter found that most young people think of the loss of one's virginity as giving "a gift," something to be cherished or treasured and "given away" with great care; as "a stigma," as something to be lost quickly and even as secretly as possible; or as a "rite of passage," or something that one must relinquish in the process of becoming an adult.[16]

A second misperception is that "everybody's doing it." Students tend to overestimate the number of hookup encounters that involve sexual intercourse. In a representative study of college undergraduates at a large northeastern university, 78 percent of the students had hooked up at least once. However, among the students that had engaged in a hookup, only 38 percent ever had a hookup that culminated in sexual intercourse, while 61 percent had engaged in hooking up without such an encounter ever culminating in sexual intercourse.[17]

The ambiguous nature of the term "hooking up" often seemed to generate confusion over *precisely* what other students are doing sexually. Most students agreed that hooking up could be anything from kissing to having sexual intercourse, but, when pressed, some students seemed to favor the idea that when most students hook up it likely involves sexual intercourse. Larry and Kevin both illustrated the confusion the term "hooking up" generates.

KB: You mentioned hooking up earlier, how would you define hooking up?

Larry: Hooking up, umm [pauses] probably spending the night at someone's place, whether there's sex or not doesn't really matter. Probably spending the night at someone's place, like obviously kissing, something physical, things going on, it doesn't so much have to be sex.

KB: Could it be [sex]?

Larry: Could it be, sure, absolutely.

KB: Have you ever hooked up where it was sex?

Larry: Yeah, sure.

KB: Is one more likely than the other? Is it likely to not be sex? Is it likely to be kissing and sleeping in the same bed? What is most likely to happen?

Larry: *Probably it would be sex, I would think.* It's kind of a random short-term thing, umm if the person is getting to know you, you may be just hooking up with them, like kissing and like just some physical contact and then it evolves into sex later on [in a subsequent hookup].

KB: So, you hook up with the same person repeatedly and eventually it [leads to sexual intercourse]?

Larry: Sure. [Emphasis added] [Senior, Faith University]

KB: [Do you] have a sense of whether most people are having sex or most people are hooking up [without actually having intercourse].

Kevin: Mostly sex.

KB: Mostly sex?

Kevin: Yeah.

KB: Okay. Even on the first encounter?

Kevin: Yeah. [Senior, Faith University]

Later in the interview, Kevin described a number of hookup situations that did not seem to include intercourse. Therefore, I asked him to clarify whether a hookup generally culminated in sexual intercourse.

KB: You've been using the term "hooking up" a lot but you had said earlier that you thought sex was more common than [just] hooking up [without actually having sexual intercourse].

Kevin: Did I? Are you sure?

KB: Yeah.

Kevin: Usually people are having sex. I will still stick with that.

The ambiguous nature of the term is undoubtedly part of its appeal. Individuals are able to share with others that they did something sexual without necessarily specifying what happened. The problem is that this ambiguity leads to confusion over what other students are doing sexually. Some students seemed to favor the idea that hooking up must mean sexual intercourse in the majority of cases. However, very few students indicated that when they hooked up they always had sexual intercourse. It was always *other* students who, they believed, actually had intercourse every time they hooked up. Gloria, a freshman at State University, illustrates the idea that it is other students who "go farther" sexually during a hookup encounter.

Gloria: You kiss them [a guy at a party] and then they'll be like: "Come back with me to my place, sleep at my place." And you'll either say yes or no.

KB: Do you ever have guys come back to your room?

Gloria: No. Maybe once. I'm really good with that, I don't know, just my morals. I had one guy come over but it wasn't even for me, he had a girlfriend, he just stayed over. But I have friends and they have guys sleep over all the time. Sometimes they'll wake up and say: "What did I do?" and sometimes it's nothing . . . *most girls, granted they'll have sex with them* and the next day they'll regret it.

KB: By sex [do] you mean literal sexual intercourse?

Gloria: Yeah.

KB: So you've talked about what you've done . . . kissing mostly, and you've talked about these other people who have had sex, what about . . . there is a lot of in between.

Gloria: Yeah, I guess there is a lot of fooling around, oral sex, but mostly these people will be with people in their rooms and they are drunk. They won't just fool around and then stop; they'll have sex . . . not that many people . . . just fool around.

> *KB*: Usually they go all the way?
> *Gloria*: Yeah. [Emphasis by interviewee]

It is possible that the students I interviewed were correct. That is, perhaps the volunteers for my study were less sexually active than the general student body. However, I think this is unlikely. Even students who were very sexually active with many different partners believed that other students were leading more promiscuous lives.

A third misperception is with regard to the number of hookup partners. The college women I interviewed, in particular, tended to believe that other students had a greater number of hookup partners than they did. This led many of the women I interviewed to think that they were less sexually active than other students on campus. For example, I asked students how many different people a typical student would hook up with in a semester if he or she was not in an exclusive relationship. Many women believed that their total number of hookup partners was less than their classmates.[18]

> *KB*: If someone was single how many different people would they hook up with in a semester?
> *Lynn*: Umm, [pauses], seven.
> *KB*: Is that about what you think you would do?
> *Lynn*: Umm, [pauses], when I was in high school I hooked up with a lot of people and then I kind of grew out of that stage because you kind of get tired of it, you know nothing is going to happen with it so it's kind of like what's the point. So . . . I still do [hook up], but just not frequently.
> *KB*: So . . . were you single last fall?
> *Lynn*: Yeah.
> *KB*: Do you remember how many people [you hooked up with]?
> *Lynn*: Umm, two. [Sophomore, Faith University]

> *KB*: In a typical semester, if someone did not have a boyfriend, how many different people might you or one of your friends hook up with?
> *Violet*: It all depends on how active they are going out to different parties. I have had friends hook up with five people in one night at a party.
> *KB*: When you say hook up are you talking about just kissing?

Violet: Yes.

  KB: So they just kiss people at the parties?

Violet: Hmm-mm.

  KB: So in a semester it could be a very high number if that were the case.

Violet: Yeah.

  KB: [When you hook up] is it just kissing or would you say that it's a lot of times more than kissing?

Violet: Not for me. A friend of mine, I have a friend that will go out to parties and she will sleep with whoever she meets. And she actually had to leave school because she had slept with half of the campus. [Junior, State University]

Quantitative studies on college student populations have confirmed that students tend to overestimate their peers' level of sexual activity and number of partners. This finding is consistent with data on college students' misperceptions of their peers' alcohol consumption. Specifically, students believe other students drink more often and in greater quantities than they actually do. Alcohol researchers have found that students' misperception of their classmates' alcohol use negatively affects their own behavior. For example, many students try to "catch up" with their (false) perception of what "everyone" is doing drinking-wise.[19] Thus, in the alcohol-driven hookup culture on campus, misperceptions may play a significant role in affecting behavior.

HOW PERCEPTIONS AFFECT BEHAVIOR

Students' perceptions of their classmates, whether accurate or not, are important because it affects their own behavior. The men and women I interviewed believed that hooking up and having sexual intercourse under a variety of circumstances was commonplace on their campus. Furthermore, they consistently seemed to believe that other students were hooking up more frequently or, at least, other students went farther sexually during "random" hookup encounters. College students, then, judged their own behavior relative to these perceptions. If students believe other students are more sexually active than they are, it creates a kind of relativism whereby students define themselves as "good" because they are not as "bad" as everyone else (i.e., "if others are doing _____, then what I am doing is okay"). This point of view was consistent regardless of the sexual behavior of the student I was interviewing. In other words, whether the student had very little sexual experience or had sexual encounters with many different people, she or he believed that "other guys" or "other girls" had lower standards in adapting to the hookup script.

In some cases, students' perceptions of the norms for their peers seemed to make them feel pressure to conform.[20] For example, a couple of students referred to "getting rid of" their virginity or getting their first sexual encounter "over with" so that they did not have the status of being a virgin anymore. For these students, virginity was a source of embarrassment. Since they thought being a virgin was unusual, they did not want to be "known as one."[21] It seems that some students adapt their sexual behavior to fit in on campus (i.e., "if others are doing _____, then I should too"). Students' perceptions can also give them permission to behave a certain way. For example, if a student wants to hook up often with a variety of different people, she or he may feel entitled to do this because "everybody's doing it." Thus, some students may view themselves as merely taking part in what typical college students do (i.e., "if others are doing _____, then I can too"). The problem is that their perception of what is typical is often not accurate.

When examining the impact of perceptions on students' behavior, one should not underestimate the power of an individual's clique. For example, students who were involved in the extremes of the campus hookup culture tended to be surrounded by others who were also very sexually active. These students, who were often involved in fraternity/sorority life, generally hooked up more often than other students. Their perceptions of classmates were influenced by their circle of friends. These men and women perceived other students to be extremely sexually active, which, on any given night, might include engaging in indiscriminate sexual encounters. Stephen, a 27-year-old alumnus of State University, described an incident that occurred when he was a college fraternity member.

KB: So you would not necessarily talk to people about your hookups?

Stephen: No, I do. We do. Guys bullshit and talk. Guys are more flagrant when they talk about hooking up [than girls are].

KB: Graphic?

Stephen: Yeah. They are more graphic. They get into great detail.
[Laughs] It is funny I am just thinking back to funny stories.

KB: Tell me one.

Stephen: Oh God. I'll tell you this story. . . . It was finals week my
junior year and I was done finals on a Wednesday. So I had
Wednesday, Thursday, Friday with nothing to do. Everyone
else is still taking finals. So I went out for some drinks. We
went to this [bar nearby]. I knew the bartender so he started
giving me shots. I was with one of my friends. There were
these two girls there and the bartender started feeding her
shots and next thing you know I started talking to her. The
bar wasn't crowded at all. Next thing you know we are back
at my frat house, she's like, she can't even walk, she is really
messed up. So, we start hooking up, nothing major. She's coherent, she knows what is going on, but she is really drunk.
So we are hooking up and we are sleeping together and she
gets sick on me. She's on top of me and throws up on me. So
I had a water bed, I think that is why she got sick. I push her
aside and run out to my living room, I am covered in throw-
up and I'm like: "Somebody has got to help me." There were
two guys out there watching TV. I'm like: "One of you guys
has to help me." First of all, the girl she doesn't look good
and I'm covered in puke and my room is covered with
throw-up. So my one friend he runs back there.

KB: And you are naked, out in the frat house?

Stephen: Yeah I am naked. I am out in my living room. And he runs
back there and he takes one smell and he starts throwing up.
So he is getting sick. So my other friend he comes back, we
put her in the shower and she is like all out of it. We wash her
off, we try to take care of her; we [continue to] wash her off.
. . . I had a bunk bed and I was on the lower level of the bunk
bed and my friend that was helping me out tried to help me
clean her up a little bit, I put her up on his bed. Because my
bed [had vomit on it so] I had to take the sheets off and
everything. So I put her up on his bed, I go out in the living
room and am just talking to those guys for a little bit. Then I
go back in and she's totally fine, she is totally coherent. So we
start "going at it" again [laughs] and then she starts calling

me by the wrong name. So keep in mind that we are on the top bunk bed so we are close to the ceiling tiles. So she is screaming somebody else's name. I can't believe I am telling you this. And, umm, and she is screaming the name Anthony, so I am like, "Who is Anthony?" and she's like, "I mean Stephen." So that was that. I took her, that was finals week, she missed her final, I took her home and went down to the kitchen in the fraternity house to get something to eat and I didn't know that my one friend had heard us through the ceiling tiles and he just looks over at me and is like: "What's up, Anthony?" And I just looked at him and am like, "You heard that whole thing?" And he's like: "Yeah." *So that was like a typical night* at [State U.].

KB: Typical night?

Stephen: It was . . . it happened. I mean that was the first time I ever had a girl throw up on me. But that is the kind of scene that went on there. [I hope you] don't look at me any differently [now that I told you this story]. [Emphasis added]

My research suggests that Stephen's story is very unusual, yet his frame of reference on campus led him to conclude that his experience represents a typical night at State University. Thus, Stephen's (distorted) perception of what was typical gave him permission to engage in what was actually atypical (and perhaps unlawful) behavior.[22]

A STATE OF CONFUSION

Men and women draw from their peers when making decisions on how to conduct their own sexual lives. In the hookup culture, students were often confused about what other students were doing sexually, particularly with regard to how often other students hooked up or how likely they were to have sexual intercourse during a hookup (i.e., outside the context of an exclusive relationship). They also had a tendency to believe that other students must be frequently engaging in sexual intercourse with a variety of partners, even if this was not consistent with their own experience or the experiences of their circle of close friends.

KB: Would you say that most students you know are having sex?

Jen: Yes.

KB: But when people hook up you [said previously that you] generally think they are not having sex?

Jen: Generally no [they are not having sex when they hook up]. [Wait, I take that back] they probably are having sex. I really don't know. Because it's not something you ask people [if they are not a close friend]. My close group of friends, two of them are in a relationship and they are [having sex]. And then my other roommate she's not really like that. But that's just people that I know. But [I am not sure] what other people are doing.

KB: You don't know?

Jen: Right. But probably [they are having sex].

KB: When would you say that you think sex is appropriate?

Jen: Personally, I think it's appropriate when you have a certain trust established. I would not really give it a time frame. Just knowing it's someone you can trust. I wouldn't want to have sex with someone and have them not call me or ignore me or something like that . . . if they are going to be a jerk about it. [Junior, State University]

Students' confusion over what peers were doing sexually resulted in confusion over what they themselves *should* be doing.[23] For example, students often did not have strong convictions regarding when sexual intercourse is appropriate.[24] Some said sexual intercourse was appropriate only in the context of a committed, exclusive, (potentially) long-term relationship; others voiced vague standards such as "when you know you can trust the person" or "when you can tell him (or her) anything." Regardless, students hesitated to give a more concrete answer, such as a specific time frame.[25] Thus, unlike the dating era when sex was deemed appropriate only after marriage or at least engagement, college students utilizing the hookup script cannot pinpoint precisely when, or in what context, sex should occur.

The fact that the hookup script allows for such a wide range of behavior leaves students grappling with the norms of the hookup script. The lack of clarity on what others are doing when they say "I hooked up" led to a sense of normlessness. Rather than there being a standard to which individuals should aspire, students seemed to believe they were responsible for inventing their own personal standards for what is appropriate. Lee, a freshman at Faith University, discussed her views on when sexual interaction is appropriate.

> *KB*: In your view, when is sexual interaction appropriate? Are there certain circumstances or is it up to an individual to decide?
>
> *Lee*: It's hard to say. Months ago I would have said if you just had sex with someone where you were with them for a couple months it was bad. But I had sex with my boyfriend like a week and half after I met him . . . I only slept with two other people and that was very rare for me [to have sex with someone so soon]. I guess it does depend. I don't know.

Consistent with students suggesting that decision making in the hookup culture must be an individual or personal decision, some indicated that what others do sexually should be private.[26] This is ironic given how preoccupied college students were with discussing the intimate details of their classmates' lives. Thus, there is a disjunction between what college students do (gossip about one another) and what some students say they should do (mind their own business). For instance, I asked the students what advice they would give incoming freshman (of the same gender) regarding how to act with the opposite sex. Emily, a sophomore at Faith University, suggested that it is inappropriate for her to impose her personal beliefs on others.

> *KB*: Is there anything else you would say [to an incoming freshman female] regarding do's or don'ts of how to act with guys?
>
> *Emily*: Umm, I don't know . . . I think everyone has their individual values and I don't think they should be pushed on anyone else. I mean, I would say: "Don't go around sleeping with the whole campus," but you do what you want to do, you do what you think is right. And I don't think I should say to someone like, even though I think it's wrong, I can't imagine pushing my beliefs on someone else.

This excerpt from Emily underscores the ethic of individual choice to which many students seemed to subscribe to in theory.[27] In practice,

however, the college students admitted that they were constantly engaged in gossiping about, as well as judging, one another for their behavior in the hookup culture. It is naive for students to believe that the
choices individuals make in order to adapt to the hookup script are simply a matter of consulting one's own moral compass. Men and women
do not interact in a vacuum. In the campus sexual arena, students create their personal standards by drawing upon what they believe other
students are doing (i.e., what is "normal"). Students' perceptions, or
misperceptions, of the norms for the hookup script ultimately affect the
script itself. In other words, if college students perceive a certain behavior to be normative, and they conform to that behavior, then they actually shape what becomes the norm.

6

Men, Women,
and the Sexual Double Standard

Certain Hollywood actresses of the 1950s and 1960s, such as Sandra Dee and Doris Day, epitomized the proverbial idea of a "good girl." These women had a squeaky clean, virginlike image that was promulgated both on and off screen. All actresses of this time period did not fit this mold, but there was something about maintaining this image that helped propel these women to stardom. An erotic image, on the other hand, also helped skyrocket the careers of actresses like Elizabeth Taylor and Marilyn Monroe. Interestingly, both Taylor and Monroe became the infamous "other women" in the marriages of "respectable" wives like Debbie Reynolds and first lady Jacqueline Kennedy. Thus, iconic women could be characterized either as a virginal "good girl" (i.e., the marrying kind), or a sexy "bad girl" whom a man should not bring home to Mother.

The women's movement of the late 1960s and 1970s aimed to free women of this kind of labeling by encouraging all women to embrace their sexuality. This era has been called the sexual revolution because it became increasingly socially acceptable for women to have sex prior to marriage.[1] Although cultural expectations for women's sexual behavior changed after the sexual revolution, the good-girl image has remained relevant. In the 1980s, girl-next-door Molly Ringwald was the leader of Hollywood's "brat pack" and starred in a number of hit films portraying youth culture. In the 1990s superstar Meg Ryan reigned as America's sweetheart, a title some are now passing on to actress Mandy Moore. In 2005, the public rallied behind jilted wife Jennifer Aniston when bad girl Angelina Jolie stole the heart of Brad Pitt.[2] The lasting popularity of women with an innocent persona begs the question: How much have attitudes on women's sexuality actually changed? The hookup culture on modern college campuses affords young people more freedom than ever before, yet there continues to be a double standard for the sexual lives of men and women.[3]

When men and women first enter college they seem to be on the same page. Freshman year is a time when all students can test limits. Most students at both Faith and State were on their own for the first time; dorm life provided the first extended opportunity to live away from parental supervision. Both men and women enter college with ideas about what college life is supposed to be like, and they are eager to be a part of the social scene. Most students indicated that, as freshmen, they did not want to be "tied down" to a relationship because this would interfere with experiencing all that college life has to offer. Many students had had exclusive relationships in high school and they reported looking forward to having a little freedom to see "who else is out there."[4] During this time of sexual experimentation, many students, both male and female, spoke of enjoying partying and hooking up. Since they were still getting to know their fellow classmates on campus, many indicated that "random" hookups were common.[5]

After freshman year, things change. Men's and women's goals in the hookup culture diverge; men enjoy the status quo, while women begin to want something more. For many men, the hookup script worked, so they did not communicate that they wanted a different way of doing things. Men preferred a "no strings attached" approach to a hookup encounter, so they could hook up with different women whenever they had the opportunity. For men who had good social skills, the opportunities were many. Men who wanted more than "just a hookup" pursued relationships and they did not seem to have much difficulty finding them.[6] However, many men indicated that they did not want relationships during college. Other men said they might be interested in a relationship if the "right girl" came along, but they were not planning to "go out of their way" to find her. Women, on the other hand, became increasingly relationship-oriented after freshman year. While many women were still willing to hook up, they wanted hookup encounters to turn into some semblance of a relationship.

GOALS AT ODDS

Since men and women want different things from the hookup culture, the intimate side of college life becomes somewhat of a battle of the sexes. Given that many women want relationships and many men do not, boyfriends are hard to come by. Lisa, a sophomore at State University, discussed what college women want.

KB: What about girls? What are they looking for, are they look-
        ing for sex, are they looking for relationships, what are they
        looking for?
Lisa: I think, like I said, when I first came in as a freshman, I was-
        n't looking for a real relationship at all, I just wanted to go
        out and have fun and do whatever I wanted to do. And I
        think a lot of my girlfriends were like that last year too. As
        time goes on, it gets kind of old [the whole hookup scene]
        and you're like: "All right, I'm sick of just kissing random
        people; it's not really that fun; it doesn't mean anything."
        And I think people, *at least girls,* as they progress through
        college they start to really want, I know a lot of them really
        want to find someone that they really like and have a real
        relationship.
KB: Do you think that is something they will be able to find or is
        that something that's hard for them to find?
Lisa: I don't know, I mean it is kind of hard to find in college. Like,
        the guy that I'm seeing now is someone from home. [Em-
        phasis added]

Many of the women were not as fortunate as Lisa in terms of finding a boyfriend. It seemed it was easier for her to maintain a long-distance relationship than to find a boyfriend on campus among thousands of single men.

The college men were aware that some women wanted hookup en-counters to evolve into relationships. So, they developed strategies for communicating their lack of interest in pursuing anything further. Specifically, men spoke about avoiding girls after a hookup, "not call-ing girls back," or "thinking of good excuses" to get out of spending time with them. Kevin, a senior at Faith University, explained how he would get his point across without actually having to say so.

Kevin: If the next day [after a hookup] she's like: "I want to come
          over and hang out" and you didn't want to hook up with her
          again you'd be like: "Oh, I got practice tonight." Or I was the

head of intramurals too . . . I'd be like: "I've got intramurals, I've got to run tonight over at the gym," that would be an easy way to get out of it. The other way [to get out of hanging out with girls] is to just not talk to them.

KB: And why would you not want to talk to them again?

Kevin: If all I wanted was a hookup.

KB: But you didn't like the person?

Kevin: It's not that I didn't like them; I did not want to lead them on. I didn't want them to think that there might be something more [when] there's not.

For some men, hinting that they did not want a relationship did not work, so they had to verbalize it. This was the case with Brian, a sophomore at Faith University.

KB: Of all the girls you've met at [Faith University], whom have you liked the most?

Brian: I don't know, I really don't know. I thought I liked . . .a chick last semester and then she just went crazy on me. Like she wanted the relationship, she wanted everything and I was just kind of like: "Oh I can't handle this right now." So I kind of backed out. . . . But, I mean, hooking up . . . can sometimes make things awkward.

KB: The girl last semester that you said went a little bit crazy, what happened? What did she do?

Brian: She started asking me out and I was like: "Uhhh, I'm not, I'm not [interested]."

KB: To be your boyfriend or asking you out on dates?

Brian: Yeah, to be her boyfriend. She's like: "Are you my boyfriend?" and I was like: "No." And she was like: "All right, well we're not hooking up unless you are my boyfriend." I was like: "All right." And that was the end of that. [Laughs]

Through experience, women learned that they could not expect a hookup encounter to turn into a relationship. Many of the women found that men's desire to avoid relationships often forced hookup partners to remain just that. Two women explained their disappointment in this way:

KB: And, it seems like [casual hookups] were a problem for you ... because you seem like you wouldn't be interested in that in the future?

Susan: Yeah, it was a problem. [The guy I was hooking up with] ... he would sleep in my bed and everything and we wouldn't do anything [sexual], like he wouldn't even kiss me. ... But then, um, we hung out more and we started kissing and everything and then he never talked about ... having it be a relationship. But I wanted ... in my mind [I was thinking] like: "I want to be his girlfriend. I want to be his girlfriend." ... I was like looking for a boyfriend, looking for that connection, looking for that dependency that I had [in a previous high school relationship]. And I found it [with] him, but he wasn't [interested in a relationship] ... I didn't want to bring it up and just [say] like: "So where do we stand?" because I know guys don't like that question. So, it eventually led to sex and we only had sex once and then he continued to still want to talk and hang out with me but he never really brought up the "where do we stand" thing. That kind of pushed me away because I just didn't want to just be casually having sex with him and it not meaning something to him. So that stopped there. [Freshman, Faith University]

KB: If people are [hooking up], is it usually with the same person repeatedly or is it more of random kind of one time thing?

Diane: Um, [for] some people it's random. [For] some people I know it's from a week to week basis, [they] hook up or get with somebody they don't know. Not that they don't know them, but they're not like in a relationship with them. Some people will consistently hook up with the same person but then something will happen and ... they'll stop but then they'll ... find like another person and like consistently be with them [for hooking up].

KB: What typically happens to have one thing stop and another thing start? What kind of stops things?

Diane: Usually the girl gets ... girls are crazy you know [if they found out the guy they were hooking up with] was [also] talking to somebody else. She'll be like: "Wait, are you talking to them?" ... girls are like very predictable ... if they're hooking up with someone for a while, they're going to want a relationship. They're going to want like some type of like title, not title but like . . .

KB: Commitment or something?

Diane: Right. Exactly, commitment. And usually guys don't want it.

KB: Why don't they want it?

Diane: Because they don't. They're in college, they don't want a girlfriend. They basically just want to get ass.

KB: So girls are looking more for relationships? Guys are looking more for a sexual relationship?

Diane: Yeah. [Sophomore, Faith University]

Perhaps the concept of "hidden power" can help explain why Susan did not even want to ask her hookup partner if he would consider being in an exclusive relationship with her. Social scientist Aafke Komter, who studied the power dynamic between married couples, found that many hidden power struggles go on beneath the surface of purported equal relationships. In some cases, wives would not even bring up issues that were bothering them in the relationship for fear of "rocking the boat" and consequently jeopardizing the relationship. In Komter's analysis, the fact that women were afraid to even raise an issue that a man might "not like" shows that men have greater power in relationships. Similarly, in my study, although women were more likely to initiate "the talk" about the status of a relationship, in some cases they did not bring up the issue at all in anticipation of a negative reaction.[7]

WHY WOMEN SEEK RELATIONSHIPS

Students were not always cognizant of why women sought relationships more than men. Some cited psychological reasons, such as women are "more emotional" or women "need that kind of connection." Some women talked about wanting a relationship due to their affection for a particular man. However, there are likely reasons beyond psychology and personal biography. One possible reason why some women seek relationships during college is that they are interested in marrying a few years after graduation. The women I spoke with often wanted to be married by age 25, and the latest they were willing to consider getting married was 29. Men, on the other hand, seemed willing to wait longer to get married. Many men suggested they would not get married until their late twenties (at the earliest) or possibly even well into their thirties. Thus, men's and women's timetables for getting married are at odds. This puts their timetables for finding potential marriage partners at odds, too, which in turn puts their timetables for having serious relationships at odds. For this reason, several women indicated that they would like to have a relationship with marriage potential.[8]

> *KB*: Do you or [your] friends . . . think about marriage at all?
> *Gloria*: Yeah. We always talk about that. It's so weird, we are going to have to . . . not soon, I would like to be with who I'm going to marry for a good three years before [we get married] . . . someone I'm going to marry I'd want to be with for a long time. So I would like to meet him soon so I don't have kids when I'm like 30 or 35.
> *KB*: So you [possibly] would want to meet someone in college . . . that you might end up with [permanently]?
> *Gloria*: Yeah. I would say junior year I would like to have a boyfriend and hopefully potential marriage [partner], but I don't know. [Freshman, State University]

However, a couple of women in their junior and senior years mentioned no longer being naive regarding finding a future spouse during their college years.

> *KB*: Would any of the people that you have liked or been interested in, have you ever thought: "I wonder if this is someone I could marry?" Have you ever thought about it that way?
> *Marie*: I think about it all the time. Like anyone I have ever been serious with I'm always like: "I wonder if we could ever get married." . . . [But] I'm not that naive anymore. I know relationships come and go and you never know what is going to happen. I mean it would be nice, like my ex-boyfriend from over the summer, I really liked him a lot and I really wanted the kind of relationship my roommates have, even if it was a year or two, just something, like some stability, like you know, a possible marriage [partner], someone that you were

close to and I definitely could see him as that. [Senior, State University]

Another possible reason that women are more desirous of relationships than men is that women need relationships in order to protect their reputation. Over 30 years since the sexual revolution, there is still a double standard for male versus female sexual behavior on the college campus. In the hookup culture, men are free to choose whether to have a very active sex life or to "settle down" and maintain an exclusive relationship. Women, on the other hand, have considerably less freedom.

KB: How do people get a bad reputation, assuming there's such a thing as getting a bad reputation?

Max: Well it's kind of bad because if you're a girl and you hook up with a lot of guys, then that's looked down upon.

KB: Okay. Looked down upon by everybody or looked down upon by guys?

Max: By both genders, yeah. But, if you're a guy and you hook up with a lot of people, like from your peers, like your guy peers, they're going to be like: "Oh you're the man!" [Sophomore, State University]

KB: What does someone do that they might end up with a bad reputation?

Joseph: If you're a girl . . . I mean obvious things: sleeping around. It's that whole double standard rule that society brings down on everyone. [Senior, Faith University]

The sexual double standard leads to an environment where women need relationships in order to protect their reputations. For women who are active participants, the hookup system is fraught with pitfalls that can lead to being labeled a "slut." Rule number one for women is: Do not act like men in the sexual arena.

KB: You mentioned the term "slut" a minute ago. How do people get that kind of label?

Kyle: Just being dirty . . . being more like a guy when you are not supposed to be. [Senior, State University]

Larry: The perception is that if a girl sleeps with a lot of guys she's a slut. If the guy sleeps with a lot of girls he's a stud . . . I mean, I see it every day. I mean, like I said, I bartend [and] I do go out to bars when I go out.

KB: So when you say it's a perception [is it] a true perception?

Larry: A complete true perception. It happens every day and you can ask anyone on campus randomly, and they would say that would be the perception. A girl sleeps with a lot of guys she's a slut. A guy sleeps with a lot of girls he's a stud. [Senior, Faith University]

Prior to the sexual revolution era, women were expected to have sex, particularly intercourse, only with their husbands.[9] Since then, sex prior to marriage has become the norm for both men and women.[10] On the campuses I studied, most students assumed sex would be part of a committed, exclusive relationship; yet, students were also aware that sex (including intercourse) was often part of the hookup script. Students evaluated their peers, particularly their female peers, based on the context in which sex occurs.[11] In the hookup culture, men and women are permitted to (and do) engage in sexual encounters that are, by definition, outside of the context of a committed relationship. However, there are prejudices against women who are seen as being too active in the hookup scene.

THE RULES FOR HOOKING UP

There are very few restrictions on sexual behavior for college men. Both male and female interviewees said college men were free to hook up as often as they had the opportunity to do so. For men, there is no stigma for engaging in "heavy" sexual activity. In fact, men are congratulated by their male peers for sexual conquests. Stigmatization occurs only for men who cannot "get any" (i.e., they are virgins or have difficulty getting women to hook up with them). However, such men were believed to be few and far between. The idea that men are free to engage in hooking up, including sexual intercourse, with a variety of women without risking their reputation was a point raised by many.

KB: Are guys ever considered to be too loose sexually, or a pig?

Emily: Oh, *I don't think so.* If you hear a guy who had sex with all these people, you're like "Hmm," but I think it's still much more for girls. [Emphasis by interviewee] [Sophomore, Faith University]

Gloria: Guys . . . don't get reps for hooking up with girls or having sex with girls. [Freshman, State University]

Kyle: [Guys] can [get a reputation for what they do sexually] but it's more, with my friends, it's more like a joke. [Senior, State University]

According to Ed, a senior at State University, men were aware that they were free to do as they please when it comes to hooking up.

KB: So, is there any kind of standards among the people you know of what's acceptable and what's not acceptable to do as far as hooking up and sexual behavior?

Ed: All the guys I know have no "don'ts."

Some students mentioned that a man who was very active in the hookup culture would be known as a "player."[12] Although this term was considered derogatory by some students, others indicated that the term "player" also had somewhat of a positive connotation. An alternate description of a promiscuous man is "man-whore" or "male-slut." However, most students indicated that these terms are used as more of a joke than as a derogatory label per se.[13]

For college men, there are virtually no rules, but for college women it is a very different story. In fact, there is a host of norms for the hookup script that, if violated, lead women to get bad reputations.[14] Many of the men I interviewed mentioned that women would get a bad reputation if they hooked up too often with too many different partners.

KB: For people that aren't in relationships, do you think that guys or girls have more partners as far as hooking up or sex?

Robert: I think guys have more partners overall because they can do it more discreetly. A girl does it and a guy knows about it, the girl has a nickname or has this connotation about her. All the guys know who "puts out" [sexually] and who doesn't. Guys know that and want to steer away from girls that do it all the time. Whereas guys try to go for the trophy ones that hook up with people seldomly or with a select few.

KB: So a trophy girl is someone who doesn't hook up as much?

Robert: Correct.

KB: So that would be someone sought after because it is more of a challenge?

Robert: Yeah. As opposed to someone who sleeps with a lot of people. That is gross, everyone has been there, done that.

KB: If girls are treated negatively if they hook up with or sleep with a lot of people, why do you think they do that?

Robert: I think it goes back to the need factor. They want to be needed or loved and it's a quick fix or immediate gratification for them, the desire to be wanted or needed or [to] feel pretty. [Sophomore, Faith University]

Despite men insisting that women should not hook up "too often" or with "too many partners," they were unable to offer a convincing operational definition of these terms. In other words, men had a sense that it was not acceptable for women to "get around," but they did not seem to know what "getting around" would really entail. When I pressed them to explain what "too often" or "too many partners" meant, they always resorted to giving a somewhat preposterous definition. Larry, a senior at Faith University, seems to have trouble identifying what qualifies as "a lot of guys."

KB: You [said] "If a girl sleeps with a lot of guys she's a slut." How many would be a lot, in your opinion?

Larry: Umm. In a short amount of time, it would be like twelve guys. If she was just randomly doing that and had like no . . . but just did it and was like: "Okay next." You know, something like that.

KB: Okay.

Larry: And would do it like that, sleep with five guys in a week. One every night, that would be like a slut.

The problem with Larry's explanation is that the behavior he defines as that of a "slut" does not generally happen. Rarely do college women sleep with "five guys in a week" or "twelve guys" in a short period of time. Even among the most sexually active college women, such behavior would be considered exceptional. None of the quantitative data on the sexual behavior of American women indicates that young women engage in this level of sexual activity with multiple partners.[15] Yet, many of the men I interviewed gave answers similar to Larry's about what women do in order to get labeled "sluts."

This raises the question: Why do men consistently give such extreme examples when asked to explain what a woman might do that would lead to her being labeled a slut? The answer ties to an issue discussed in chapter 5. That is, although there are many norms governing the hookup script, there is simultaneously a sense of confusion, which is, in part, generated by the ambiguous nature of the term "hooking up." The rules for sexual behavior within the hookup script do not seem altogether clear and, to complicate matters, college students often have distorted perceptions of what others are doing sexually. Therefore, it is not surprising that students had difficulty articulating what constituted a rule violation when they were not entirely clear on what the rules were in the first place. An alternate explanation is that male interviewees felt awkward telling a female interviewer their thoughts on what behavior they consider "slutty." Perhaps men were afraid to cite less extreme behavior as promiscuous, given that they do not know anything about my beliefs (or behavior). However, I believe that the distorted perceptions of what others were doing is most likely behind the extreme examples cited by several men.

Another potential pitfall for women is hooking up with two different guys who know each other well. This is particularly problematic if the two different men are friends or fraternity brothers. The time span between the hookups is also a critical consideration. The men indicated that if a woman hooked up with two different men who knew each other without a reasonable amount of time between the hookup encounters, she would be labeled a "slut." Again, it was difficult to pinpoint what men considered a "reasonable amount of time." However, men seemed to object particularly to encounters that happened in the same month or even in the same semester (which generally equates to a three and a half month span of time).

Kevin: If she has a reputation then we know who she is. And she would know who we were if we were a group of guys that were all friends. If she blew three or four guys, of course she would get a reputation.

KB: What if it was just [a] hookup [which did not involve oral sex]?

Kevin: Still, that's her writing her own fate.

KB: So it's a no-no to hook up with several people in the same clique?

Kevin: You are only making yourself trouble. . . . If one girl would hook up with me and then my friend and so on, of course she'd get a reputation.

KB: Even if it was just kissing?

Kevin: Bad idea. How do you expect these people not to talk [when] they're friends? "Did you hook up with Susan?" "Yeah, I hooked up with [her]." "Yeah, me too." She would have to realize that these guys are close buddies and of course they are going to know. I'd almost say that would be her fault. I would not put myself in the situation. [Senior, Faith University]

At State University, where fraternities were a more prominent feature of campus life, men indicated that the cardinal sin for women was hooking up with two or more men within the same fraternity. The same issues regarding hooking up with men who are friends applied here. However, the fraternity dimension seemed to add insult to injury.

Kyle: If they have multiple partners in the same fraternity, I know other girls in other houses, even girls at our [fraternity] house who have hooked up with six or seven different guys. And you are like: "Maybe she'll hook up with everybody and we'll put her picture on the wall or something." [sarcastic tone] Everyone knows her business and I think it is detrimental to her . . . reputation.

KB: So, hooking up with people that are friends or in the same fraternity is not a good idea?

Kyle: No. Because I think everyone talks about them. [Senior, State University]

In addition to the problems for women regarding how often they hook up or with whom, there were also a number of other behaviors that could potentially lead to being negatively labeled. Several men mentioned how some women at their college dress, particularly how they dress for parties, bars, and other social gatherings where hooking up takes place. When women dress too seductively, they were often labeled "easy" or "stupid." In some cases, men indicated that girls who dressed in a seductive manner were purposely sought after by men looking for an easy, one-night hookup. Jack, a sophomore at Faith University, said "If I want it to be something for one night, then I'm looking for someone that's showing a little midriff." Ed, a senior at State University, made a similar point:

KB: Are there people on campus that have high status?

Ed: I think that a lot of the girls on campus, I definitely don't want to be picking on the whole Greek system, but I think that a lot of sorority girls seem to dress the same and even the girls that aren't [in sororities] seem to dress . . . the same, in a really seductive manner. And I think that they're more sought after for the casual sex kind of thing rather than relationships.

Another pitfall for college women was constantly hanging around a particular fraternity house. A couple of male fraternity members I interviewed mentioned that there were some girls who were always at their fraternity house. These girls became friends with some of the brothers in the fraternity and they started hanging out at the house even when no party or other social gathering was happening. These women were seen as the lowest of the low. In fact, one fraternity member said that these women were referred to by the fraternity brothers as "houserats."

Kyle: We also have houserats . . . who always hang out [at the fraternity house]. They don't have to knock on the door; they come right in and sit down. There [are] usually people over the house or whatever.

KB: Are they friends with the brothers or why are they there?

Kyle: Friends . . . I guess, yeah, [but] they hook up too. [They are] kind of like special friends or friends with benefits. A lot of times they get stigmatized too. "I don't want to hook with her, she hooked up with three of my brothers," or "I know what she did last weekend."

Thus, "houserats" were stigmatized not only for what they did sexually within the hookup script, but also for their behavior outside the sexual arena. Kyle went on to explain that he did not treat houserats the way he would treat other girls. For example, he felt no need to "watch what he says" or extend any other kind of traditional courtesy toward them.[16]

Women's conduct in the hookup scene can also lead them to be negatively labeled. The men I spoke to said that women need to "watch themselves" in terms of flirting, drinking, and "letting go" at parties or bars where hooking up might take place.

KB: Are there people that have bad reputations?
Trent: Yeah.
KB: [How does someone get] a bad reputation?
Trent: Just doing stupid stuff. If you hear stories about them, you're going to think less of them.
KB: What would be a story that would earn someone a bad reputation?
Trent: This one girl was at this thing called "Mrs. Faith University" . . . for one of the frats. . . . It was this contest down at this one motor lodge place and they had to chug beer and do this drinking contest and the "dream girl" would be the one who won the most. But, this one girl comes out with this real short skirt and no underwear on and just starts flashing people and she was a mess and ever since then people just look at her and are like: "That's disgusting, what are you doing?" It's dirty. She's branded with that for the rest of her time here [at Faith U.]
KB: At the time, were you there?
Trent: No, I wasn't there.
KB: So, the story kind of got around?
Trent: Yeah . . . people were just telling me about it and everyone looks at her and is just like . . . and I found out the next day, so you know the whole campus knew within the week.
KB: So, in that case it's not a bad reputation from something she did . . . with somebody else or sexually, but it was just how she was acting?
Trent: Yeah, in that case it was how she was acting. But, then you always hear stories about girls who will sleep around and you'll get a bad reputation that way [too]. [Senior, Faith University]

• • •

Kyle: I think [freshman women] are a lot different than other women you encounter on this campus.

KB: Why are they different?

Kyle: Because they don't have a clue. They have no idea. They don't know what they are doing. . . . They can't get beer. They maybe feel out of place. . . . I just find that a lot of them hadn't drank a lot in high school and they go to a party and get sloshed, and then, it's funny to look at them sometimes.

KB: So you could almost spot at a party who is a freshman?

Kyle: Yeah. Definitely. And also they'll get . . . real sluttily dressed, I find. They wear those black sex pants and there will just be fifty of them rolling up to your house and you are just like: "Oh man, I don't want to drive anyone to the hospital tonight."

KB: Because they are going to drink so much?

Kyle: Or they just don't know how to handle themselves.

KB: What do you mean handle themselves, besides the drinking?

Kyle: That is what I mean. They drink too much and get themselves in trouble. Throw up all over the place, take their clothes off, or something stupid that they normally wouldn't do and I don't think they would do if they were a senior and had been exposed to the college culture and drinking. A lot of the time it is like letting a kid out of a cage. Your parents in high school, they are like: "Oh be home by 1:00 A.M." You bring the kid to college and it's like no cage, go nuts, run wild.

KB: Do freshman males do that also or is it specifically girls?

Kyle: I think males do it too. It's just displayed differently. Guys would get drunk too, but maybe a guy would do something he wouldn't normally do like get in a fight or something, not like take his clothes off [the ways girls do].

KB: Would you say then that females change more over the four years [in college] than males do?

Kyle: Yeah. Definitely. Females change a lot more. They come to college and figure it's a big school and no one is going to find out what they do and then [they learn this is not the case]. [Senior, State University]

Kyle refers to several of the ways women can get negatively labeled: how much they drink, what they wear, how wildly they behave, and so on. However, Kyle also noted that men did not have these same concerns. Men may need to learn their limits with drinking and to avoid starting fights, but men were not being judged in the same way as women. Moreover, women's behavior is specifically being scrutinized and sexualized. As Kyle points out, drinking may lead to guys getting in fights, but it is girls who "take their clothes off."

Just because these unwritten rules for women within the hookup scene exist does not mean all women follow them. The guidelines are sometimes vague and they may not be known to all women on campus. As Kyle and many other men I spoke with indicated, some women had to "learn the hard way" over time what is acceptable within the hookup script. This is particularly true for freshman women who may be naive about the rules at the outset of their college careers. Other college women may know the rules and flout them intentionally. However, most of the women I interviewed said they were aware of these rules and they "watched" their behavior accordingly.

BREAKING THE RULES

For women who break the rules there are consequences. One consequence is that students will label women who are seen as promiscuous. Being labeled a "slut" goes well beyond hurt feelings. Some students indicated that some women on campus were severely stigmatized. In my interview with Emily, a sophomore at Faith University, she reveals how a label can overtake a woman's identity.

> *KB*: Are there people who have bad reputations for how they act with guys?
> *Emily*: Yeah, I think so, like . . . supposedly there's a girl named "Blow Job Jen" and supposedly she gives a lot of blow jobs, I don't know, but when I see her I think about that so I guess there are [people with bad reputations].

In addition to women being labeled by others, women also evaluate their own behavior by the standards set by their peers. As Adrienne, a senior at Faith University, put it:

> Guys talk about girls like this, like it's a number. It's like: "What did you do with this girl? Oh, she was hot." But I think for girls, if they like

the guy or whatever [they hope it's not just a one-and-done hookup].
Or maybe it's because then [girls] don't feel like as much as a slut too
if they can talk to the guy the next day. If they never talk to the guy
again, then it's like: "Oh yeah, I hooked up with him one night and I
haven't talked to him since." I think that [makes them feel like]: "Am
I a slut for doing that?"

Another consequence for breaking the rules is being ostracized.
Several women spoke about close female friends who were severely
stigmatized for their behavior within the hookup scene. For instance,
Gloria, a freshman at State University, had a friend who "could not be
seen" at a certain fraternity house because she had sex with a few different fraternity brothers during the course of a semester.

Gloria: I have a few [female] friends that have a rep, like a bad rep.
First semester we couldn't go to certain frats because they
were like with too many guys.
  KB: What do you mean you couldn't go?
Gloria: Like she wasn't wanted there. She would have sex with this
guy and then this guy [at some later point] and they'd be
three frat brothers. They obviously don't want this girl at
their parties.
  KB: I don't understand why that is obvious . . . why would they
not want her there?
Gloria: I don't know. Maybe she would feel . . . stupid going there.
Say she had sex with this guy, she would get there and they
would not acknowledge her. They would not talk to her, not
even look at her . . . they would be . . . laughing at her [rather]
than like [saying]: "What's up?"

It seems likely that a woman labeled this way (and treated accordingly) is affected both emotionally and, in turn, behaviorally. Sociologists argue that labeling can affect behavior by altering one's sense
of identity and thereby ultimately creating a self-fulfilling prophecy,
whereby people live up to the labels imposed on them.[17] If this is
true, a young woman who is labeled the "campus slut" is likely to
continue a pattern of behavior that will lead to further confirmation
of the label.[18] However, in some cases, life on campus might become
too difficult. For instance, Violet, a junior at State University, had a

female friend who ultimately transferred to a different college in order to escape the negative label imposed on her.

> KB: Do you know people that have a bad reputation on campus?
> Violet: I know . . . one friend who was at another campus. She had to leave [school because] she had a bad rep.
> KB: When you say "she had to leave" is it something she felt she had to [do] because she had a bad reputation? What made her leave?
> Violet: Because she slept with a lot of people on campus . . . people look at her as though she was a slut. And I think it made her feel like people were looking down on her so she had to leave to make herself feel better.

Another consequence for women was that men indicated that they would not be willing to be in a relationship with a woman who has a reputation for being highly sexually active. Interestingly, even men who were highly sexually active themselves said that they would refuse to be involved with a woman who behaved in the same way. For instance, Tony, a senior at State University, indicated that he had sexual intercourse with over forty women, but he would not want to be in a relationship with a woman who also had a high number of past sexual partners.

> KB: When you say that you know people who might hook up with twenty different people in a semester, are you talking about guys or do you know girls who do that also?
> Tony: [Laughs] Well, the one girl I was telling you about before, that's one of the girls that does it. She's like a guy, like she'll go out and she'll just like, she *loves* sex.
> KB: So, she hooks up with a lot of different people?
> Tony: Oh yeah.
> KB: Would you be willing to be in a relationship with a girl who was like that?
> Tony: *No way,* no way.
> KB: But, you were involved with her before?
> Tony: Yeah, I was involved with her freshman year, when I first got to know her. . . . What was the question, you said: "Would I be involved with someone like that [a girl who had hooked

up with a lot of guys] after I knew she was [with a lot of different guys]?" For that reason alone, I mean I don't want to date somebody that's been with a hundred guys. [Emphasis by interviewee]

This does not mean that the men I spoke with would not hook up with a woman who had a bad reputation on campus. Rather, men will not consider *relationships* with women who are known as "sluts." In my interview with Jack, a sophomore at Faith University, he discussed his current relationship status. Specifically, Jack mentioned a girl with whom he was pursuing a relationship. Importantly, Jack said that he wanted a relationship with this young woman because he had respect for her (unlike others on campus).

KB: Are you single now?
Jack: Trying not to be.
KB: So, you're trying to be in a relationship?
Jack: Yes.
KB: Is she a [Faith University] girl?
Jack: Yes. She's actually one of the few girls on campus that I actually have respect for. I'm just very picky when it comes to women.

Thus, women who are not worthy of "respect" will likely have difficulty forming relationships with men on campus.

BOYFRIENDS, BENEFITS, AND BOOTY CALLS

As a result of the sexual double standard, participating in the hookup culture can be risky for women. Most college women were aware of the rules imposed on them and the consequences of breaking those rules. Although they may not have been cognizant of it, being in an ongoing relationship of some kind was a way for women to manage their reputations on campus.[19] In the context of a relationship, college women are free to engage in sexual activity without the risk of being labeled or shunned.[20] The students I spoke with often referred to women initiating "the talk" with men (i.e., a conversation to try to turn a hookup partner into a boyfriend).[21] This was one way for women to try to gain control in the hookup scene, which is so fraught with pitfalls for them. Adrienne, a senior at Faith University, had this to say about "the talk":

> *KB:* So were you [and your current boyfriend] considered exclusive at some particular point? When did things transition to that?
>
> *Adrienne:* I'd say . . . we don't really have an anniversary. We don't really subscribe to that, either. But like, um, I made it mid-June. That's when I have my own personal [anniversary] just to keep track. [Laughs] So, about mid-June going into junior year.
>
> *KB:* So what changed in June?
>
> *Adrienne:* Um, basically I'd come up [to visit him during the summer and] we had like a really fun time and I really liked him and he acted like he liked me. But he's always like, he kind of did this like pull away thing. . . . But, I was like: "Look I'm really, I'm really starting to like you and I really just don't want to get hurt. Like you tell me yes or you tell me no." He's like: "Oh, of course, you know, I really like you." And then we kind of made it I guess official. So then I started, I kept coming up on the weekends [to visit him over the summer break]. . . . So we hung out.

In the case of Adrienne, "the talk" worked; however, many women were not as successful with this strategy, as is evident in the following exchange with Patrick, a junior at Faith University.

> *KB:* If you could have anything you wanted going on in terms of the opposite sex, what would be your ideal situation?
>
> *Patrick:* I think I would want a girlfriend, I think I would want to be in a relationship, but I'm like really sociable. So, when I was almost in a relationship, the girl [I was hooking up with] was upset because I would always be talking to other girls. So basically I would want somebody who would realize that I would want to be with one person but I would still like, like talking and hanging out and being close friends with other girls.
>
> *KB:* Okay, so tell me about that girl that had a problem with it. How did you meet her and how did things evolve?

Patrick: We met first semester sophomore year and like we hooked up a couple times like we really never talked about a relationship until she brought it up the one time. And I'm like: "Well . . . yeah we could . . . like I'm not saying like I don't want to start dating and seeing you exclusively but it would be nice to like . . . maybe just see what it's like." And then when I would see her at parties [and] I would be talking to other girls and she would be all upset. I'm like: "Well, you know if that's going to get you upset, something small, just me talking to other girls, I mean I don't think we would be able to work this out." [But hooking up with her has] gone on. Like I still talk to her now and we still . . . hook up. But, I think she realizes that if we started seeing each other exclusively that I would still be talking to other girls and like being sociable to them. I wouldn't hook up with them but I just think that she . . .

    KB: She gets jealous?

Patrick: I guess, yeah.

    KB: But it's been two years now that you guys have been hooking up off and on?

Patrick: Yeah.

    KB: But you have freedom to hook up with someone else if you want to?

Patrick: Yeah.

    KB: And she does?

Patrick: Yeah.

    KB: And do you both take advantage of that freedom?

Patrick: Yes.

    KB: Typically if people hook up with people repeatedly, would they talk on the phone in between or do they usually just run into them when they're out?

Patrick: I would say [they] run into them when they're out. That's when they're just hooking up. When it becomes more serious I would say they talk to each other on the phone.

    KB: Okay, so what about you [and the girl you have been hooking up with for the past two years]? What do you do mostly?

Patrick: I haven't talked to her on the phone at all. I talk to her like on IM [instant message] every once and a while. But like I don't like call her up and say: "Hey what's going on?" I don't.

> *KB*: Okay, so you just see her in the course of things?
> *Patrick*: Hmmm-hmm [yes].

Like Adrienne and the woman Patrick refers to, many women indicated that they either want boyfriends or at least "something" beyond hooking up. Women who were able to find boyfriends could avoid hooking up altogether by being in an exclusive relationship (where hooking up with someone else would be considered cheating). However, for most women, boyfriends are not easy to come by during college.[22] Generally, college men resist committing to an exclusive relationship in favor of remaining free to hook up with other partners.

For women who were unable to find men who were willing to be exclusively committed to them, there were other avenues they could pursue that would help protect them from the negative labels they might get from too much hooking up. A "friends with benefits" arrangement was one way to avoid acquiring "too many" new hookup partners.[23] A friend with benefits refers to a man or woman who has someone of the opposite sex with whom he or she has sex on some level; however, they are not in an exclusive romantic relationship with that person. Friends with benefits are defined from the outset as "just friends"; the twist is that they are friends who are attracted enough to each other to want to engage in some version of a sexual relationship.[24] Friends with benefits is not a step toward a romantic relationship and this is agreed upon in advance. Gloria, a freshman at State University, talked about her friend with benefits.

> *Gloria*: I have a friend who is like my best friend and we hook up every time we are out and pretty much drunk . . . we'll hang out during the day, he is my best friend, and we won't kiss or anything [during the day]. We have fun. But when we're drunk, we hook up. But I guess you see that person out a lot and you hook up with [him] . . . [we] just kiss. Like I get really drunk and flirty, you hang on them, but it's funny . . . it's just like funny, friendship.
> *KB*: You talked about this person you hooked up with repeatedly. Does he call you, do you call him?
> *Gloria*: The guy that I hook up with repeatedly, we talk everyday, five times a day. He lives far away from me so we don't really hang out that much. He lives in dorms [across campus].

KB: You don't think of him as your boyfriend?

Gloria: No, not at all, because he wants the same thing, just [to be] single. [We] can hook up with [other people], that way we don't get mad at each other.

KB: So you don't care that he hooks up with someone else at all?

Gloria: No. I don't care. I wouldn't be like mad but I would be like: "Oh, how is she?" You know what I mean, kind of jealous, but not like mad at all.

KB: And same for you . . . he doesn't care if you hook up with someone else?

Gloria: Yeah. I mean he'll say: "Oh, who'd you bring home tonight?" [just] kidding around. He gets . . . jealous, but not mad.

As Gloria indicated, friends with benefits represent more than "just a hookup." Someone who is just a hookup partner is not necessarily someone with whom you spend time beyond the night you hook up. Also, someone who is just a hookup partner is not necessarily someone you know that well or care about in any significant way. Thus, a friend with benefits relationship may represent a middle-of-the-road option for those who do not feel comfortable repeatedly hooking up with what some students referred to as "randoms" (i.e., people they did not know well). The advantage of friends with benefits for women is that, unlike a casual hookup partner, at least the man is supposed to care about them as a friend (just not as a girlfriend).

In addition to the positives for women, men may also find friends with benefits to be an attractive option. Many men indicated that finding hookup partners involves a certain degree of "work" or "skill." Having a friend with benefits provided a "steady hookup" option for those nights where finding a new hookup partner was not worth the effort. At the same time, friends with benefits does not imply an exclusive relationship; therefore, individuals are free to pursue other people whenever they choose. This level of freedom may make friends with benefits a very attractive option to many college students, particularly men.

Although both parties may agree that a friends with benefits relationship is not exclusive, the arrangement does not always play out so easily. Despite the positive spin that Gloria puts on it, many students talked about the potential problems inherent in these relationships. Men were concerned that the woman would end up wanting more, while women were at risk for developing romantic feelings.

KB: Did you ever have an issue where someone wanted a relationship with you and you didn't want it?

Joseph: Yeah I had . . . one.

KB: Okay and how did that happen?

Joseph: We had something set up kind of where we were really close friends, we always had been, and one night we went a little further [sexually] than we probably should have. And [at first] we said that probably we shouldn't do that again. And then we were like: "Oh well, we can probably keep doing that but we can't let it go any further. We can't get attached."

KB: Kind of a friends with benefits thing?

Joseph: Yeah. That's how we agreed on, like if one person was going home with somebody that night, we can't be mad or anything like that. There wasn't a relationship. It was strictly, if for some reason we needed [each other], the other person was there. [But] she got attached and that's when things kind of went [wrong]. And I don't even talk to her anymore.

KB: So she wanted it to be a relationship?

Joseph: Yeah.

KB: Did you ever have an incident, a fight or something that blew up? Was she mad that you left with someone else or whatever?

Joseph: Yeah, that's kind of what started the whole thing because she got mad and I didn't understand why because I thought we had that agreement. I guess I'm kind of dumb when it comes to that stuff. So I thought we had an agreement, so I didn't understand why and then that's what kind of finished off that. Then she wouldn't talk to me the next day. [Senior, Faith University]

Ed: More girls than guys are looking for relationships, but not necessarily a permanent relationship, just something that's more than just a couple hookups or casual sex.

KB: And does that create issues that girls are looking for relationships more than guys are? Do you see that creating problems?

Ed: Yeah, yeah, because the next time you see them it's . . . very uncomfortable [and] awkward.

KB: So, you've had that issue where you thought girls were looking for a relationship [when you were not]?

Ed: Right.

KB: And how can you tell that they're looking for a relationship, do they tell you?

Ed: Yeah, yeah. Or they'll just, like I had one where [the girl] assumed that it was a relationship because we hooked up once. [She] just assumed that meant that suddenly you're girlfriend and boyfriend and she just took it way too fast.

KB: And how did you let her know that wasn't the case [that you weren't really her boyfriend]?

Ed: I just told her.

KB: How did she take it?

Ed: Then she was like: "Well, *can we still do that friends with benefits thing?*" And I was like: "No, I don't want to do that." Like I said before, I don't want to be that guy who is seen as using somebody and I also don't want to have this turn into something where you get all crazy and weirded-out. What I was afraid of is if she was at the same party and she saw me talking to another girl and then she came up and made a big scene about it. That would be very awkward and embarrassing for everyone involved so that's what I try to avoid. [Emphasis added] [Senior, State University]

Many students suggested that women may be more likely to get "emotionally involved" with a friends with benefits arrangement. Even Gloria, who suggested she was happy with her friends with benefits situation, admitted that her male friend is also "her territory." In other words, Gloria's female friends were not permitted to hook up with her particular male friend. Thus, for women, there is an emotional or territorial dimension that factors into friends with benefits arrangements.

KB: Are people that have a "friends with benefits" thing going, are they allowed to hook up with other people?

Violet: Yes.

KB: And does that ever create problems or issues? If you have . . . a female friend that has a friend with benefits [arrangement] and then she sees him hooking up with someone else, does that bother her?

Violet: I think it bothers girls more than boys. Because a male friend of mine has a girl [and] they were just friends [but] they would sleep together. And then he met somebody and she got very upset about it. And [she] was like: "What is he doing?" and I am like: "I thought you guys weren't together?" and she's like: "Oh no!" I think girls get more emotionally involved with it, even though they are [supposed to be just] friends. [Junior, State University]

Another pseudo-relationship a number of students talked about was "booty calls." A booty call is a late-night phone call placed, often via cell phone, to an earlier hookup partner, inviting him or her over for another hookup encounter.

Kevin: My friend would always have . . . he would fool around with a girl, but then he always had this one [other girl] where . . . what did we call her?

KB: Plan B?

Kevin: No, it's his late-night call, no matter what. If he was going after some other girl all night, he could pick up the phone and call this girl and she would come over to his room.

KB: And sleep with him?

Kevin: [Yes] and sleep with him.

KB: Okay. You don't remember what the term was that you called her?

Kevin: I want to say "late night . . ." [wait it's] "booty call." That's your booty call! You pick up the phone and go: "Why don't you come over?" and not even say sex or anything, just: "Why don't you come over." She knows exactly what she's coming over there to do. [Senior, Faith University]

KB: What does [booty call] mean?

Lisa: Like someone, well usually it occurs late at night when you're, like everyone is usually drunk or whatever and someone calls you and [says] like: "Do you want to come over?" And you both know what's going to happen. Like it's usually a friend or something like that and they basically just want to hook up and that's why they called you. Or computer IM's [Instant Messenger], they happen now too.

KB: You [can] do a booty call over the IM? (Laughs)

Lisa: Yeah. [Laughs] [Sophomore, State University]

Students suggested that booty call partners often have an ongoing relationship, albeit not a romantic one.

KB: What about "booty call"? Does anyone use that term?
Brian: [Laughs] Definitely, definitely. I mean it's just, you use it jokingly. Like my one friend this past weekend was like: "Oops, booty call" and then left [the place we were hanging out]. Like, but I mean he's been hooking up with her for a while. She's a good friend of mine from home. So I guess everything there is cool. But, yeah, I mean you're not really just like: "Oh, I got a booty call" and you leave and like come back an hour later. I mean if it's a booty call, it's usually someone you're hooking up with for a while. It's not just [at random]. [Sophomore, Faith University]

A very interesting gender dynamic occurs with regard to booty calls. In this type of relationship, men often placed the call or sent the text message; women accepted their invitation.[25] On the face of it, it would seem that such an invitation would not be particularly attractive to women. Booty calls were a man's last-ditch effort to find someone to hook up with for the evening. The man was often drunk when he placed the call and the woman generally would have to walk or drive over to his place late at night by herself. This does not seem like a very appealing combination. Yet, the students said women often took men up on their invitation. Why? One explanation is that women were on the same page as men. That is, the woman came home from a party or bar without finding someone else to hook up with that night. Thus, she was happy to have the opportunity to have a sexual encounter. Given how women are negatively labeled for having too many hookup partners, a repeat encounter with a previous hookup partner has its advantages. Consistent with this explanation, some students described this type of relationship as all about the sex.

KB: What about "booty call," does anyone say that?
Diane: Uh-huh [yes].
KB: How would someone use that in context?
Diane: Friday and Saturday night you get a call at 2:00 in the morning saying "Come over." Both of you are drunk.

KB: Does that, do you see that happening around [Faith University]?

Diane: Uh-huh [yes].

KB: And why do you think that happens?

Diane: Because they come home, they're alone, they're drunk, they're horny, they want ass. That's basically it. [Sophomore, Faith University]

KB: What does [booty call] mean?

Kim: Um, that implies sex.

KB: What kind of scenario would that be? How does sex happen in that scenario?

Kim: I mean I think it's pretty much synonymous with friends with benefits. I mean, you know the person, you may be friends with them, but, you don't have a significant relationship and you just want your sexual needs to be fulfilled.

KB: And why do you think people end up in those kinds of situations?

Kim: Because they like sex.

KB: Yeah?

Kim: [Laughs] I mean, I guess. [Sophomore, Faith University]

Another reason why women might agree to a booty call is that maintaining any kind of ongoing relationship is better than randomly hooking up. Additionally, since women are often looking for committed relationships, any attempts by a previous hookup partner to pursue further contact may seem like a step in the right direction toward evolving into "something more."

KB: Do people in your circle of friends [use the term booty call]? . . . Is that something people say?

Marie: Yeah. I'm not going to say that I've never done that or been used like that, but sometimes you don't realize that you're doing it. Like, the guy I was with for seven months . . . he started to get weird and I like . . . wasn't realizing that basically the only time he was calling me to come over (his place) was like one [o'clock] in the morning. But, I had liked him so much that I was like: "That's just how we are." But, that's basically what it was [a booty call relationship] . . . *he was just using me* when he felt like having me come over. . . . Guys love that [laughing]. If you're cool with that, guys are like: "That's a great girl!" [Emphasis by interviewee] [Senior, State University]

Although, as Marie noted, "guys love" having someone available as their booty call, women who were hoping the relationship would develop romantically were usually disappointed.

WHY NOT OPT OUT?

For those on the outside looking in, it may appear that men and women are on an equal playing field in the hookup culture on campus. Upon closer inspection, however, it becomes clear that college men are in a position of power. First, men are able to sustain the hookup system on campus despite the fact that it is not working for the majority of women. Most of the students indicated that college men favor casual sexual encounters or casual relationships, whereas women prefer more committed relationships. Therefore, while the hookup system works for men, it does not provide a good way for women to get what *they* want. Men's power in the hook up culture is also demonstrated by the fact that men control the intensity of relationships. They are able to keep most women as "just a hookup partner" and they decide if and when the relationship will turn into something more serious.

In addition to women's struggle to get the type of relationships they want, they also have difficulty navigating the hookup system. On one hand, the norms for hooking up (or at least the perceived norms) call for women to be sexually active. On the other hand, if women behave "too sexually" or are otherwise out of line with the unwritten rules for hooking up, they can be negatively labeled and treated accordingly. It may be that women seek relationships to avoid this dilemma.[26] Entering into an exclusive relationship, in particular, is a way for women to manage the double bind that they face. Since full-fledged boyfriends are hard to come by, women often agree to other options, such as friends with benefits and booty calls. However, more often than not, these arrangements do not work to women's advantage.

Given the inherent problems for women, why don't they refuse to partake in hooking up? The answer seems to be that there is no clear alternative. If a student opts out as an individual, then she is no longer part of the mainstream on campus. Students who buck the system have few other options for engaging in sexual encounters and forming relationships. Theoretically, college women could ban together and refuse to participate in hooking up. However, this never occurred to any of the women I interviewed. Most college women did not necessarily object to hooking up per se; rather, they objected to how often it ends up leading to "nothing." They seemed to accept hooking up as a given and alter their expectations accordingly.

> KB: Ideally, what would you want right now? I know you [mentioned that you] don't want a serious relationship, but what would be your ideal for what could be going on with you in terms of guys right now?
>
> Emily: I think that right now I would like to meet someone who, like I'm starting to want to get into a relationship . . . but I want to get to know someone and like take it a step at a time before we get into a serious relationship, like . . . hook up, talk, maybe like hang out just as friends and then get into it [a relationship]. That would be ideal, but I don't know what will actually happen.
>
> KB: You said before regarding hooking up that people know that nothing will come of it. Are there ever problems where the guy and girl aren't on the same page and one of them wanted more, I know you said you had a situation like that.
>
> Emily: I think it happens both ways because I had that before, but even like the beginning of this year I hooked up with this kid who I liked. . . . I talked to him in the summer and he didn't feel the same way and I was like: "Okay, fine," you know, but I think that totally happens. But, I think people have to deal with the fact [that a hookup implies] an understanding. That is the way it is; he never made a commitment to you even though he did hook up with you. [Sophomore, Faith University]

When I asked college women what their ideal scenario would be for meeting someone and getting together, it gave them pause. It was as if an alternative to hooking up had never crossed their mind. However, most revealed that they would want something different than the typical hookup scenario. Some women said that they would prefer to meet a man and "get to know him" without the first encounter involving sexual activity. Others suggested it was better to be "friends first" with a man and get to know him that way. Some women seemed to want to turn back the clock and go on dates.

> KB: What would you like to have going on? Are you happy with male / female interaction on campus or if you could dream up [something else] what it would be like?
> Lynn: I wish the guys would ask girls out. . . . I don't mind hooking up, but I know guys [who] like girls, but [they] are just too scared or something, like I don't understand it, but they won't ask girls out. [Sophomore, Faith University]

> KB: Ideally how do you think meeting and getting together with the opposite sex should work if you could design it?
> Jen: It would be very honest with no game playing. You just . . . meet somebody, you like them, you tell them [that you like them], you have everything out on the table. I would appreciate that. Have somebody not go home with you that night, but call you up the next day and ask you if you want to do something. Try to think of different things to do instead of just going to the bar . . . just getting to know you before anything sexual [happens]. [Junior, State University]

College women who yearned for something different than hooking up may not have long to wait to get their wish. As the twenty-something college graduates I interviewed told me, life after college begins a new phase for sex and relationships.

7

Life after College

A Return to Dating

MTV's hit reality series, *The Real World*, places seven 18–24-year-olds in a house where cameras film everything they do over a four-month period. The men and women who are chosen to be on the show come from various parts of the country and are previously unknown to one another. These strangers are then thrust together, sharing everything from bedrooms to bathrooms. The seasons are fairly predictable with episodes depicting the housemates: getting drunk, developing crushes, making out, arguing, partying, and having sex. This is certainly not the real world, but it does seem a lot like the way many of the people I interviewed described college life. Millions of young men and women will never get the opportunity to be on this show, but they can choose to have that kind of experience (minus the cameras) as a resident on campus. But, inevitably, the college students who graduate each year must abandon their college campus to enter the *real*, real world.

Across the board, recent graduates I spoke with talked about the transition from college life as a major change in their lives. After graduation, many moved back to their parents' homes; others moved to apartments, which they shared with friends from college. For some, leaving school meant no longer residing in the state where the college is located, and those who did remain nearby were nevertheless removed from campus. Graduation also signified the start of their postcollegiate careers. Many got their first full-time jobs and were taking on financial responsibilities for the first time. New work demands and living in a new place meant a dramatic change in the graduates' day-to-day activities and social lives. No longer were masses of their peers around all the time. The lack of camaraderie and leisure time after college made the transition very difficult for some. Many felt their lives changed overnight, and others described the change as a process that took a few years before they felt the full impact. As Lucille, a 23-year-old alumnus of Faith University, told me, "Everybody that I have ever seen leave college and enter the real world has gone through a transition. I think that was my transition period, too."

My exchange with Clark, a 25-year-old alumnus from State University, further illustrates this point:

KB: What about since you graduated from college a few years ago, did social life change since you left?

Clark: Yes, greatly.

KB: How has it changed?

Clark: For one thing I [cannot] go out almost every night. I think for me . . . since I am working full-time and I am living on my own, I am spending a lot more time by myself, to be honest. Living in a residence hall on campus: your friends are next door, your friends are upstairs. You open the door and there are always people around, there are always things going on not related to a work situation. There are people sitting in the lounge playing cards [or] throwing a Frisbee in the hallway. You can sit outside and have a cigarette, something like that. . . . And I think being removed from that was a big adjustment for me personally.

KB: Do you feel like your life changed overnight or did you think it was a process over time of changes?

Clark: I'd say it was a process. Since graduation a lot of my close-knit friends did stay either associated with the university or at the university as graduate students working there [and they still lived in town]. Since [that first year after graduation] that has decreased. So I was still always in town [the first year out]. On the weekends I would go down there and crash, sleep on people's couches. I would hang out in town; we still went to football games. I went to homecoming two years ago. Since then there are other "adult demands" quote / unquote [that] have crept into the schedule. And even for my close friends, their schedules have gotten more complicated too. My friend got married. They own a house now. So he spends a lot of time with her and [her] family. It's not my schedule pulling me away; it is everyone's schedule pulling them in a different direction.

As individuals became immersed in their new environments, they found new rules and expectations for their social lives. During college, most of the alumni I spoke with had been immersed in the partying and hooking up scene. After college, they continued alcohol-centered socializing, primarily in small groups at bars. However, in terms of the opposite sex, men and women largely abandoned the hookup script in favor of formal dating.

THE SHIFT TO FORMAL DATING

The men and women I interviewed from both Faith and State universities said that, after college, going on dates was the norm.

> *KB*: Does the hookup scene still exist now like it did in college? Can you go to a bar and go home with someone [to hook up]?
>
> *Will*: I think it definitely changes. There are more dates now . . . where you meet someone in a bar [and] they are a complete stranger, they don't know your personality at all so you are more likely to have a conversation, have a great time that night, maybe hang out with them for a couple hours. *Sometimes* maybe a girl goes home with a guy [to hook up] . . . but I think that's a small percentage now. I think it's mostly you exchange phone numbers or make plans [to go on a date]. [Emphasis by interviewee, a 24-year-old alumnus of Faith University]

> *Elizabeth*: It is kind of funny because no one has really ever asked me out before. [During college] I never had a random guy say: "Can I have your number? Can I call you?" And then it's like six or seven people asked me out. Within two months I would say seven people asked me out . . . it was weird having people be like: "Can I have your number and maybe can we go out sometime?" [25-year-old alumnus of Faith University]

> *Carol*: Like I said in college no one dated, really. . . . Now I would say people do go on dates . . . they actually do date someone. [24-year-old alumnus of Faith University]

Alumni stressed that dating was completely new for them. As college students they only went out on a formal date *after* they had hooked up with someone repeatedly and that person became their boyfriend / girlfriend. Since many hookup partners never reached the point of a committed relationship, many had never been on a date at all.

Carol: He asked me for my phone number and he called me the next day and we talked [on the phone] a couple days and [then] we went out for dinner . . . we went out on [one] date and that was it.

KB: What was that like when you hadn't done that much?

Carol: It was a little weird. Like I said, in college I never went out on dates, the [only] dates I ever went on was with my [college] boyfriend, so it was weird. [24-year-old alumnus of Faith University]

The only major similarity between hooking up in college and dating after college is the location where men and women meet. The alumni I spoke with indicated that they still primarily meet people at bars or parties; however, what happens after the initial meeting changes.[1] Rather than departing from the bar or party to hook up, as they did in college, generally the man asks the woman for her phone number and subsequently contacts her to arrange a date.

When college students hook up, more often than not nothing develops between the two parties beyond the night of the hookup. However, in cases where the hookup partners do become involved after the initial hookup, students would refer to their relationship status as "seeing someone," "talking," "dating," or "hanging out." This represents an in-between stage, beyond a one-night stand, but not a full-fledged relationship. Men and women who are in this type of relationship do not actually go on formal dates. Instead, the pair hangs out in the dorms or meets up at a bar near campus with their friendship circle. For alumni, dating someone means something entirely different. I asked Raquel, a 24-year-old alumnus of State University, to elaborate on this shift.

KB: What is the difference between hanging out and dating? How do you know it's a date?

Raquel: When my [current] boyfriend . . . and I first got together, when we first started dating, he came to my apartment and picked me up. We went out on a date; he took me out to dinner and he brought me back and dropped me off. . . . I say: "He takes me out on dates." I don't call it ["hanging out"]; he and I don't hang out. But in college [people] hung out. We don't do that anymore. [Hanging out] is something you do in college. It's not something I do now.

   KB: Why is it different from college now?

Raquel: In college . . . you don't really have any money so you don't go out and do nice things. [My current boyfriend] will take me out to very expensive, fancy restaurants and we sip wine and have a nice meal and then maybe rent a movie or go out to a movie afterwards. That to me is a date. Going to [a bar in college with a guy] is not a date. A date is when . . . a guy picks you up and takes you somewhere. . . . [In college] we really didn't [go on dates] that much. We would just hang out at the apartment and watch movies or play games, drinking games, stupid things like that.

WHY THE SWITCH TO DATING?

Dating replaces hooking up as the primary script after college because the environmental factors that made hooking up easy on campus are no longer in place. The alumni I spoke with said that one major change since college was that they were no longer socializing in the "safe haven" of campus. During college, they felt as though they knew everyone and could trust them, even though most of their fellow classmates were technically strangers, particularly at larger schools such as State University. If a female student was at a bar or party and was interested in someone she did not know as a hookup partner, she would at least have a classmate who could vouch for the unknown person. In other words, everyone was a "friend-of-a-friend." After college, this sense of familiarity is gone.

   KB: [From what you have told me], hooking up seemed to be a common part of college. . . . And it seems that maybe [hooking up] isn't common after college. Why not?

Shana: I think, I know for me, it is hard to trust someone. I would-
n't feel comfortable with a stranger. In college you felt so
safe. Everyone knew one another. It was somebody's roommate. It was [a] comfort zone. It was safe. "You want to go
home and hook up with him, all right." Because it is somebody's roommate [or he] has a class with someone. Now
it's not that security or comfort zone you had in college. It's
kind of nice walking into somewhere in college and everyone knowing your name. . . . It is comforting. You don't
have that once you graduate. You are out there with all
these new people. . . . I don't trust people that easily. So,
that is why I don't hook up. [25-year-old alumnus of Faith
University]

   KB: So you really feel most comfortable [going on a date with
someone] when it is that friend-of-a-friend connection?
Claudia: Yes. I think it's easier because I have some kind of background. Otherwise it's like: "I don't know anything about
this person." Nothing.
   KB: What are you concerned about if they are a stranger?
Claudia: I don't know. I always think too much about things. I think
of every worse case scenario. But I guess I am more comfortable if I know something about them. [Otherwise] there is
not that level of comfort off the bat. [25-year-old alumnus of
Faith University]

Female alumni were more cautious about going home with "strange
men" than their college counterparts.[2] During college, if a woman
wanted to go home with a man to hook up, they could merely walk
from one part of campus to another. After college, if a woman meets a
man at a bar and she is interested in a hookup, she would either have
to get in a car with the man to accompany him somewhere or the two
parties would have to follow one another in separate vehicles to someone's "place." The men and women I spoke with indicated that women
were very reluctant to do this. Thus, the postcollege environment presents logistical difficulties that do not merely make hooking up incon-
venient, but actually serve to exacerbate a fear of strangers. Twenty-
seven-year-old Stephen, an alumnus of State University, touched on
this point.

KB: Would you say that the hookup scene, as it was in college, doesn't exist anymore?

Stephen: I think it has definitely died down a lot.

KB: Why do you think that is?

Stephen: Girls are reluctant to go home with just some random guy that they meet at a bar. . . . Now it is more along the lines of [someone saying]: "If you are interested, here is my number, give me a call and we will go out sometime."

At first glance, it may seem that men still might want to hook up, but women are just unwilling because of their fear of strangers. While there may be some truth to this, it is not the whole story. In fact, alumni men also revealed concerns about strangers. Some indicated that dating was almost a screening process to "make sure you know what you're getting" and to avoid, as one man put it, "crazy psychos." Matthew, a 28-year-old alumnus of State University, discussed why he thought hooking up was really not a feasible option after college.

KB: How is the hookup scene now compared to college?

Matthew: Now it's more date oriented. You don't get to do that research, generally speaking. If you are dating someone in the [big city where I live] it is a lot different than dating someone who is going to State University. First of all [there are thousands of students at State] and [the city where I live now] has several million people in the metropolitan area. So you don't really know what you are getting into now.

KB: So you don't feel you have that common ground that you had in college?

Matthew: Yes. You may have commonalities but you don't find them out until you are out on a date with that person.

KB: So do you ever just go to a bar and go home with someone the way you would in college?

Matthew: Not nearly as frequently [as during college], maybe one-tenth of the time.

KB: So why, other than not knowing the people as well, why do you think [you hook up one-tenth as often]?

Matthew: I think logistically it is a little more difficult. Because as you grow older . . . you have to drive, everywhere we went in college you walked. It was so much easier. Everything was in such a confined area. But if you met a girl you really liked and maybe you did want to hook up, but what if we were in [the city] and I live in [the suburbs] and she lives [on the other side of town]? Logistically, it could be a nightmare.

KB: Do you even try for [a hookup] and it doesn't work, or you don't even try?

Matthew: I would have to say I don't even try.

KB: So if you are interested in someone what do you do?

Matthew: I would typically ask them out on a date.

Both sexes, then, seemed to realize that campus provided a safe feeling that was not present most of the time after college. Perhaps, as students, they became used to socializing primarily with other people of a similar background in terms of age and social class, whereas in the real world, most bars tend to be occupied with a more diverse clientele. As a fifth-year senior at Faith University, Kevin was in a stage between the college and postcollege setting. He described his observations of why hooking up breaks down after college now that he moved off-campus and is on his own.

KB: You described how things are in college versus after college and you were saying that people didn't date at [Faith U.], but you have now, why do you now [when] you didn't then?

Kevin: [Pauses] It's environment. Do you understand what I'm saying when I say environment? Like the environment has changed. Girls in college know that they can go home and hook up. [When it's a fellow student] . . . they know it's a guy from campus, they know if something goes wrong they can call the school. I think when you get out of this situation girls' guards go up to another level. You know what I'm saying: "Whoa! These guys at all these bars are from all over this area. I don't know where they are from." I think [their] guard comes up. So I think there is more dating that occurs because: "Okay, I really like that guy but I do need to maybe see if he knows some people I know." That's why whenever I start talking to people I say: "Where are you from?" And I know people from anywhere so I'm like: "Do you know these people?" And they are like: "Yeah." It takes the edge off right away because I already knew people that they know

too. So it's like there is a connection. I think in this setting . . .
I don't know about [a big place like] New York City, but in
[this town] where I am, girls [went to one of the] five major
colleges, and if you're [an alumnus] from the five major colleges then somehow you can connect one way or the other.
And that's how you usually end up dating [or] going out on
a date. [Also,] it's the next step, you mature. Girls aren't
going to be like: "I partied with this guy all night in his frat
house and I'm going to sleep with him," [as if they were in
college]. "Now if this guy wants to sleep with me he's got to
take me out to dinner first [so I can] get to know him and
maybe, maybe not. I'm attracted to him, I want to sleep with
him but I'm not going to let it be as easy as it was in college
where my excuse was I was drunk and I was in college and
I can do this." I think girls bring themselves down with their
school and they go kind of nuts.

KB: So they define college as a time when they can do that kind
of stuff?

Kevin: They can do some stuff that they would otherwise not do
when they get out of college.

   In the later part of my interview with Kevin, he gives another reason why alumni favor dating over hooking up. The men and women I
interviewed defined college as a time to "party." After college, everyday
life changes and a new "definition of the situation" takes hold.[3] Many
alumni were very focused on getting established in their careers.
Alumni reported working long hours during the day and being ex-
hausted at night. Gone were the days of going out socially every Thursday, Friday, and Saturday night as many reported was common during
college. Instead, many alumni suggested that they often went out socially only one night per week because they were too tired to go out two
nights in a row. The point is that this change in lifestyle leads to a
change in attitude about what is appropriate behavior. James, a 25-year-
old alumnus of Faith University, mentioned how people had an entirely
different mentality during college.

KB: Do people that you know that are completely out of college
still hook up?

James: Randomly? Not really.

KB: Why do you think that doesn't happen anymore?

James: I don't know. People change when they get out of college. Everything is just "whatever" in college. Anything goes.

KB: So . . . people think of it differently postcollege?

James: Yeah.

After college, there is a markedly more conservative mentality, especially with regard to interaction with the opposite sex. For example, two male alumni, both of whom had been heavily immersed in fraternity life, drinking, and the extremes of the hookup culture during college, spoke of the importance of being polite and respectful of women now that they are out of college. Their responses in other portions of their interviews made it clear that exhibiting courteous behavior toward women was the furthest thing from their minds during their college days. Matthew, a 28-year-old alumnus of State University, discussed how a man should behave when he takes a girl on a date: "I think the gentleman should be very polite on the date, I think it should be a little more formal. Obviously, it gets a little more informal as [the relationship] goes on. But as you're learning about someone, you want to mind your p's and q's." Stephen, a 27-year-old alumnus of State University, also shared his perspective on dating. "You have to put more effort in now [that you are out of college] . . . [if] I am going to take this girl out to dinner and have a good time and spend two hours of my night with her, then obviously I am interested in her and I want to pursue things with her . . . you are more respectful also, more respectful of women [than during college]."

Another major factor contributing to the demise of the hookup script after college is a change in relationship goals for both men and women. Many of the college women I interviewed indicated they did not plan to marry until at least their mid-twenties; for college men it was late twenties or early thirties. Thus, during college there was plenty of time to "play the field" without engaging in a serious marriage-bound relationship. After college, both men and women start to get closer to the age when they would like to marry. As a result, they are increasingly looking for relationships with marriage potential. According to alumni, hooking up was not a good way to find "the one" (i.e., the person he or she will marry). Clark, a 25-year-old alumnus of State University, discussed how people cannot find a "quality" relationship by hooking up; therefore, he chose to go on dates instead.

> *KB:* Why does everyone abandon [the hookup system after college]?
> *Clark:* I don't know. [After college] you are looking for more [of a]
> relationship. I know this person, I can trust them, I can share
> things. If I have a bad day, they will listen to me, those kinds
> of concepts. Meeting someone in a bar, buying them drinks,
> getting them drunk and hooking up in your car, there is no
> quality there at all. You don't even know if that is their real
> name they gave you. . . . As you get older, you . . . want some-
> thing more solid.

Other alumni echoed Clark's sentiments. Alumni did not believe that hooking up was conducive to finding "solid" relationships and a potential marriage partner. Twenty-four-year-old Will, who graduated from Faith University, said that "after college you are possibly looking for that person that you want to spend the rest of your life with so I think it's a long process [of dating] until you actually realize if that is the person you want [to marry]." Thus, with the campus environment no longer in place, hooking up breaks down after college. Alumni no longer exclusively socialize in close proximity with "familiar" people of similar backgrounds. They also largely shift out of party mode and, with marriage more imminent, a formal dating script emerges.

HOW DATING HAPPENS

Dating is different than hooking up in many ways. The hookup calls for sexual activity from the outset, while dating is a process of getting to know someone en route to potential sexual interaction. Additionally, the goal of forming a romantic relationship takes on greater significance for both men and women. Although formal dating was not something alumni practiced in college, the dating script they followed after graduation encompassed a host of traditional customs.[4] According to alumni, the man generally was the one to ask the woman for her phone number. In other words, the man initiated the date by first asking for the phone number and then following up with a phone call to ask for a date. Shana, a 25-year-old alumnus of Faith University, recounted a typical scenario for how two people meet and end up going on a date. "I met him that night and nothing happened, noth-ing physical, we danced on the dance floor; that was it. He asked for my [phone] number, called a couple days later. We went to a concert."

Several men I spoke to, 25-year-old alumnus Will of Faith University among them, mentioned that women prefer the man to be the one to initiate the date.

KB: And as far as getting phone numbers, is there a typical way [it works]?

Will: [Laughs] I would say 75 to 80 percent of the time the girl wants the guy to call; the girl wants the ball to be in the guy's court.

According to the alumni I spoke to, the entire date follows a fairly traditional format. Not only do men initiate the date, but they also generally drive unless the woman suggests meeting somewhere. Once the man picks the woman up at her home or apartment, the two generally go to a public place, such as a restaurant or movie theater. When the check comes, it is generally the man who pays.

KB: When you say you take people out on dates and you said you would say: "I'd like to take you out," [then] do you pick them up [and] do you pay [for whatever you do on the date]? Is it kind of traditional?

Stephen: Yeah.

KB: Is that what it is always like?

Stephen: In my eyes, yeah. I can't speak for all men but if I ask somebody out, I expect to pick them up, unless they want to meet [out somewhere]. . . . [Sometimes] they feel more comfortable meeting because some women prefer that. But other than that, I expect to pick up the bill and I wouldn't ask her to go out and then have her pay, [that's] not my style. [27-year-old alumnus of State University]

Although the man generally pays for the date, sometimes the woman will offer to split the check or she will offer to pay for part of the date. For instance, the man pays for dinner and then the woman offers to pay for a movie. However, most alumni indicated that even if the woman offers to pay for something, the man will usually insist on paying for everything himself.

Claudia: Usually they insist on paying. I always offer money though. I just feel like . . . [if] I know they don't earn a lot of money [then I should offer to pay for something]. I always make an offer and I am usually shot down. [Laughs] [25-year-old alumnus of Faith University]

Jake, a 28-year-old alumnus of State University, confirmed this.

KB: So, you [said that you] call and ask them out to dinner and then do you drive, do you pay, how does that work?
Jake: I am old-fashioned. I take care of it all.
KB: Do they usually offer to pay?
Jake: Some have. I say, "Are you nuts?"
KB: Is that typical of people you know, that the guy would pay?
Jake: I am more old-fashioned. Some girls will go: "Let's split it." But I think the girls today still want the guy to treat them to dinner. They may say: "Let's go dutch," but . . .
KB: They are thinking: "You pay." [Laughs]
Jake: *Exactly*. [Emphasis by interviewee]

Despite men and women being immersed in a decidedly nontraditional, hookup culture during college, the postcollege environment facilitates a radically different, yet traditional, type of behavior. After college, men seemed to interact with the opposite sex as one might expect their grandfathers would have done.[5] In addition to some of the obvious indicators of traditional dating (i.e., the man initiating the date, driving, and paying), men also exhibited other signs of chivalrous behavior. For instance, several alumni mentioned that men hold doors open for their date or open the car door on the passenger's side to see the woman safely to her seat. By their own admission, chivalrous behavior was not something exhibited by these same men during their college years. Interestingly, many men suggested they behaved in a traditional way during a date because they personally were "old-fashioned." However, given that alumni across the board indicated that they behaved this way, it is apparently not as unique as they believed. Rather, men were playing their part.

SEXUAL EXPECTATIONS

It is not surprising that the men and women I interviewed were already familiar with the dating script upon leaving college. Since the dating era, "the date" has been a part of our culture, portrayed in movies and on television for decades. Recently, HBO's popular comedy series *Sex & the City* followed the dating exploits of four thirty-something single women in New York City. The show's depiction of the contemporary dating culture is one where there are virtually no rules. The characters are highly sexually active: they frequently have sex on the first date or go home from bars with strange men. This scenario makes for good entertainment, but its accuracy is questionable. Recent college graduates paint a much tamer picture of the dating scene. The people I spoke to were not only wary of strangers, but regarding first dates, they were very clear: anything more than a goodnight kiss was totally inappropriate.

> *KB:* What would physically happen on a date, okay [let's] say you didn't just meet [the girl], you already met and [then] you went on a date. Do you kiss at the end of the date? Do you have to wait until the second date?
>
> *Clark:* I don't think there is a standard for those kinds of things. I have gotten a kiss goodnight; I have given a kiss goodnight. Never more than that on a first date. . . . [On the] third date, probably [things] get a little more physical. But definitely not the first time you go out. The first time you went out, if you had a good time, I'd hope to get a kiss goodnight.
>
> *KB:* You say "get a" as though they would give it to you.
>
> *Clark:* Oh, I would probably instigate it and hopefully she would accept. [25-year-old alumnus of State University]

> *KB:* What about [what happens] physically at the end of the night. Did you ever get physical with someone at the end of a date?
>
> *Carol:* I would just kiss them goodbye before I got out of the car. [24-year-old alumnus of Faith University]

State University alumnus Jake, 28 years old, agreed with Clark and Carol.

> *KB:* What about the end of a date, how do they usually end?
>
> *Jake:* Usually I will just kiss them goodnight and that is it. I don't expect anything else.

KB: And why is that?

Jake: Because if you were too aggressive then you are wasting your time because they are going to be turned off. But I don't know; it's not going to work, [you should] take things slower.

Alumni stressed how important it is to "get to know" someone before anything sexual happens. To this end, many suggested that it is not only common for nothing sexual to happen on the first date, but even on the first few dates. This represents an abrupt change from the norms of the hookup script. In college, students indicated that it was permissible to go home with someone that you had never dated, or in some cases never met, and engage in a sexual encounter. Suddenly, the same people who hooked up in college now believe men and women should find out more about each other before anything sexual happens. However, if the two parties are going to continue dating, things must escalate sexually at some point, but when? Although their answers varied, the consensus seemed to be "the later, the better."

KB: Do you remember how far into your relationship with your fiancé you guys slept together?

Carol: Six or seven months . . . I don't think there is any right time to have sex or not to have sex. I think a month or two is really soon. I don't think you really know someone well then. But then some people might think six months isn't [a long time, either]. It depends also on how often you see and talk to the person. If you are seeing someone for six months but you see them every other weekend and talk to them three times a week, I don't think that you know that person as well as someone [who] talks to each other every day on the phone and sees them three times a week. . . . I think that [at] six months we had met each other's family. . . . [By then] I felt like I had known him for much longer than six months. And so I think that if you really know someone, I can only [have sexual intercourse] with someone if I can tell them everything.

KB: Did you feel like it was both of your decisions to wait until the six month mark or he was ready and you decided when?

Carol: I think it was more that I did decide when, but he never tried to get me to [have sexual intercourse] earlier. [24-year-old alumnus of Faith University]

Clearly, alumni had not reverted back to the script of the dating era with regard to when sexual intercourse should occur. Most of the men and women I spoke with were not adhering to the guideline of waiting until marriage (or engagement) for sex. Instead, they made decisions about sex in light of more contemporary standards (i.e., premarital sex is expected). However, it should not be inferred from the excerpt from Carol that six months, or any other particular time frame, constitutes a norm for when sexual intercourse takes place in the postcollege dating scene. Rather, the point is that delaying sexual intercourse beyond the initial dating phase is regarded as the "right thing to do." Raquel, a 24-year-old alumnus of State University, was also in a very serious relationship at the time of the interview. She was not engaged, but she was living with her boyfriend. Like Carol, she thought it was better to "wait" before having sexual intercourse. However, Raquel's version of how long to wait differed significantly from Carol's.

> *KB*: Do you remember with [your current boyfriend] when things escalated sexually?
> *Raquel*: I made him wait a long time. I made him wait.
> *KB*: So he wanted to [have sexual intercourse] before you [did]?
> *Raquel*: Oh yeah, he did. He wanted to from the beginning, but I made him wait a long time. I made him wait like a couple months, which for me was a long time.
> *KB*: Okay. When you say you made him wait, do you mean for intercourse?
> *Raquel*: Yeah.

It was not only women who believed delaying sexual intercourse was the appropriate course of action. Will, a 24-year-old alumnus of Faith University, was also in a serious exclusive relationship at the time of the interview. In the excerpt below, Will discussed what he thinks is appropriate to do sexually on the first date and thereafter. Again, although there is no specific time dimension, waiting until the relationship progresses and both parties are on the "same page" seemed to be critically important.

> *KB*: What do you think is appropriate to do with someone physically or sexually in the dating realm now that it is postcollege? Do you have standards as to what you think is appropriate?

Will: Umm. As far as a first date goes?

KB: Yeah.

Will: I think the first couple dates I wouldn't even expect any-thing, after a kiss that's it. All you do is kill yourself if it's anything more than that. Why would you want to do that? You are just getting to know the person. After college you are possibly looking for that person that you want to spend the rest of your life with so I think it's a long process until you actually realize if that is the person you want and you get a good enough feeling that's what she wants then it goes to the next level. And that could be months [or] that could be a year. For myself and for my girlfriend [just kissing] lasted a while.

KB: Just kissing?

Will: Yeah. I think any more would have hurt us and I don't think I would be together with her right now.

KB: Try to explain that a little more. Why do you think that is the case?

Will: To be blunt about it, I think the guy is a jerk.

KB: The guy is a jerk if he tries for anything [sexual] too early?

Will: Maybe I am just different. I think if you really care about this person, and it's not about like holding back, it's not like I was saying: "Hey I really like this girl and I am not going to do something to screw it up." I didn't *want* to do it. I really cared about her and thought I was going to be with her for a long time. I wanted that to be special, I wanted to wait a while and make sure that us two were really connected, on the same page and that it was going to be a long relationship.

KB: Not to be graphic, but there is kissing and sleeping together and a lot of in between. Are you saying you should wait for even the in-between [sexual interaction] for quite a while?

Will: Yeah. Absolutely . . . I think my longer relationships have been when it's been a friend first, so we might meet and then hang out for a while as friends. Then we realize this is great and maybe take it to another level as far as going out by our-selves [on dates] to dinner, movies, whatever, out to the bar scene maybe meet up with people. Then obviously you have feelings for each other, so there is kissing going on, a good-night kiss [and eventually that] might lead to something else.

> *KB:* And do you think that this is a unique standard that you
> have. Or do you think that this is what [your friends] think
> too?
>
> *Will:* I would say my closer friends feel that way. [Emphasis by in-
> terviewee]

REVISITING THE SEXUAL DOUBLE STANDARD

The change, with the dating script, to more conservative sexual norms
is ironic. Sexual behavior is no longer taking place under the micro-
scope that it once was. During college, students were able to heavily
monitor one another's actions, gossip about others, and label peers for
violating norms. Women's behavior, in particular, was under scrutiny if
they were too promiscuous. Thus, the college hookup scene contained
many pitfalls for women. After college, nobody is watching anymore.
The postcollege environment is no longer conducive to keeping abreast
of the "private" lives of hundreds of people. Therefore, with their reputations no longer at stake, it would be logical for women to feel free to
"let loose" sexually after college. Yet the opposite is true.

Generally, alumni indicated that life after college is much more isolated; they spend most of their time either at work or with a few close
friends. They became less preoccupied with one another's business. As
a result, sexual behavior became more private after graduation. The
men and women I spoke to said that they did not know the intimate details of their coworkers' or, in some cases, even their close friends' lives
anymore. Twenty-five-year-old Shana, an alumnus of Faith University,
had this to say on the subject:

> *KB:* In terms of either you or your group of friends, do you have
> a standard of what you think is appropriate [sexually] and
> when? When things can get more physical or when things, if
> ever, should advance to sleeping with someone?
>
> *Shana:* I don't think we have a standard . . . I don't think we really
> talk about it so much anymore.
>
> *KB:* Why do you think that is?
>
> *Shana:* I just think everybody is getting older and we don't want to
> say it.
>
> *KB:* It's more private?

Shana: Yeah. It's more private [than it was in college]. It doesn't have to be everybody's business.

The influence of a new, more isolated environment is also a factor, according to Lucille, a 23-year-old alumnus of Faith University. "Because we don't live in such close proximity to each other anymore [as we did in college] . . . and because we don't wake up and go to brunch or whatever, so you don't know as much [about each other's personal lives]."

Matthew, a 28-year-old alumnus of State University, believed that there is a greater degree of anonymity in the postcollege environment, and that this anonymity protects one's reputation.

> *KB*: When you said people would get reputations for [having sexual intercourse on a first encounter] in college, would they now [in the postcollege environment]?
>
> *Matthew*: No, because that is the whole logistics thing . . . it's so vast. I could literally go out and have sex with two different women on two different nights and they would never know each other. If they went home and talked to anyone they probably wouldn't know who I was. So there is anonymity to it.

If women's reputations are not on the line, why does sexual behavior become more conservative after college?

During college, women had to learn the rules as they progressed through their four years on campus. By senior year, many women had figured out that the more they really liked someone and the more they wanted a relationship with that person, the less they should do sexually. Specifically, these women learned that if they were "too sexual" during an initial hookup, the man of interest would be less likely to consider them for a potential relationship. I believe that many women take this knowledge with them after graduation and it affects how they adapt to dating. Women have more at stake than ever relationship-wise as they become increasingly focused on finding the person they will eventually marry. Even if women no longer have to worry about being labeled by their classmates, they do have to worry about what their date thinks of them and whether he will call again. This may, in part, account for the more conservative sexual behavior exhibited in the postcollege environment.

There is still a sexual double standard after college. However, sexual behavior is being evaluated by the two *individuals* on the date, rather than by the group (i.e., the inhabitants of the college campus). As in college, it is women's sexual behavior that receives the closest scrutiny and there are consequences for those who violate the sexual norms deemed appropriate for the dating script. The men I spoke with said they would not be interested in pursuing a romantic relationship with a woman who was too sexually aggressive, particularly on the first date.

James: I went out one time with a person, it was happy hour and we went to another place [together] and [then] I took her home. She asked me to come in for a drink and I came in for a drink and then it progressed a little more and I was out [of there].

KB: Why?

James: Uhhh.

KB: You thought she was trying to get too physical?

James: I didn't think she was like that first of all. You should see this girl at work, she is quiet and like all about her work. But outside of work she is totally different. It took me by surprise. I kind of weirded-out and left. [25-year-old alumnus of Faith University]

Apparently, James was under the impression that the woman he worked with was "not that kind of girl." Thus, he was surprised that she initiated more than a kiss on their first encounter. This norm violation meant the first encounter would be the last. Similarly, Jake, a 28-year-old alumnus of State University, discussed a situation where a woman was very aggressive with him on the first date. Unlike James, Jake engaged in sexual intercourse with the woman, but was never able to think of her as a potential relationship partner.

KB: Have you ever had a girl, postcollege, be aggressive with you?

Jake: Yeah. Yes I have.

KB: How did that work?

Jake: It was after dinner and we are sitting in the car and it was right out in front of the place and she jumped over the car seat and she started . . . sticking her tongue down my throat. It was pretty cool actually. It was a surprise. Yeah.

KB: [Laugh] So, did you go out on another date with her?

Jake: Oh yeah.

KB: Did that become a relationship?

Jake: No. But it did turn into sex; let me put it that way.

KB: Do you remember how many dates before it turned into sex?

Jake: It was the first date.

KB: Oh, it turned into sex that night?

Jake: Yeah.

KB: In the car?

Jake: Yes.

KB: What did you think of this girl, positively or negatively, [you said] it was kind of a surprise that she did that. Was [it] a good surprise?

Jake: Well, let's put it this way. It was good . . . from a physical standpoint, but that's all I saw her as from that point on, as [something physical]. I never took it serious[ly].

KB: Do you think she was in it for the sex or do you think she wanted you to be her boyfriend?

Jake: No, she wanted some sort of relationship. But, [oh well].

KB: So how did that end?

Jake: It just fizzled out. I just stopped calling [her].

Other men voiced similar concerns about women who were too "forward" or "put out" too much, too soon.

KB: You said that you would not try [to initiate] . . . something too sexual in the beginning if you wanted [to pursue] some sort of relationship. Suppose the girl were to try for something more sexual in the beginning. Would that actually deter you from being interested in her?

Will: Absolutely. . . . Again, I don't know who would make the first move . . . but I think that a girl that is too . . . what is the word?

KB: Forward?

Will: Yeah. A girl [that] is too forward . . . guys don't like that kind of personality. [24-year-old alumnus of Faith University]

Twenty-eight-year-old alumnus of State University Matthew put it even more bluntly: "I would never, ever date a girl I banged on the first night. *Never! Ever! Ever!"* [emphasis by interviewee, a 28-year-old alumnus of State University].

The men I spoke with were also concerned about their dates' sexual history. Jake, a 28-year-old alumnus of State University, discussed his concern about the number of a woman's past sexual partners. Interestingly, Jake says that some women are unwilling to reveal that information.

KB: What about for a girl that you would be interested in. Would you have any expectation of what their [sexual] past would be or what you would find acceptable?

Jake: What age are we talking about here? How old is the girl?

KB: Well, let's say she is your age.

Jake: If she is 28, less than [the number of fingers on] two hands. If she's in double digits [I would be concerned].

KB: Is that something you would normally talk about with a girl at some point, sexual history?

Jake: Of course. I always like to bring that up. Sometimes they will talk about it, sometimes they won't. Actually, now that I think about it . . . the girl I am with now . . . declined to answer that question.

Similarly, Matthew, a 28-year-old alumnus of State University, expressed concerns about a woman's sexual past. Matthew's concerns were particularly interesting when juxtaposed with his own sexual past.

KB: Are you curious when you first become interested in someone, what their sexual past is?

Matthew: Sure, for very practical reasons. You never know what you are going to get out there [in terms of sexually transmitted diseases].

KB: If there was no such thing as STD's, would you [still] care [about their sexual past]? . . . If previous number of sexual partners came up, is there a number a girl could tell you that would make you cringe?

Matthew: First of all, I think guys always inflate their numbers and I think girls always deflate their numbers. I think it would depend on the age. If you are talking about my age anything over 15 [past sexual partners] would make me cringe.

KB: But [you said previously that] your number is over 100 [past
sexual partners].

Matthew: Yes . . . there is a double standard. There is a certain
amount of hypocrisy to our culture. There really is.

Later in the interview Matthew explained his philosophy on what
women should do sexually in the postcollege environment.

KB: So how should things progress sexually in a best-case scenario?

Matthew: I think the less that a girl does [sexually] the better. You
don't want to play your hand right away. Because guys are
smart . . . guys know if a girl puts out too much the first
night, I don't think I am anything special. I don't think I am
the cat's meow . . . and all of the sudden after one night with
me she turns into a sexually crazed lunatic. That is the furthest thing from the truth. You have to realize if she [gets
physical] with you, who knows what she was doing last
week. So . . . a girl that can practice a little self-restraint, I
think is the one you are looking to keep.

THE ROLE OF ENVIRONMENT

In 2003, the movie *Old School* premiered, featuring comedians Will Fer-
rell, Vince Vaughan, and Luke Wilson as thirty-something friends who
buy a house close to a college campus and start throwing fraternity-
style parties that attract herds of students. The story reveals that the
men enjoy the license that the pretext of college gives them, and, regardless of their age, they start behaving like students themselves. The
point is that environmental context facilitates behavior. The alumni I
spoke with participated in the hookup scene while in college; after
graduation, they began following the dating script because the environmental factors that sustained hooking up were no longer in place.
This does not mean that the alumni never hooked up since graduation.
In fact, there were circumstances, which mirrored campus life, where
alumni would revert back to the hooking-up script.

According to alumni, after college, the only major exception to formal dating is when they spend time at the beach (also referred to as "the

shore").[6] Going to beach towns is very common among young heterosexual singles on the East Coast. Several alumni I interviewed spent
many weekends during the summer at beach towns located a couple of
hours from their full-time residences. Generally, they rent a beach property along with a large group of friends and acquaintances. When they
are at the beach on weekends throughout the summer, they hook up;
from fall to spring, they go on formal dates. A look at environmental
context explains why the sexual script changes with the change of a sea-
son. Carol, a 24-year-old alumnus of Faith University, mentioned how
she hooked up a couple times when she was at the shore. During the
rest of the year when she was operating out of her home, she did not
hook up (but did go on a few formal dates).

> *KB*: Are you talking about dating and hooking up as two sepa-
> rate things or the same thing?
> *Carol*: Two separate things. Like dating, I would actually go out
> somewhere like to dinner or to the movies.
> *KB*: Give me a scenario, one of a hookup and one of a date. What
> are the differences?
> *Carol*: Well, one of the hookups was [when I] met a guy at a bar, but
> I actually had known him [before that]. This was at the
> shore, he walked me home and I kissed him. Then the next
> time I saw him same thing, he'd walk me home [from a bar
> and] I'd kiss him.

In Carol's case, her hookups at the shore culminated in "just kissing."
However, for several of the alumni I interviewed, hookups at the shore
culminated in greater sexual intimacy on the first encounter. This is not
surprising given that the hookup script allows for a greater degree of
sexual intimacy even during an initial encounter.

> *Jake*: I met her three weeks ago down the shore and things pro-
> gressed pretty quickly.
> *KB*: When you say progressed quickly, what do you mean?
> *Jake*: Well we hooked up both nights that weekend [when we
> met]. And she came back down this past weekend and we
> hooked up every night, four nights in a row.
> *KB*: Are you sexually involved with this girl fully?
> *Jake*: Not fully yet. Oral sex, not sex-sex.

KB: Not intercourse?
Jake: Yes. [28-year-old alumnus of State University]

At first glance, interacting one way with the opposite sex for three-quarters of the year and then interacting a different way for one-quarter of the year (i.e., during summer weekends) seems inexplicable. However, when one considers the similarities between the shore and campus environments, it becomes clear why both these environments facilitate the same script for behavior. First, like college, the shore scene contains many familiar faces. Everyone is a friend-of-a-friend, so fear of strangers is nullified. Second, the landscape of the shore is similar to college insofar as you can walk anywhere you want to go.

Will: Yeah, I definitely miss college. I think [that is] one of the [reasons] people of our age . . . look forward to the shore. I think the shore is kind of an extension to college.
KB: And why is that?
Will: Because you have a group of people living together, you are all living within a certain mile radius, where you can forget the car thing. Once you get down the shore for the weekend you can park the car and it's not going anywhere. You can go out to a bar scene that is all young people and you are again in that college atmosphere. [24-year-old alumnus of Faith University]

Matthew: The beach is the only exception to the [formal dating] rule. It's kind of like a fantasy land down there almost.
KB: So what do you think is so similar, what do you think about the beach makes it more similar to college than here [in the city / suburbs]?
Matthew: It's the same concept of logistics. Everyone is packed into one small town. There is a sense of familiarity . . . you can meet people and recognize people. So any night you can go out to a bar [at the beach and] I'll know at least thirty people at that place. Whereas if I go out to a club in [the city], I might run into one, maybe two people that I know. That's that whole meeting people through other people deal. [28-year-old alumnus of State University]

In addition to the logistical advantages and sense of familiarity at the shore, there is also a different definition of the situation. Recall that many students believed college was "time to party." The shore scene encourages a similar mentality. The men and women I spoke with felt that they worked hard during the year and they deserved a break when they are on "vacation." Stephen and Jake, both 28-year-old alumni from State University, said the following in separate interviews:

KB: Would you say the shore is any different than [your] social life up here [where you live] in terms of [male/female interaction]?

Stephen: Hmm-mm. I think it's . . . more [of a] laid-back mentality during the summer. That so-called "it's summertime I want to do my thing." You see a lot more of that [at the shore] than you see up here during the wintertime.

KB: Would you say that the shore is more like college than up here?

Stephen: *Absolutely.* The shore is definitely closer to college than the city [where I live] is. [Emphasis by interviewee]

KB: Is the summer [beach] scene different than during the year?

Jake: No doubt about it. Yes.

KB: Why is that?

Jake: Girls are much more liberal, they are much more of interest, talkative down the shore. [At home] there is more dating, I'd say fall through spring. [During the] summer, everybody goes down [to the shore] just to have a good time.

KB: There is more of like a hookup college scene [at the beach]?

Jake: Totally.

KB: What do you think of that? Do you like the summer?

Jake: Yeah, of course. [Laughs]

It seems that alumni actually engage in what can be referred to as "script switching."[7] In other words, they utilized the formal dating script during the fall, winter, and spring; however, during the summer (when they were at the shore), they utilized the hookup script. Although some of the men I interviewed were enthused about the opportunities for hooking up at the shore, not everyone held the same view.

KB: You spent some time down the shore during the summer. Is anything different down there than it is during . . . September to May up here?

Elizabeth: It wasn't for me.

KB: Did you have the same thing of guys asking you out down there?

Elizabeth: It was almost like being back in college. [I was like]: "What? No! I am not going to make out with you at the bar. What is wrong with you?" [Laughs] Maybe it's because, I don't know what it is, but it felt like being back in college. In a crowded bar or party, everyone is drinking and I don't know. It was weird because I kind of felt like am I the only one who is past this now. You know? But there [were] some [who asked]: "Can I have your number?" But, there was also lots of [me thinking]: "Can you stop breathing on me." [25-year-old alumnus of Faith University]

Unlike Elizabeth, not all men and women simply "age out" of hooking up. In other words, the shift to dating after college is not just due to people maturing. When the environmental factors are in place, many return to the hookup script.

THE SEARCH FOR RELATIONSHIPS

Men and women find themselves playing new roles in the dating script. During college, men were often sex driven, primarily interested in women whom they found physically attractive. In the dating culture, men redefine themselves as more conservative and old-fashioned; interactions with women take on a more serious tone. They now seek romantic relationships and desire more substantive qualities in a partner.[8] For most women, their objective postcollege did not change. They continue to pursue relationships, but their sexual behavior becomes more reserved. On the surface, it appears that men and women are on the same page. Unlike their college years, both spoke of wanting relationships, including serious ones; however, their timetables for "settling down" are still at odds. Men can afford to take their time to find "the one" via dating, while women, who generally want to marry sooner than men, often have difficulty finding a serious, marriage-bound relationship as quickly as they desire. Coming to the realization that they would not be married as soon as they hoped was very disillusioning for some of the women. Elizabeth, a 25-year-old alumnus of Faith University, addressed this issue.

> I want to have kids now. I am like: "Obviously that is not going to happen." I didn't want to be, and not that it is bad for anyone who is but, I didn't want to be thirty. Maybe I will have kids in a few years, [but] I wanted to have them young. Soon. Now I am like: "Wow! That is not happening." I mean like even if I met someone right now and dated someone for a year and a half at least, get engaged for a year, get married and [be] married for a year, I am thirty. "Let's have kids now," that is what I wanted. And I don't even see that happening soon. So I am like "Great! Okay, [my plan is] out the window!" [I guess I'll have to move to] Plan B. [Laughs]

Lucille, a 23-year-old Faith University alumnus, offered the following:

Lucille:My main group of friends is very, I call it boy crazy. They want a boyfriend so bad they can taste it. [There are] lots of tears when they get drunk. They get very emotional about it.
   KB: About guys?
Lucille:Yeah.
   KB: About what aspects, [what] brings them to tears?
Lucille:When they get drunk they get very emotional. [Crying voice] "I don't have a boyfriend and I just want a boyfriend. Why can't I find someone?" That type of thing.

Claudia, a 25-year-old alumnus of Faith University, described a common difficulty:

   KB: Would you say that you are happy with the social life that is available to you post-college and the dating opportunities? Is what's out there good or is it a struggle?
Claudia: Socially it's good. I am happy with my friends. Good group of people and we always have a good time. But dating, there is not really a whole lot out there. Like two of my good friends, unbelievably handsome men, very intelligent, very fun, and of course they are both gay. [Laughs] Of course you

got to wonder if they are really good looking and intelligent, if they work, if they are employed, that is always a good one [laughs], and you're not going to support them, they are usually gay. It's unfortunate [that many men of interest] are also married. So that is a struggle. There is not, I don't see a bunch of great guys, even a bunch [of] mature or even nice guys. A lot of them are very self-centered, it's almost like a lot of them are, I guess the term is "players." They will just date as many girls as they can. And they are like: "I got to do it now before I get married." I think too many are like that. Others are just not, there is no, what is the word, real emotion. They just kind of go through their day and then it's just another thing on their list: work, date. I haven't met too many really okay, decent guys. If I have, they are usually gay or married. I mean I know they are out there somewhere, maybe it's just like I don't know the areas they are in. I assume there are some out there.

For the women, finding someone was only part of the problem. Like their college counterparts, alumni women were also eager to turn casual relationships into more committed ones and to hang on to boyfriends once they found them. Thus, the struggle between men and women over what they want from relationships continues after college.

THE HOOKUP ERA

The college hookup scene has lasting effects on alumni. First, graduates share a hooking-up background. After college, men and women enter a dating scene that is new to them because the hookup culture on campus is all that most of them have known. Despite being thrust into dating, some alumni yearn for a return to the hookup scene whenever circumstances permit. Their shared experience allows the hookup to reemerge sometimes (e.g., summertime at the beach). The fact that the postcollege environment utilizes both the dating and hookup scripts could lead to some confusion among singles when two parties might not be on the "same page." This scenario was played out many times in alumni accounts of one person trying to go too far sexually (according to the hookup script) when the other party was thinking of it as a date (and behaving more conservatively as a result). In other cases, alumni, such as Elizabeth, spoke of being irritated that some men were still in hookup mode when she wanted to be asked out on dates.

Second, the focus of the social scene remains (as it was in college) on friendship groups. After graduation, alumni go on dates, but spending time with groups of friends and engaging in alcohol-centered socializing is the centerpiece of social life for many. Although dating replaced hooking up as the primary means for beginning romantic and sexual relationships, it is not as central to social life as hooking up was during college. On campus, partying and hooking up went hand in hand. That is not to say that every student hooked up after every party, but hooking up was going on every weekend. The alumni I interviewed went on dates, but they were not immersed in a dating culture the way they were immersed in a hookup culture in college. Even the most active in the singles scene do not go on dates on a weekly basis.

The infrequency of dating was a problem for some of the men and women who were looking for a relationship but having difficulty finding one. Many were not satisfied with trying to find dates via the bar scene. This may account for the popularity of internet dating, speed dating, and other organized attempts to help singles find dating partners.[9] Even a cursory look at the profiles on Web sites such as match.com reveals that men and women turn to these resources because more traditional avenues are not working for them.

Thus, hooking up is not just a meaningless phase that young people go through in college. Rather, the sexual and romantic lives of men and women who come of age in the hookup era are continuously shaped by their past experiences with the campus hookup culture.

8

Hooking Up and Dating

A Comparison

In *The Way We Never Were*: *American Families and the Nostalgia Trap*, historian Stephanie Coontz challenges those who lament the loss of "traditional family values" by debunking myths about families of the past.[1] Coontz contends that the images of ideal family life that many people conjure up resemble a hodgepodge of old television shows' depictions of a bygone era (i.e., *The Waltons* [1930s], *Leave It to Beaver* [1950s], etc.), which often misrepresent the realities that families faced during those time periods. Thus, sentimental views of the past are often presented using revisionist history. Likewise, many critics of the hooking-up phenomenon have compared it to the rose-tinted version of dating, emphasizing the deterioration of courtship customs since the glory days of the dating era.[2] This raises the question: How significant is the shift from dating to hooking up? In *Dating, Mating and Marriage*, sociologist Martin Whyte states that "the topic of continuity and change in premarital relations is a 'blank spot' in the study of social change in America."[3] With this in mind, let's consider the similarities and differences between the traditional dating script and the contemporary hookup script in college.

SEX

The most notable difference in the shift from the dating script to the hookup script is how sexual behavior fits into the equation. But it would be a mistake to assume that men and women in the dating era were any less interested in sexual interaction than those in today's hookup culture. In some cases, a man asking a woman on a date was a thinly veiled attempt to see how much she would "put out" sexually.[4] Therefore, one of the primary objectives of a date was the same as that of a hookup (i.e., that something sexual would happen). Although men and women in both the hooking-up and dating eras had sexual objectives, the timing has changed. With traditional dating, sexual interaction occurred after the two parties had gone on a date or series of dates. With hooking up, the sexual interaction comes first; going on a date comes later, or not at all for those who never make it to the point of "going out" or at least "hanging out." Marie, a senior at State University, discussed what typically happens after an initial hookup. "Most [girls] who hook up initially get a lot of bullshit, like a lot of guys will be like: 'Yeah, I'll call you,' but they don't. You know, so it might take them a while to see you out and then hook up with you more before they really, you know, want to like call and hang out."

Some college women I interviewed said they would prefer to "get to know someone" before engaging in sexually intimate acts. The hookup script does not preclude getting to know someone prior to the first hookup; however, it does not require it, either. The dating script did require it.

The content of what can fall under the rubric of a "sexual encounter" has also changed with the shift to the hookup script. Most college students during the dating era restricted their sexual experimentation on dates to so-called "necking" and "petting."[5] Oral sex was not a part of the sexual script for the majority of people during the dating era.[6] The sexual possibilities are much greater for the contemporary hookup script. According to the college students I spoke with, hooking up can mean "just kissing," "fooling around" (i.e., petting), "oral sex," or "sex-sex" (i.e., sexual intercourse).[7] Although "going all the way" was not unheard of during the dating era, it was not the norm. There is evidence that many women had sexual intercourse prior to marriage, but most did so only with the man they would eventually marry.[8] In the hookup era, intercourse is not limited to exclusive, marriage-bound relationships. The hookup script includes the potential for a wide array of sexual behavior, including intercourse, even in the most casual encounters.[9] This represents a significant departure from what the dating script allowed.

THE RULES

In the dating era the rules were clear: young people, especially women, were not supposed to have sexual intercourse prior to marriage.[10] Religious leaders played a primary role in communicating this standard to the American public. Since the sexual revolution, Americans largely re-buffed religious reasons for delaying sexual intimacy, and attitudes to-ward premarital sex became more lax.[11] For example, most approve of sexual intercourse prior to marriage, but only in the context of an on-going, exclusive relationship.[12] Most of the college men and women I interviewed indicated that neither their religious affiliation nor their re-ligious beliefs had a major effect on their participation in the hookup culture. Adrienne, a senior at Faith University, considered herself a practicing Catholic. She also indicated that her religious beliefs affected her day-to-day behavior; however, these beliefs did not prevent her from hooking up or engaging in premarital sex with her boyfriend.

KB: Do you think that [Faith University] is any different because it's a Catholic school with regard to male-female stuff?
Adrienne: Not really. I don't think so . . . well, obviously they don't like hand out condoms. And I don't think you'd be able, like I don't even know if you had a problem with your birth con-trol or anything, I don't even know if you could like say any-thing to the health people. I think that might make people a little more like apprehensive to go [to the campus health cen-ter]. I mean you might have [some people who] come here that want to wait until marriage [to have sex] and stuff like that. . . . Once a year you might see a poster or something [that says] like: "Wait until marriage" or something. But it's not like anything else [is different than any other school]. Like [I said before] there's not condoms in the bathroom or anything like that. But I think the girls and the guys, they pretty much hook up, they just hook up the same [whether they are at a Catholic college or not]. Because I think you can still be like religious, like I said before, I'm religious, but I still engage in like premarital sex. But I don't think that's wrong necessarily. So I think that's where a lot of people are right now.

The change in the script for sexual behavior on the college cam-pus is part of a larger trend toward increased premarital sexual experi-ence throughout our culture.[13] In one of the most comprehensive stud-ies on sexual behavior of men and women in the United States, Lau-mann et al. found that the median age at first sexual intercourse decreased throughout the twentieth century, particularly for white women. In the latest birth cohort, the median age at first intercourse was approximately 17 for white men and women.[14] This change, coupled with the increased age at first marriage, has led those who came of age in more recent years to accumulate more sexual partners than those in the pre-sexual-revolution dating era.[15] Changing times and circumstances have led to a change in society's standards regarding premarital sex. In the dating era, "waiting for marriage" meant delaying intercourse for a relatively short period of time. In the hookup era, men and women spend more time being single adults, so delaying intercourse for marriage has become an increasingly difficult standard to achieve. Therefore, in the hookup era, society does not strictly dictate that men and women wait for marriage, and any religious regulations to that effect are not staunchly followed.[16]

Although the contemporary ideal may be for intercourse to occur only in committed relationships, on the college campus many students were willing to have sex under other circumstances when the ideal was not available or, in the case of some college men, when the ideal was not desired. The increased sexual possibilities with the hookup script may seem to create more options for college students. In other words, while those in the dating era were not supposed to engage in sexual intercourse on dates, those in the hookup era can choose to have sexual intercourse or choose to abstain (until they are in an exclusive relationship or married). However, increased choice has also brought about a sense of normlessness.

The fact that there are no clear standards has led to confusion for students trying to decide when sex is appropriate. Many students believe that having sex is simply a matter of personal choice. The problem is that students' "personal" choices are affected by what they perceive "everybody else" is doing sexually. Unfortunately, students' perceptions are often distorted. For example, if students perceive other students as being highly sexually active under a wide array of circumstances via the hookup scene, they may not want to be left behind. This helps explain how virginity, at least for women, went from a "treasure to be safeguarded" (in the dating era) to a "problem to be solved" (in the post-sexual-revolution hooking-up era).[17] In fact, some college students spoke of virginity as something to "get rid of" to avoid being "known as a virgin."[18]

KB: Do you know any people that are virgins?

Larry: Very few. Very few.

KB: How is that viewed? Is it males or females that you know that are virgins?

Larry: I'd say I know both and it's very shady. People that are virgins I've found, I find out that they are virgins because they won't come out and tell you. They kind of seem a little shameful of it. They haven't "done it" yet, if you want to put it that way.

KB: Guys are embarrassed about it or girls are embarrassed about it too?

Larry: Both.

KB: Okay. Is that something people would get teased about?

Larry: Sure. Sometimes [people will say] like: "You haven't done it yet, what are you waiting for?" I've seen that before. [Senior, Faith University]

Rebecca: I know a lot of people who just want to get the sex thing, well one person, who just wanted to get the sex thing over with. She didn't need it really to mean a lot, she just needed it to be over, so she could have her virginity gone, you know [laughing]. [But losing your virginity is] supposed to be a special moment kind of thing. [Sophomore, State University]

The lack of a clear standard in the hookup era has also led to some problematic behavior. For those students who believe "anything goes," college social life can take the form of excessive drinking and exploitive sexual encounters. In 2006, the media spotlight turned to Duke University when rape allegations were made against three members of their lacrosse team. Although this scandal held the attention of the public for a variety of reasons, it underscored the problem many college campuses face with regard to the extremes of the hookup culture. Regardless of the outcome of the criminal investigation, it was clear that members of this team were engaging in heavy alcohol consumption and creating a sex-charged atmosphere by hiring two exotic dancers. It is this type of behavior that has concerned many scholars who have studied binge drinking, fraternity life, and rape.[19]

Students define normal sexual behavior relative to their peers. Those who get caught up with certain groups on campus, who define their college experience as the characters did in the movie *Animal House,* might have trouble distinguishing the behavior of their friends from that of a typical college student. With no firm guidelines decreeing when, where, and with whom sex is appropriate, some students can engage in lewd behavior and think it's permissible because there are no rules saying otherwise.

WHAT'S LOVE GOT TO DO WITH IT?

Along with the rule forbidding premarital sex, the conventions of the dating script pertaining to the emotional side of relationships also wavered in the shift to hooking up. In the dating era, the script offered an opportunity for men and women to learn about their dating partners. While there may have been plenty of cross-sex interaction generally, going on a date represented a distinct time where the pair could get to know each other. While the dating script dictated that men and women spend "quality time" together, hooking up does not. Although the hookup script does not preclude two people from getting to know each other (aside from sexually), it does not require it, either. Liz, a freshman at Faith University, began hooking up with someone she met in the first weeks of school. Although hooking up continued for months and eventually led to sexual intercourse, it never became a romantic relationship. When Liz's partner began to show less interest in frequent hookup encounters and the sexual aspect of the relationship fizzled, she found that there was not much of a foundation for a relationship. Even building a close friendship was a struggle.

> *KB:* If you could paint an ideal scenario of how you would meet and get together with someone, how would it be?
>
> *Liz:* Well, I guess . . . seeing them at a party or something and having a nice conversation, realizing that we have something in common or that we seem to hit it off. And then, um, like maybe he would get my number and then we'd talk or I would see him on campus or something. And then we would hang out the next weekend and see where it went from there. I don't like jumping into things because that always ends up bad, I feel like.
>
> *KB:* Why do you think it does?

> *Liz*: Because you don't give it a chance to become friends with someone or you don't really know someone [if you hook up with him right away]. I think that's what happened to me in the beginning [of this year] because we just jumped into it so fast and . . . we're just starting now to like become like real friends. . . . Of course we were friends before, but it was more on like a physical level and now that it's backed off [and we don't hook up as often anymore] it's kind of like upsetting. Like I feel bad for myself, you know, that I let that happen. Like, I don't want to be like that. I don't want to just like meet someone and jump right into something because it doesn't give it enough like . . . like um . . .
>
> *KB*: The time to develop the friendship aspect?
>
> *Liz*: Yeah, yeah, things just like, yeah. I don't know, and when things fizzled with that person it was like: "What are you left with?"

Men and women in the hookup scene seem to have to work harder to build a relationship of any kind. Thus, to the extent that relationship formation is a goal, dating offered a better script for doing this. This point was emphasized by many recent graduates. After college, the men and women I interviewed became increasingly focused on finding a boyfriend/girlfriend, and in order to do so, most virtually abandoned hooking up in favor of traditional dating.

Getting to know someone, via the dating script, was also a way for men and women to ascertain whether or not they had romantic feelings toward their dating partner. Presumably, if feelings got stronger as the couple continued dating, sexual intimacy would also increase. Thus, in the dating era, there was some expectation that the degree of sexual intimacy would match the degree of emotional intimacy. In other words, two people would become increasingly sexually intimate as they grew "closer."[20] In fact, during the dating era there was a level of sexual intimacy deemed appropriate for each stage of the dating process.[21] Ideally, young men and women would initially limit their sexual interaction to kissing.[22] Within an ongoing dating relationship, necking and petting were hallmarks of the dating experience.[23] Sexual intercourse was supposed to be reserved for marriage, but often took place with dating couples once marriage was imminent.[24] These rules were not always followed, but there was a standard sense of appropriate behavior for each stage of the dating script, and love or a strong romantic attachment was a part of the equation.

Sexual intimacy in the hookup era is no longer as symbolic of relationship status as it was in the dating era. There is still a sequential pattern for relationships: hooking up, seeing each other, and going out, but it is not altogether clear what the corresponding sexual behavior is for each stage. Sexual intercourse is expected in many of the "going out" relationships; however, it is less clear what one should do sexually in the other contexts.[25] The students I spoke with were vague in response to questions about when certain degrees of sexual intimacy were appropriate. Some suggested one should wait (at least for sexual intercourse) until "it feels right" or "until you can trust someone." Interestingly, none of the men and women mentioned love as a prerequisite for sex.

It is safe to say that in the hookup era the degree of sexual intimacy is often unrelated to the level of commitment to the relationship. In fact, many of the college students, particularly women, indicated that they were more likely to "go farther" sexually with someone during a hookup if they did not like the person that much or believed there was no relationship potential. This is not to say that romantic feelings are absent among hookup partners, but that the hookup script does not dictate an emotional attachment.

THE GROUP

Perhaps the decreasing importance of emotional attachment between sexual partners in college derives from the increasing importance of friendship groups among students. In the shift from the dating era to the hooking up era, the focus went from the pair to group-oriented socializing.[26] The dating script called for a couple to go out together and the man and woman would each play a strict gender role. According to advice books from that era, men and women were supposed to play opposite but "complementary" roles in the dating script.[27] Men were expected to initiate the date and "take the lead" throughout the evening; men were also responsible for any expenses incurred on the date.[28] Women, on the other hand, were supposed to wait to be asked out on a date, let the man determine the plan for the date, and so on. The dating script did not allow much room for altering the roles played by men and women. In the hooking-up era, college students are more focused on groups of friends going out together. Of course, those who end up engaging in a hookup encounter pair off at the end of the night, but the evening's socializing is done among a gathering of classmates.

The shift to group socializing also means that no one is forced out of the social scene. Although there may have been some "mixers" where singles could go to socialize in the dating era, weekends were often reserved for "date nights." There also may have been occasions where a person would go "stag," but socializing was done primarily in dating pairs. The hookup script does not dictate that one must hook up in order to socialize in places where hooking up is possible. On any given night there are many more students out partying or bar hopping than will actually hook up. In fact, many of the men and women I interviewed who were in exclusive relationships still went to campus parties and bars with their friends at least some of the time. Thus, although the dating script left many students sitting at home while their classmates went out on "hot dates," the hookup scene promotes a form of interaction where, at least theoretically, anyone can join the party.[29] To be sure, there are men and women in the hookup scene who are more sought after than others (just as there were in the dating era). The difference is that the men and women who do not rate high on the desirability scale are less likely to be shut out from being a part of the social scene altogether.[30]

Group socializing is also central to men and women after college. Although alumni switch primarily to a dating script, the dating pair is not at the center of social life as it was in the dating era. As a result, the men and women I interviewed revealed that they primarily intermingle among friends at parties and bars, with dating an outgrowth of the way they socialize in general.

UNDER THE INFLUENCE

As group partying became increasingly central to the lives of students, so did the significance of alcohol to the sexual script. During the dating era, drinking was not a major focus of the typical date.[31] It is well documented that many contemporary college students consume a great deal of alcohol.[32] Many of the students I spoke with, including Liz, a freshman from Faith University, indicated that drinking and hooking up went hand-in-hand because hookup encounters generally occur after a night of partying.

KB: If somebody was interested in someone else, how would they have something happen with them? How do you get from A to B?

Liz: Probably alcohol would be a big factor and like the parties and stuff. Like it's just, like if something's going to happen it will be like at the party or things will evolve [from there and] you'll hang out with them one on one [later].

The hookup culture and the alcohol culture on campus are so inextricably linked that students who choose to forgo the party and bar scene are also excluding themselves from the hookup scene. Since hooking up is the primary means for finding potential sexual and romantic partners, those who do not participate struggle to form relationships.

KB: So what do people do then . . . if most hooking up happens when you're drinking and you don't really drink much, then how can people like you have something going [relationship-wise] . . . or would it be really difficult?

Kim: I kind of feel like in college it's more difficult just because that's what everybody does . . . that's been my experience. I mean, it's fine; it's not hard to meet people through classes and through organizations and stuff. But, I really feel like a lot of relationships do start at parties and stuff. So . . . maybe I am missing out on that right now. [Sophomore, Faith University]

The connection between hooking up and alcohol-centered socializing on campus is not insignificant. Researchers have demonstrated that alcohol consumption is correlated with the decision to have sexual intercourse as well as engaging in so-called risky sexual behavior, such as having casual sex.[33] Many college students I interviewed recognized that, at times, alcohol "made them do things" that they would not otherwise do, particularly with regard to hooking up.[34] Brian, a sophomore at Faith University, said, "Usually when you're hooking up . . . [both parties have] probably been drinking. You know, it's just like: 'Oh we're doing this cause we're both drunk and we're both kind of horny,' to be honest with you."

Although alcohol consumption may lead to hooking up, the link could also be reversed; that is, perhaps the hookup script requires alcohol.[35] In other words, alcohol appears to be a desirable social lubricant to aid the hookup process. Although hooking up is often a desired outcome for students after an evening at a party or bar, for the most part it is not clear who is going to hook up with whom. During the dating era, it was clear to everyone who someone's date was for the evening. If a sexual advance was going to be made, the person, generally the man, knew who would be the target: his date. The hookup scene carries a lot more uncertainty. Students must utilize many nonverbal cues in order to indicate interest to a potential hookup partner; however, there is a great deal of trepidation about getting one's signals crossed. As Robert, a sophomore at Faith University, put it:

> The likelihood of [hooking up] happening when you are totally sober is very unlikely, I would say. It is only when people start loosening up by drinking, I call it liquid courage. Most guys are shy about going up to pretty girls, [so that is why] I call it liquid courage. They got enough courage up to go up and talk to the girl. And if she was the same status regarding alcohol consumption, then the two people that are attracted to each other will just go ahead and [hook up].

Drinking alcohol makes navigating this difficult system easier for the participants. If one person indicates interest in another and the feeling is not mutual, the party of the first part can easily claim, "I was drunk, I didn't know what I was doing," rather than admitting, "I was rejected." This also holds true for a regrettable hookup encounter.[36] Thus, the awkwardness and uncertainty of the hookup script may encourage participants to use alcohol in a way that the dating script did not. Indeed, the alumni I spoke with dramatically reduced drinking when they went on formal dates because it was defined as "inappropriate" for the postcollege dating script.

UNDER COVER

Alcohol use may be one strategy employed by students trying to cope with the hooking-up system, which has made male-female interaction more covert. In the dating era, many aspects of a date were out in the open. It was socially acceptable for a man to ask a woman out on a date anywhere and at any time (i.e., a grocery store in the afternoon), and the invitation for a date was direct and verbal. The man had to ask the woman if she would like to go out with him and risk that she might say "no." If she accepted the invitation, the man had to put some thought into where he would take the woman, how they would get to their destination, and so forth. The date itself would take place somewhere in public, such as at a restaurant or theater. Regardless of the precise location, the woman was the man's date (and vice versa) for the evening, something that was readily apparent to onlookers. Thus, the public nature of the date, coupled with the "work" the man had to put in to make the date happen, insured that the dating partners could not easily disclaim any affiliation with each other.

The hookup era allows for much more private and spur-of-the-moment interaction. For example, the advent of Web sites such as MySpace and Facebook, where students can create personal profiles and converse with others by posting messages on their Web page, has revolutionized the way young people interact. Although these profiles are often accessible to anyone (and therefore far from private), the internet has made connecting with the opposite sex more anonymous and secretive. Contemporary college students can be "socializing" with others while sitting alone in their dorm rooms or apartments. Other technological advances, such as cell phones, have also made waiting at home for a suitor's phone call a thing of the past. There is no longer a need for advance plans when today's students can call or "text" each other to make last-minute arrangements to get together to "hang out."

Additionally, unlike a date, a hookup encounter typically begins at the end of the night with nonverbal cues between two people who have been drinking. If one party is not proud of their hookup partner (due to appearance or some other reason), he or she can act like it never happened. A number of men I interviewed said they were careful about admitting whom they hooked up with for fear of being teased or getting their "balls busted" by their friends.[37] Moreover, both men and women who are immersed in the hookup scene occasionally use alcohol as an excuse for having engaged in a hookup with someone they later considered undesirable.[38] Thus, the public nature of dating made it a less anonymous way of getting together. Someone of the opposite sex was your date for the evening, he or she was the person "on your arm," and there was no easy way to pretend otherwise.

Outward signs of romance also accompanied the dating script. Traditional symbols of wooing a partner, like flowers and candy, are no longer part of the early stages of a romantic relationship in college. In the hookup era, these types of gestures are reserved for special occasions, such as Valentine's Day, among men and women who are already a couple. Thus, those who participate in the hookup script do not use the customary trappings of courtship that, in the dating era, were public signs of affection among romantic/sexual partners.

MONEY, STATUS, AND WORTH

Gestures such as flowers and candy may also have become passé as money became less significant as a status symbol in the hookup script. In the dating era, the script called for the dating pair to go out together, which often involved men paying for entertainment of some kind. However, it was not just a matter of men needing money to date; rather, with dating, men and women began to determine what the other was "worth."[39] A woman could determine a man's worth by what kind of car he drove, by his family name, and by what kinds of dates he could afford or was willing to "spring for."[40] A man determined how much a woman was "worth" by considering the "assets" she had that would make it worth it to take her on an expensive date.[41] In many cases, a woman's worth was determined less by intrinsic or individual qualities than by her popularity or reputation as a sought-after date.[42] Indeed, the discourse surrounding dating indicated that women, in particular, were treated as commodities.[43] This point is clearly demonstrated by the comparison often made between women and cars during the dating era. According to social historian Beth Bailey: "The equation of women and cars was common in mid-century American culture. Both were property, both expensive; cars and women came in different styles or models, and both could be judged on performance. The woman he escorted, just as the car he drove, publicly defined both a man's taste and his means."[44]

Since hooking up does not involve a pair going out together, there is no reason to directly spend money. Although financial costs are still associated with collegiate social activities, they no longer consist of men spending money on their dates the way they did during the dating era. According to the college students I interviewed, both men and women generally "pay their own way" for admission into an event, such as a party that has a cover charge to gain entrance. Thus, women are no longer subject to being evaluated in terms of how much they are "worth" as they were during the dating era, and men are less often judged by the size of their wallet (or their family's bank account). The fact that finances have been taken out of the equation for the hookup script in college creates an atmosphere that is less money focused. Jake, a 28-year-old alumnus of State University, discussed the difference in money and status during college and after.

KB: You mentioned that sorority girls only seemed to want to be involved with fraternity guys. Why do you think it worked like that?

Jake: Because that's the way it always is. Girls want the football guys. They want the jocks or whatever. That's the way it has always been, probably always will be.

KB: So they just want people with high status and certain people have high status?

Jake: Exactly. If you are not in, you're out. Just like in the real world there are certain things that girls want, if you don't have it, you are out.

KB: Okay. Do you have it?

Jake: [Laughs] Do I have it? Now I do. Back then [in college] I didn't.

KB: So you weren't an athlete or fraternity member [during college]? What do you have now?

Jake: See what happens is, and this is from everybody I hear, and this definitely includes myself, when you're out in the working world for a few years and you start making a few bucks, you start learning how to dress, you get better friends, you get a nice car, you start to put things together. You figure out who you are, in college you don't have a clue. . . . But that's pretty much what happens, you get a job, you get some experience.

KB: So now you have the car, the clothes, the job, is that what [women] are looking for? What makes you in better shape now than other guys?

Jake: The smart guys [in college who got] straight A's or whatever, finance [majors], the payoff isn't until after they graduate and until they start making some money. That's the payout. In college, money doesn't matter. Everybody is equal. Everybody is living off of Mommy and Daddy anyway, so money

is no big deal. Of course if somebody is richer than somebody else it helps, but not until you get out in the real world
do girls start to wake up . . . once their [biological] clock
starts to tick, once they hit twenty-five. Then the roles reverse; the guy is more mature and the girls are starting to
panic. A flip-flop.

POSTPONING ADULTHOOD

In Jake's observation on the difference between students and alumni, he
mentions college students' dependence on parents. Since most college
students are of legal age upon entering college (a traditional marker of
the beginning of adulthood), it raises the question: Do contemporary
college students see themselves as adults? In the dating era, most considered marriage as the most important factor in the transition to adulthood. With the average age at first marriage in the 1950s dating era 20
for women and 22 for men, students were likely to be considered by society, and to think of themselves, as adults during their college years.[45]
In recent decades, men and women have been postponing marriage and
many other role transitions (such as parenthood and home ownership)
and college students have become less likely to think of themselves as
adults.[46]

In the hookup era, students tend to view their college years as a last
chance to "live it up" before settling down into their postcollege career.
The men and women I spoke with defined college as a time to have fun
and referred to graduation as a time when "real life" and adult responsibilities began. This mentality greatly affects their attitude and behavior in the realm of sex and relationships during their college years, al-
lowing contemporary college students more freedom to experiment
and "play the field."

BATTLE OF THE SEXES

Although there are many differences between the dating and hooking-
up scripts, there are also important similarities. One thing that has not
changed with the shift to hooking up is that men continue to hold most
of the power, as they did in the dating era. When the calling system was

abandoned in favor of dating, there was a shift in power from women to men.[47] In the calling era, young women and their mothers had the power to invite men to call (i.e., come to their home for a visit). If a man was interested in a woman, he had to hope for this invitation. However, when dating became the dominant script, only men could initiate a date.[48] Men were responsible for paying for the date, so the decision was in the hands of the man to figure out what he could afford and then ask a woman of interest to accompany him for the evening. This often left women waiting by the phone for a man's invitation.[49]

With the hookup script, the power to initiate is less gendered; both men and women can signal interest in hooking up. So, with regard to initiation, women in the hookup era may have more power than women had in the dating era. However, in the hookup era, it is not the power to initiate, but the ability to ultimately get what they want that demonstrates men's continuing dominance.[50] Many of the women I interviewed indicated that they wanted "something more" than just a one-night hookup encounter. Women do not necessarily object to hooking up per se; rather, they object to how often hooking up fails to evolve into some semblance of a relationship. Moreover, women feel that men have the power to decide whether a hookup turns into "seeing each other" or "going out."[51] Thus, women have a great deal of difficulty obtaining what they want via the hookup script. This is not the case for men. Many of the men I interviewed indicated that they could choose to be in a relationship if they wanted to; however, they often preferred to hook up with no strings attached.

KB: You didn't want to be a steady boyfriend?

Tony: No, definitely not.

KB: Why not?

Tony: Because then you get into that whole other world and it's a fucking mess. [Laughs]

KB: So, why are relationships a mess? Why do you like the other way of interacting?

Tony: Well, they [relationships] can be cool, don't get me wrong, like I loved being in relationships before, but as far as right now, that's not what I want and I think a lot of people don't want that just because they're graduating. Like why hang out with a girl right now, this is actually [a] pretty good [thought], why hang out with a girl right now when you

have one semester left before you're graduating? So, a lot of
my time is going into hanging out with my good friends and
I hate to lose that and invest it into a girl, which I'm probably more than likely not going to marry, you know. So, this is
the last couple of months with my best friends; why would I
invest my time with someone that I'm not going to hang out
with that much [after college].

KB: You mentioned marriage [earlier]. Do you picture yourself
getting married at any particular age? Or do you ever think
about that?

Tony: Definitely. Probably like around late twenties. [Senior, State
University]

Although Tony did "go out" with someone for part of his college years,
he often terminated relationships before they got to the point of being
serious or exclusive. Many of the men I interviewed, like Tony, were active members of the hookup scene, but were not utilizing it for the purpose of finding a relationship. They were able to have satisfying sexual
encounters via the hookup script without offering commitment in return. During the dating era, a man often had to spend a great deal of
time with a woman before she was willing to become sexual with him.
Moreover, the man often had to ask a woman to marry him before he
could hope to have sexual intercourse.[52] This is no longer the case in the
college hookup scene. Although this is a difference between the hookup
and the dating scripts, the commonality is that men have a greater share
of power in both eras. During the dating era, men held the power because only they could initiate dates, while women played a more pas-
sive role. During the hookup era, both men and women can initiate
hookup encounters, but it is men who still have the power to control the
intensity of the relationship.

As in the dating script, as described in Waller's study of Penn State
University students in the 1930s, relationships today are governed by
the "principle of least interest."[53] This means that the person with the
least interest in continuing the relationship holds all of the power or
has the upper hand. In the dating era, this could be either the man or
the woman. In the college hookup scene, men typically are the ones
with the least interest in a continuing relationship. The college men I
interviewed talked about the feeling of having many women to choose
from, so there was no need to hold on to a particular woman. Most of

the college women I spoke to, on the other hand, were interested in turning hookup partners into boyfriends. Violet, a junior at State University, relayed an example from her own experience.

> KB: Have you ever had a situation where you wanted a hookup to turn into something more and they didn't want it, or vice versa?
>
> Violet: Yeah. I had a friend of mine who I hooked up [with] one night and it was the kind of scenario where we were friends and I wanted something more out of it and he didn't.
>
> KB: And how did he know you wanted more and how did you know he didn't?
>
> Violet: Well, like I called him after we hooked up and he was like: "Hey, what is going on?" And I was like: "If you want to go out sometime give me a call." And he was like: "Yeah, okay." And he never called me. And we would see each other [sometimes] . . . and he'd just be like: "Hey." And it never came to anything; [it was] just that one time.

Liz, a freshman at Faith University, encountered a similar issue.

> KB: You said that you're not really sure why things fizzled out [between you and the guy you have been hooking up with repeatedly] but do you feel like it was more one person's doing than the other? Was it more him or more you?
>
> Liz: It was more him. We had this talk once because people started labeling us as like "together." And that freaked him out because, I don't even know why. He didn't [want that]. He was like: "Whoa! I just got here. I don't want a girlfriend. I'm not hooking up with anyone else right now, but I don't want to be labeled as like hooking up with just one person." You know what I'm saying? [He didn't] want it to be like: "Oh, there's Liz and oh where's [your boyfriend] John?" Whatever.

Both in college and after, women were interested in pursuing relationships with marriage potential sooner than men were interested in doing so. The idea that a woman's "clock is ticking" while a man has "all the time in the world" fundamentally affects who holds the power.

Thus, the hookup era's power dynamic carries over postcollege. Many of the alumni women I spoke with discussed the challenge they faced in trying to get the men in whom they were interested to commit to them.

KB: How did you know you were together [in a relationship]? Did you verbalize it?

Raquel: I had been calling him my boyfriend from the very beginning . . . but he's very handsome and . . . he had a bunch of women he was juggling in the beginning and they fell by the wayside and I was the one still standing . . . he would not call me his girlfriend until one day in August when we went out to dinner and ran into somebody and he introduced me as his girlfriend. That was the first time I ever heard those words, and I was like: "Thank God!" He was a battle in the beginning; he never wanted to have a girlfriend . . . I had to work hard for this relationship. I was like: "I don't know what to do." He will only see me once every two weeks and only call me once every two weeks.

KB: So you were hoping, almost from the beginning, that it would develop more and were kind of waiting until he was ready?

Raquel: Yeah.

KB: When you said he was a battle and you put a lot of work in [during] the beginning [of the relationship], other than waiting and hoping he was going to ask you out more, what else did you feel like you were doing to put in work?

Raquel: It's putting in the brainpower and working to mold him into thinking I am his girlfriend and keeping myself back and not bother[ing] him . . . I had to really bite my tongue and try hard not to nag him. [I had to] let him take his time and make his decision about whether I was right for him. . . . I didn't want to hound him, or ask too many questions. I just wanted to be the sweet, nice person that I am. It was like working really hard to prove to him that I was someone he wanted to be with. It did work out and I knew he and I would be good together, but I had to work hard at not pushing too hard. I was like: "What can I do to make this decision easier for you?" He said: "Keep doing what you are doing. Everything you are doing is great." [24-year-old alumnus of State University]

Many of the women I interviewed had a story similar to Raquel's: a woman who was involved, sexually and otherwise, with a man often wanted that man to be in an exclusive relationship with her. When the two parties were not on the same page, women struggled with whether to keep "hanging on" with the hope of a happy ending or to "move on" and start searching for a new partner. These women found it very difficult to end a relationship, even when they were not satisfied with its quality. For college women this sometimes came in the form of booty-call relationships or repeat hookup relationships with a man they were hoping would eventually agree to a committed relationship (i.e., "seeing each other" or "going out"). Unfortunately, these women were often disappointed when hooking up failed to evolve into something more than that. This difficulty became amplified for alumni women who were looking for a boyfriend and ultimately a potential lifelong mate. Despite women's interest in finding boyfriends, many reported that the men they were interested in pursuing a relationship with were hesitant to be in an exclusive relationship. Several alumni women indicated that this problem led to an "on again, off again" relationship while the tug-of-war over commitment was fought.

Shana: He's not ready to commit. He wants to keep playing and I just can't sit around anymore because it hurts too much. All of his like, other people.

   KB: Other girls?

Shana: Yeah.

   KB: So he wants to be involved with you, but wants it to be a nonexclusive thing?

Shana: [Right, so] . . . then it comes to the point where he says: "We have to talk." And I am like: "Oh great! [sarcastic tone] Here we go." . . . We are famous for having talks. [He says]: "I want to make sure we are on the same page, that you realize that I am still not ready to commit to you. I can see us in the future together, but not right now." A relationship with someone is not in his plan. He needs to accomplish some things in his career and be settled. He is very analytical and logical and he thinks he can be analytical and logical when it comes to relationships. But I keep trying to tell him that: "No, [it doesn't work that way]."

   KB: What did you say to him when he gave you this talk?

Shana: Just that I feel like I am either setting myself up for the biggest fall of my life [if I wait it out and we don't end up together] or the chance for my dreams all coming true. And it's like—do I take that chance? Am I going to end up being 35 and single still waiting for [him] to come around? [24-year-old alumnus of Faith University]

Carol: So before me he dated people for like two months, then he'd move on. He wouldn't ever let it get serious; he just did it to date but not to get more involved. He's told me now that [our relationship] was serious to the extent that we weren't dating anyone else. He was my boyfriend. But any time he thought it was getting too involved, like I was being too dependent on him . . . he would just say: "I am not ready for this." [He would] get scared . . . and he would always say to me: "I am breaking up now because I can't do this to you farther down the road." The last time we broke up . . . I realized, not what I was doing wrong but, I was kind of pushing him away a little bit, scaring him off. But also it was because of him. He would make me so insecure.

KB: Give me an example of something you might do to scare him off or [something] that would show that you are too dependent.

Carol: It was just little stuff. He said now it wasn't so much me being dependent on him, it was just that he wasn't ready to be [in a relationship]. Like I would call him and ask his advice on something and he would think: "Why is she calling me to ask me that?" I would ask him [advice] now and he would answer me. I don't think now that I was being as dependent as he was saying. He wasn't ready for me to ask him his advice or to do the full couple thing. But we should have been [ready]. We dated for nine months; it was serious dating. We weren't seeing anyone else; we saw each other every weekend and even during the week and we talked every day. He was my boyfriend. It was one of those things where we just weren't on the same page at the same time about what we wanted and stuff like that. [24-year-old alumnus of Faith University]

One can clearly see that Waller's "principle of least interest" is still (60-some years after he coined the phrase) largely dictating who holds the power among young singles. Given the relationship struggles that many women go through, it is obvious why advice books, such as *He's Just Not That Into You*, end up being best-sellers.[54]

WALKING THE LINE

Men's greater control has led to the sexual exploitation of women in both the dating and hooking-up eras. According to Waller's study of the dating era, exploitation occurred when one party was more interested in a continuing relationship than the other and thereby she or he was willing to give in to the other's demands. Among dating partners during this time, women might exploit men by "gold digging," while men could exploit women for sexual favors or "thrills."[55] Therefore, in a case where a woman had stronger feelings toward a man and was trying to secure him, she might offer more sexual favors. In the hookup era, sexual exploitation continues to be an issue for women. Since hooking up does not involve men spending money on women, college men have no fear of gold digging.[56] Women, on the other hand, must be cautious about being used. Many of the college men I spoke with were aware that women were desirous of more committed relationships, yet men were often able to keep a woman as just a hookup partner.

Exploitation was an issue not just for women in some version of a relationship, but for those seeking relationships, too. Throughout the dating era, women who had a reputation for "putting out" might be asked on dates by a variety of men, each having the purpose of seeing how much he could get sexually.[57] Certain women might be sought after for dates because they were defined as being sexually available merely due to their social class or occupation.[58] For example, student nurses were stereotyped as a "good time" by college men. Thus, college men sought dates with student nurses in order to "get a little" sexually.[59] Some college men in the hookup era who are interested in accumulating various hookup partners do so by going after certain women, as men did in the dating era. For example, several college students mentioned that freshman males have a great deal of difficulty getting into campus parties unless they know one of the hosts personally, while freshman women are granted free admission. This practice increases the likelihood of upperclassmen being able to hook up with freshman women who are a target because they are naive about the unwritten rules of the hookup scene.

Like women of the dating era, college women in the hookup culture must walk a fine line between being exploited and being excluded. Those who choose to take part in the script not only risk being used for sex, but also risk their reputations. There are a host of norms to which contemporary college women must adhere in order to avoid being labeled a "slut." College women can be negatively labeled if they hook up too often or with too many different partners. Indeed, women must be careful not even to appear to be conducting themselves in an overtly provocative manner or they will be perceived as "easy." Kyle, a senior at State University, summarized it this way: "One night can screw up a girl's reputation."

Another pitfall for women is going "too far" sexually during a hookup. Many of the students I spoke with took for granted that it is a woman's responsibility to decide "how far" a sexual encounter will go. Lee, a freshman at Faith University, explained this attitude: "Because I think guys will always try to make [sexual] advances and it's up to the girl to go along with that or not. And I think girls are scared to say no and to say that they are not into doing that because they don't want to look stupid. . . . But I think ultimately it is up to the girl."

In the hookup culture, college women's reputations can be affected not only by their own behavior, but even by whom they associate with on campus. For example, certain sororities on the campuses I studied were given nicknames having a sexual connotation. Similarly, an article in *Rolling Stone* magazine about Duke University quotes an anonymous blog entry entitled "How-to Guide to Banging a Sorority Girl," which ranks the women of the "Core Four" sororities on campus in terms of their attractiveness. The blogger contends: "I would include a ranking for sluttiness, but in general all four are equally slutty." The blogger goes on to say it may be difficult to have sex with women in one of the "hottest" sororities, "unless you are part of the lucky group of dudes that pass these bitches around."[60] Although this blogger's point of view may be more extreme than that of most students on campus, it demonstrates how college women exist in a fishbowl, for others to watch and judge.

In the dating era, women's sexual behavior was also scrutinized.[61] Women were permitted to allow some necking and petting, but were absolutely supposed to maintain their virginity. Advice books were filled with suggestions for women on how to conduct themselves in sexual matters.[62] These books suggested that women were responsible for playing the "gatekeeper" role during sexual interaction on dates.[63] The 1958 advice book *The Art of Dating* warned young women about what men really think about girls who go "all the way." It suggested that if a girl allows a guy to go all the way, afterwards he is haunted by the question: "If she went all the way with me, how can I be sure there have not been others?" It continues by saying that men do not want to get "stuck with a tramp" for a long-term relationship.[64]

Although the dating script and the hookup script differ with regard to specific sexual norms, women's sexual conduct continues to be scrutinized in a way that men's behavior is not. Thus, the sexual double standard, which prevailed during the dating era, is still very much a part of the hookup scene. This scrutiny makes navigating sex and relationships in the hookup era difficult for women. Women want "romantic" interaction with men, but there are many pitfalls for them in doing so. The catch is that a woman needs to hook up in order to find someone with whom to have a potential relationship, yet her very participation in hooking up can mean that she is not taken seriously as a potential girlfriend, is exploited for sex, and/or is labeled a slut. Women of the dating era faced the same dilemma. For example, student nurses found themselves in a difficult situation because of the stereotype that they were promiscuous.

> If she is not cooperative and does not meet the college boys' expectations of sexual permissiveness, she is likely to be dropped immediately and have no further dates. If she is cooperative, she easily builds a reputation and becomes fair game for her current dating partner and later his friends and fraternity brothers. The authors suspect that more girls than not choose to solve the dilemma by being more permissive than they normally would, just in order to keep dating.[65]

Despite this dilemma, women actively participate in hooking up, as they did in dating. Why? Because the prevailing script in any era is seen as the only way, or at least the most likely way, to get together with men and feel a part of the social scene of their peers.

CONCLUSION

In the final analysis, much has changed since the dating era. Some of the changes can be seen as an improvement, and others can be viewed as negative. One of the most interesting things to examine about the shift from dating to hooking up is its impact on women. Since the emergence of hooking up can be traced back to the sexual revolution period, it begs the question: Have the goals of the women's liberation movement been met? If the objective of women's rights activists was for women to be able to have sexual experiences without having to barter exclusive sexual access in exchange for a wedding ring, there is evidence that it has been realized. Women's sexual behavior has changed more than men's since the 1960s, and on several key indicators women are reaching "parity" with men. For example, historically men had their first experience of sexual intercourse earlier than women; today, it is roughly equal.[66] Historically, men also had a higher number of sexual partners than women; however, in more recent decades gender differences are less pronounced.[67] These changes were precisely what many architects of the women's liberation movement had in mind.

However, even as similarities between men and women increased, the double standard remains. On the campuses I studied, contemporary college women may be permitted to engage in a wider variety of sexual behaviors under a wider array of circumstances than their dating-era counterparts, but there are no clear rules guiding what they should do and under what conditions. The ostensible lack of rules in the hookup script may seem to be liberating, and perhaps it can be, but it is also problematic because there are many unwritten rules that women must learn as they go along. These unwritten rules continue to limit the options available to women who are interested in pursuing sexual relationships.

Despite the double standard, women do have more sexual freedom today than they did in the dating era. But, it was not only women who gained sexual freedom since the sexual revolution; men did also. Since "respectable" women were not supposed to have premarital sex in the dating era, men who wanted to engage in sexual intercourse

(while society looked the other way) had to do so with women of ill re-
pute.[68] In the hooking-up era, men have many more women to choose
from for potential sexual encounters. For better or worse, men also do
not have to put forth the amount of effort (e.g., phone calls, flowers, expensive dates, etc.) that their grandfathers did for sexual interaction to
take place. Men today also do not have to propose marriage or walk
down the aisle in order to have regular access to sexual intercourse. Indeed, men can have sex without entering into a relationship at all. Thus,
hooking up is a system whereby men can engage in sexual encounters
without the pretext of a relationship and where no guarantee of an ongoing or future bond with the woman is required. In a sense, it can be
argued that men are the ones who really benefited from the sexual revolution. Robert, a sophomore at Faith University, opined:

Robert:It almost seems like [the hookup scene] is a guy's paradise.
　　　No real commitment, no real feelings involved, this is like a
　　　guy's paradise. This age [era] that we are in I guess.
　KB:　So you think guys are pretty happy with the [hookup] sys-
　　　tem?
Robert:Yeah! I mean this is what guys have been wanting for many,
　　　many years. And women have always resisted, but now they
　　　are going along with it. It just seems like that is the trend.

Clearly, women's rights activists who called for sexual equality with
men did not intend to promote a form of interaction that would be considered a "guy's paradise."

Despite the increase in sexual freedom since the dating era, the
hookup culture is not as out of control as some observers (and college
students) believe. Hooking up is dominant on campus, but it represents
a wide range in terms of level of participation and sexual behavior.
There are many students who do not take part in hooking up at all and
others who, for various reasons (e.g., they are in a relationship), have
only hooked up a few times.[69] For those students who have engaged in
hooking up, many encounters involved nothing more than kissing. Although a hookup can involve casual sex between two parties who just
met that evening, a hookup could also mean two people kissing after
having a crush on each other for a year. Likewise, a hookup encounter
may happen only once or evolve into repeatedly hooking up or even become a relationship. The point is that hooking up can mean different

things, and it is too often assumed, by scholars and commentators alike, that it refers to only the most promiscuous scenarios.

This is not to say that extreme behavior is not happening in the hookup culture. For some students, college life can become an endless spring break. These are the same students who consume a disproportionate amount of alcohol on campus and hook up with different partners on a weekly basis. This behavior raises a variety of health concerns, particularly with regard to the level of binge drinking and the potential for STD transmission or rape. It is students caught up in the extremes of the hookup culture who, to the exclusion of their more moderate classmates, have captured the attention of critics. Although this behavior needs attention, it can also distort the reality of life on campus for the student body as a whole.

Acknowledging the variation in the hookup culture is important not only for students generally, but also for understanding differences between genders. Although I chose to highlight the differences between men and women throughout the preceding chapters, there is, no doubt, as much variation within gender as there is across it. Just as not all students fit the mold of the most raucous partiers, not *all* men want sex and not *all* women want relationships. I spoke with some men who preferred being in a relationship over hookup encounters with new partners. I also spoke to some women who enjoyed the freedom and experimentation of the hookup scene (at least during freshman year). Therefore, it would be unfair to oversimplify the behavior of the sexes. However, I found that women's interest in hookup encounters evolving into some semblance of a relationship and men's interest in "playing the field" was a theme that fundamentally affects the dynamic between men and women in the hookup culture.

Given that there is a wide range of possibilities available to men and women coming of age in the hookup era, it would seem that there is an almost endless array of choices an individual can make. For example, if a student wants to go to parties and hook up every weekend, he or she can choose to do so. Likewise, if a student wants to be part of the hookup scene, but as a more moderate participant, he or she can do that too. However, in many ways, the hookup system creates an illusion of choice. Although students have many options about how they conduct themselves within the hookup culture, they cannot change the fact that hooking up is the dominant script on campus. An individual student may decide to abstain from hooking up altogether, but they are more or less on their own to figure out an alternative. In other words, no other script exists side-by-side with hooking up that students can opt to use instead. Emily, a sophomore at Faith University, put it this way: "If [hooking up] is not what you're looking for, then I guess it is hard to escape it."

Students who would prefer to go out on traditional dates every weekend cannot change the fact that they did not enter college during a time when that was the "in" thing to do. Thus, students can use their own moral compass to make personal decisions on how to use the hookup script, but their decisions are constrained by their environment and the time period. The modern college campus is conducive to hooking up, and no individual can change that.

It is my hope that readers have gained a better understanding of the hooking-up phenomenon. I believe that the stories of college students and young alumni presented here provide a look into the world of campus life and single life after college as many young people experience it today. The information in this book can be useful for those on the outside looking in at campus life, particularly college administrators and parents seeking to guide students through their college careers. I hope that they, and other commentators, will come away with an appreciation for the systemic issues that impact individual experiences.

I also hope that my work will be useful to researchers who study social problems on the college campus, such as binge drinking, STD transmission, and sexual assault. Understanding the relationship between hooking up and these issues is crucial because, I believe, these campus problems grow out of a larger context of how students socialize and form sexual and romantic relationships. Without understanding this context, it would be difficult to find any effective solutions.

For recent graduates who are trying to make sense of a new singles scene, this book can provide insight into where they have been, where they are going, and why things change (almost overnight) after they leave the campus environment. Although hooking up ceases to play the dominant role in social life that it did in college, it has lasting effects for alumni. After college, individuals must learn to adapt to a new script (i.e., formal dating), yet prepare to switch back to the hookup script when circumstances make it possible to do so. I hope alumni readers will find the views of other twenty-something singles insightful.

Most importantly, I believe that college students who are learning to navigate the hookup system will find the information in this book helpful. Many students I interviewed spoke of having to find out how hooking up works as they made their way through college. By sharing their experiences of college life, they have given current students a point of reference on the hookup culture. Although students may not identify with all of the individuals in the preceding chapters, I think that the stories of some men and women will resonate with each reader. Understanding others' perspectives on hooking up will allow students to see how their intimate lives fit into the bigger picture. I hope my work will give students the opportunity to reflect on what they are doing, why they are doing it, and will ultimately help them to make informed, and possibly better, decisions about their lives.

Methodological Appendix

In order to obtain interviews for the college portion of the study, I solicited professors at both Faith and State universities to ask for student volunteers to participate in the study. Some professors permitted me to contact their students via e-mail so a description of the project could be sent to them; however, most professors gave a handout to their students with a description of the project and information on how to contact me if they were interested in volunteering for the study. Importantly, only professors who had a diverse group of students in terms of gender, grade level, and major were asked to help me obtain interviewees. For the college portion of the study, I interviewed 33 women and 18 men. I also interviewed students of all grade levels, including 8 freshmen, 20 sophomores, 11 juniors, and 12 seniors. Given that many aspects of students' social lives change throughout their college career, it was important to include the experience of students from freshmen through seniors.

I recruited interviewees through a number of means. For the college portion of the study, I asked professors from a variety of disciplines to hand out an interview solicitation in class. For the alumni portion of the study, I found interviewees via an alumni Web site as well as by mailing an invitation to participate in the study to homes of recent graduates within a two-hour radius of their undergraduate institution. I avoided snowball sampling because it might have led to misleading data. Snowballing would inevitably lead to interviewing people from the same crowd or clique. Since perception of the behavior of other members of the college community was a part of the college portion of the study, it was important to vary the type of students being interviewed.

To obtain alumni interviews at the faith-based university, I utilized a Web site containing alumni e-mail addresses. At the state university, I utilized the alumni office to reach graduates from the previous 10 years who lived in surrounding zip codes (i.e., within approximately 60 miles). I contacted alumni ages 23–30 and asked if they would volunteer to meet me for an interview. For the alumni portion of the study, I interviewed 16 men and 9 women.[1]

The interview solicitations given to both college students and young alumni were deliberately vague. The terms "hooking up" and "dating" did not appear in the solicitation. Instead, prospective volunteers were asked if they would be willing to be interviewed about "their experiences and observations of campus social life, particularly male/female interaction on campus." The alumni were asked the same, but for "their college and post-college years." I utilized the phrase "male/female interaction" in lieu of something more precise in hopes that a wider range of "types" would volunteer for the study. For example, I did not want only those who were completely immersed in the hookup culture to volunteer; I also wanted to talk to those who did not hook up or rarely did so. Importantly, I did not assume that students or alumni utilized any particular script to interact with the opposite sex. Instead, I asked them to describe how men and women typically get together and form relationships. Then, I asked them whether their experience was similar or different from what they believed was going on around them.

All potential interviewees were informed that the information they conveyed to me would be kept confidential and anonymous. To ensure privacy, I conducted most interviews in an office on campus or a private library study room.[2] Furthermore, interviewees were assured that their real names would not appear on the audiotape or in the transcriptions. Interviewees were also informed that they could stop the interview at any time or skip a question they did not wish to answer. The Institutional Review Boards at both of the universities in the study approved the study design, solicitation form, interview guide, and informed consent form.

I began data collection in November 2001 and continued through May 2006. The interview format was in-depth and semistructured. I audiorecorded and transcribed all of the interviews, each of which ranged from approximately one to one and a half hours in length. After the first ten interviews, themes began to emerge. I recorded each theme and then used what I learned from these initial interviews to refine the interview guide. Despite using interview guide questions during each interview, the interviews took on a more conversational style. I found that this style allowed interviewees to open up about intimate aspects of

TABLE 1
Breakdown of Interviewees by Institution and Sex

	Male	Female	Total
Faith U. undergrads	11	20	31
State U. undergrads	7	13	20
Faith U. alumni	7	6	13
State U. alumni	9	3	12
Total	34	42	76

their lives. I analyzed and coded the data utilizing Straus and Corbin's grounded theory method.[3] In other words, the data analysis is grounded in the experiences and perceptions of the interviewees. Data collection continued until I reached theoretical saturation.

LIMITATIONS

Although I attempted to interview a wide range of students and young alumni, my sample was not diverse in terms of race/ethnicity.[4] As I indicated in chapter 1, the lack of diversity partially reflected the campuses I chose to study, but was also by design. Given that previous researchers have found that the script for interaction varies by race, it was virtually impossible for me to fully explore how "minority" men and women initiate sexual and romantic relationships without at least doubling the number of people I interviewed. Although I did interview a couple of African American students as well as a couple of people of Asian descent, several other racial/ethnic groups are left out entirely, such as Hispanics, Indians, and Native Americans. It seems likely that the intimate behavior of these groups vary not only from the dominant white culture, but also from one another. This makes studying them an even greater challenge, yet it is a challenge that I hope researchers will undertake soon.

In addition to the lack of racial diversity, interviewing students and alumni from two primarily residential four-year colleges inevitably reduces the social class diversity. Most of the students on the campuses I studied were middle or upper-middle class. This raises questions about how men and women interact and form relationships if they attend a commuter college or if they do not attend college at all. I suspect that hooking up still goes on, but to a much lesser degree (similar to what I found among alumni once they leave the college environment). However, this is only speculation and empirical research is needed to examine this issue. My study was also limited to universities on the East Coast of the United States. Although some national data on hooking up has been gathered, more is needed to see if there are regional variations in how the hookup script operates on campus.

I chose a qualitative methodology for this project because I believed it was the best way to capture what is really happening in the intimate lives of college students and young alumni. Hopefully, the richness of the data I collected came through in the many interview excerpts provided throughout the preceding chapters. Although my data were able to show what hooking up is, the range of experiences it encapsulates, and so on, my data cannot tell us how many students are engaging in various activities along the spectrum of hooking up. Therefore, more representative quantitative studies are needed to determine how often students are engaging in various behaviors within the hookup script.

Finally, hooking up was the dominant script for forming sexual and romantic relationships on the campuses I studied, but not "everyone" was doing it. As I indicated in chapter 4, there were many groups or individuals who did not engage in the hookup culture. Although I attempted to have their voices heard, I realize that their stories were not completely captured. Future research should consider how students who abstain from hooking up navigate their sexual and romantic lives as well as how they are affected by the dominant hookup culture that surrounds them.

Notes

NOTES TO CHAPTER I

1. Wolfe 2000, book jacket.
2. Bailey 1988.
3. See Miller and Gordon (1986) for a discussion of the decline of formal dating in high school.
4. Bianchi and Casper 2000.
5. U.S. Department of Health and Human Services, National Center for Health Statistics 2001.
6. U.S. Department of Education, National Center for Education Statistics 2002.
7. The findings from this national study were presented in a report to the Independent Women's Forum. Although the study was nationally representative and conducted by scholars, the findings, to my knowledge, have never been peer reviewed.
8. Glenn and Marquardt 2001, 4.
9. For evidence of the decline of dating on college campuses, see Horowitz 1987; Moffatt 1989; Murstein 1980; Strouse 1987.
10. For a discussion of the connection between hooking up and rape on the college campus, see Armstrong 2005, Sanday 2006. For an examination of the effects of divorce on college women's involvement with hooking up, see Glenn and Marquardt 2001.
11. Sherman and Tocantins 2004; McPhee 2002.
12. See C. Wright Mills's *The Sociological Imagination* (1959) for his classic statement on seeing personal troubles as public issues.
13. The term "hooking up" has appeared in other studies using college student samples. However, these studies were focused on subject matter outside of consensual intimate interaction, for example, sexual assault on campus (Boswell and Spade 1996) and drug use among college women (Williams 1998). These studies, as well as two nonrepresentative studies that did focus directly on the subject of hooking up (Lambert, Kahn, and Apple 2003; Paul and Hayes 2002) will be discussed in later chapters.

14. Bell and Buerkel-Rothfuss 1990; Bettor, Hendrick, and Hendrick 1995; Cohen and Shotland 1996; Cupach and Metts 1995; Felmlee 1994; Gilbert et al. 1999; Hogben, Byrne, and Hamburger 1996; Laner and Ventrone 2000; Mongeau, Serewicz, and Therrien 2004; Mongeau and Johnson 1995; Morr and Mongeau 2004; Seal, Agostinelli, and Hannett 1994; Smith, Byrne, and Fielding 1995; Sprecher 1990; Sprecher and Sedikides 1993.

15. Baldwin and Baldwin 1988; Carroll and Carroll 1995; Cooper 2002; Dermen, Cooper, and Agocha 1998; Desiderato and Crawford 1995; Hammer et al. 1996.

16. Paul, McManus, and Hayes 2000.

17. Paul, McManus, and Hayes 2000, 79.

18. Paul, McManus, and Hayes 2000, 84. The Paul, McManus, and Hayes (2001) College of New Jersey study used a narrow definition of hooking up that represents only a portion of what hooking up encompasses. Their definition states that hooking up occurs between "strangers or brief acquaintances" and usually lasts "only one night." However, my data suggest that hooking up covers a much wider set of scenarios in terms of how hookup partners meet and whether there is an ongoing relationship after the initial hookup. The major drawback of the Glenn and Marquardt (2001) Institute for American Values study is that they only examined the sexual attitudes and behaviors of college women.

19. Glenn and Marquardt 2001, 4. Despite the contribution of these first scholarly studies on hooking up, they have many limitations. Because both studies were primarily based on quantitative methods, they could not, by design, analyze the hooking-up phenomenon in depth. In fact, many studies on sexual behavior rely on quantitative research. For example, see Laumann et al. 1994. Findings from this type of research identify rates and trends of sexual behavior (i.e., what people are doing.) However, statistics cannot reveal the meanings men and women give to a sex act and the context in which sexual activity takes place (i.e., why people are doing it). Thus, survey findings alone cannot fully reveal the complexity and variations in how the hookup system operates on campuses.

20. Vaughan 1986. Inspired by Diane Vaughan's classic 1986 work, *Uncoupling*, I designed my research as a qualitative study.

21. By contrast, in both prior studies on hooking up, the researchers supplied the definition of hooking up used in their survey instruments. Although both studies used focus groups or interviews to inform their definition of hooking up, they were not fully able to capture the variations in how hooking up works from the definitions they employed. See Bogle 2005 for a full discussion on this.

22. The Institute for American Values study focused only on college women in the United States.

23. The first wave of data collection consisted of 58 interviews for my doctoral dissertation (November 2001–March 2003). A second wave of data collection began after my degree was conferred in January 2004 (N = 18). These interviews were added to ensure that theoretical saturation was reached (Glaser and Strauss 1967).

24. Glenn and Marquardt 2001; Williams 1998.

25. Examining how homosexual college students and recent alumni sexually interact and form potential relationships is an entire study in itself and beyond the scope of the present study.

26. Eble 1996; Murray 1991.

27. Goffman 1959.

28. Gagnon and Simon 1973. See also Simon and Gagnon 1984, 1986, 1987.

29. According to scripting theorists, cultural influences do not merely socialize individuals to learn how to constrain their "natural" sexual urges; rather, "sexual scripts specify with whom people have sex, when and where they should have sex, what they should do sexually, and why they should do sexual things" (Laumann et al. 1994, 6). Thus, sexual behavior is scripted in the sense that a given culture defines what is sexual and how sexual behavior should commence (Gagnon and Simon 1973).

30. Gagnon and Simon 1973; Laumann et al. 1994.

31. Gagnon and Simon 1973.

32. Ibid.

33. Kass and Kass 2000. See Carpenter (1998) for a discussion of how scripts for sexuality and romance are presented to teenage girls in *Seventeen* magazine.

34. See Laws and Schwartz (1977) for a discussion of how scripting theory can be used to understand the "social construction of female sexuality."

35. Bailey 1988.

NOTES TO CHAPTER 2

1. Lipson 2002.

2. Prior to the twentieth century, although a particular script generally dominated a society, there was also quite a bit of variation in the local practices for intimate partnering. The local variations likely persisted because of the lack of mass communication throughout this time period (Shorter 1975).

Scholars have had to look to other sources, such as diaries, letters, and medical and other expert texts. Although these sources of data are important, they are largely written by and for members of the middle and upper class who had the ability to read and the means to write. Thus, these sources tend to enlighten us more on the script for intimate behavior for the middle and upper class or "elite" than for society as a whole. Despite this difficulty, many sociologists and social historians have undertaken this task (Bailey 1988; Coontz 1988; Gordon 1973; Lystra 1989; Murstein 1974; Rothman 1984; Shorter 1975; Whyte 1990). Importantly, some quantitative sources of data, such as census data and local records of births, marriages, and the like can help fill in some of the gaps left from the qualitative sources.

3. Bailey 1988; Murstein 1974; Shorter 1975.

4. Rothman 1984.

5. Shorter 1975; see Adair (1996) for an alternate view of the role of parental and community involvement in intimate partnering.

6. Bailey 1988.

7. Rothman 1984.

8. Shorter 1975. See also Coontz (2005) for a thorough discussion of the historical circumstances that led to love and romance playing a greater role in mate selection.

9. Sexual attraction remains paramount in the contemporary hookup script..

10. Bailey 1988.

11. Bailey 1988; Rothman 1984.

12. Specifically, the first usage of the term "dating" in this context was in 1896 (Bailey 1988).

13. Bailey 1988.

14. Bailey 1988.

15. Rothman 1984.

16. Rothman 1984.

17. Bailey 1988, 19.

18. Waller 1937.

19. Although courting may not always have culminated in marriage, the idea was that it would lead to marriage, or at least that it might. With dating, there is no explicit or implicit intention to marry one's date (Murstein 1974). Although dating is viewed by some as a process of whittling down potential mates until one's life partner is found (Whyte 1990), many scholars agree that dating has much more of a recreational tone (Waller 1937; Schwartz and Lever 1976). See Baruch (1980) for an interesting discussion of the "politics of courtship."

20. See Gordon (1981) for a critical examination of Waller's rating and dating complex.

21. See Horowitz (1987) for further evidence that dating is the key to women gaining status on campus during the 1920s and beyond.

22. See McComb (1998) for more on how young women were commodified during the "rating and dating" era.

23. Unfortunately, Waller does not describe exactly what would constitute an "indiscretion."

24. Waller 1938.

25. Waller 1938.
26. Bailey 1988.
27. Bailey 1988, 28.
28. Bailey 1988.
29. Bailey 1988.
30. Bailey 1988.
31. Bailey 1988.
32. Cate and Lloyd 1992.
33. Bailey 1988, 51.
34. Bailey 1988.
35. Bailey 1988; Rothman 1984.
36. Bailey 1988.
37. Bailey 1988.
38. Bailey 1988. See also Bromley and Britten (1938) and Fass (1977) for more on college students' sexual behavior during the "rating and dating" era.
39. Bailey 1988.
40. Bailey 1988, 80.
41. LeMasters, quoted in Bailey 1988, 80.
42. LeMasters, quoted in Bailey 1988, 80.
43. Bailey 1988; Rothman 1984.
44. Rothman 1984.
45. Bailey 1988.
46. Whyte 1990.
47. For example, Whyte (1990) found continuity in the age that dating began (i.e., 16 years of age). Whyte also found that parents of all generations "hover at the sidelines" of their children's dating relationships, doing their best to exert their influence without outright controlling their children's choice of dates (Whyte 1990, 39). See also Bruce (1976) and Leslie et al. (1986) for a discussion of parental involvement in the "courtship activities" of children.
48. Whyte 1990, 26.
49. Gagnon and Simon 1973.
50. Whyte 1990.
51. Bailey 1988; Horowitz 1987; Murstein 1980.
52. Horowitz 1987; Moffatt 1989; Strouse 1987.
53. Moffatt 1989, 49.
54. D'Emilio and Freedman 1988.
55. Laumann et al. 1994.
56. Gagnon and Simon 1987.
57. Laumann et al. 1994.
58. Cate and Lloyd 1992; Gagnon and Simon 1973.
59. Rubin 1990.

60. Gagnon and Simon 1973.

61. Modell, quoted in Arnett 1998, 301.

62. Bailey 1988.

63. Poulson and Higgins 2003.

64. See Lance (1976) for a discussion of the effect of sex-integrated dormitories on college student sexual permissiveness.

65. Surra 1990.

66. Bianchi and Casper 2000.

67. U.S. Department of Health and Human Services, National Center for Health Statistics 2001.

68. Cate and Lloyd 1992.

69. Glick 1975.

70. U.S. Department of Education, National Center for Education Statistics 2002.

71. Horowitz, 1987; Moffatt 1989; Murstein 1980; Strouse 1987.

NOTES TO CHAPTER 3

1. Most dictionaries do not include an entry on hookup or hooking up where the definition refers to a form of sexual interaction. This omission includes many dictionaries focused on slang terms or sexual terminology. An exception is Eble's (1996) book on slang among college students. In a study on the use of slang terminology among students at the University of North Carolina from the 1970s to 1990s, Eble found the term "hooking up," defined as "to find a partner for romance or sex" or "to kiss passionately," to be commonly used since the mid-1980s.

2. From this point forward, I will often refer to "college students"; however, I am referring only to the white, heterosexual, traditional-aged college students at the two East Coast universities I studied. As I indicated in chapter 1, the interviewees were not chosen via probability sampling; therefore, the results cannot be generalized to all college students.

3. See Manning (2005) for a discussion on middle and high school students' participation in "nonromantic sexual activity."

4. Stepp 2003.

5. See Bogart et al. (2000) for a discussion on college students' interpretations of what scenarios count as "sex." See also Sanders and Reinisch (1999) on the debate about what counts as "sex." See Rosenblatt (1998) for a journalistic account of this debate.

6. Notably, oral sex has become an increasingly common part of the sexual script for young heterosexuals over the last several decades. For a complete discussion of this change in sexual practice and its implications, see Gagnon and Simon (1987) and Laumann et al. (1994).

7. This point is confirmed by Carpenter's (2005) work on the meaning assigned to virginity loss. Specifically, she found that men often perceive virginity as a "stigma" that they strive to hide from friends and have to get rid of as soon as possible.

8. I will return to this issue in chapter 6 with a discussion of why women feel the need to protect their reputation because of the sexual double standard.

9. College students traveling in groups to parties and other social events has been taking place since at least the 1970s (Horowitz 1987; Moffatt 1989; Murstein 1980; Strouse 1987).

10. See Holland and Eisenhart (1990) for a discussion of college women's preoccupation with beautifying their appearance in order to appeal to men during cross-sex interaction at parties, bars, sporting events, and so on. See also Grazian (in press) for a discussion of college women's (and men's) preparations for a night out.

11. See Greer and Buss (1994) for a discussion of what tactics college students use to promote sexual encounters and how these tactics vary by gender. See Moore (1995) for how adolescent girls utilize facial expressions and gestures to signal interest in boys.

12. See Armstrong (2005) on how "in-network strangers" affect socializing on a college campus.

13. What determines who is attracted to whom is a complicated matter. However, Laumann et al. (1994) shed light on this issue with their discussion of human capital and the sexual marketplace. They argue that people possess a collection of qualities that place them on a continuum of desirability in the sexual marketplace. Interested parties are, in a sense, shopping for a potential sexual partner. However, not everyone will meet a shopper's criteria for a potential match. Importantly, which qualities are valued in potential sexual partners depends not only on individual preferences, but also on what a given culture defines as desirable in a partner. See also Townsend and Levy (1990) on what characteristics college students look for when selecting partners.

14. Bailey 1988.

15. Martin and Hummer 1989.

16. See Gagnon and Simon (1973) for a discussion of how nonverbal cues play a role in sexual scripts in general.

17. Consistent with Gagnon and Simon (1973), the hookup script begins with nonverbal cues, which are derived from culturally agreed upon symbols of sexual interest. Some in the field of communication (see Koeppel et al. 1993) have found that there are significant gender differences in interpreting nonverbal cues. For instance, men tend to perceive women as making a sexual advance when they initiate interaction, while women perceive a male-initiated conversation as "just being friendly." My research has not uncovered gender differences in this regard; however, direct questions on this subject might have yielded different results.

18. Given that many religious denominations attempt to regulate the sexual behavior of their members, one might expect religion to have an effect on sexual behavior. Yet most of the college students I interviewed who were practicing members of their particular religious denominations still took part in the hookup script—an issue I will return to in chapter 4.

19. Paul, McManus, and Hayes 2000.

20. This finding is consistent with Glenn and Marquardt's (2001) finding, in the survey portion of their study: 57 percent of college women indicated that they felt "awkward" after hooking up with someone.

21. This finding is similar to Willard Waller's (1937) revelation that male / female interaction on campus is governed by the "principle of least interest," where the party with the least interest in a relationship holds all the power.

22. Importantly, college students' use of the term "dating" did not reflect the traditional meaning of the term. In other words, students were not referring to the traditional dating script, which would include going out to dinner or the movies or any other public place to spend time together. Instead, "dating" referred to repeatedly hooking up with one person and having some form of contact between the hookup encounters.

23. Similarly, Glenn and Marquardt (2001) found that college women generally initiate "the talk" to see whether hooking up will evolve into a relationship; however, it is generally the men who decide whether the relationship will progress.

24. Bailey 1988; Waller 1937.

25. This finding is consistent with Glenn and Marquardt's (2001) national study on college women.

26. Bailey 1988; Waller 1937.

27. Bailey 1988.

28. Bailey 1988.

29. Bailey 1988.

30. The crucial role that alcohol plays in facilitating hooking up has been documented by other researchers as well. According to Glenn and Marquardt, "A notable feature of hook ups is that they almost always occur when both participants are drinking or drunk" (2001, 15). Similarly, Paul et al. found "the overwhelming majority of hook up experiences included alcohol use by both partners" (2000, 85).

31. Moffatt 1989; Strouse 1987.

32. Bailey 1988.

33. Bailey 1988; Whyte 1990.

NOTES TO CHAPTER 4

1. In chapter 7, I will discuss what circumstances must be in place for young alumni to hook up. For a discussion on middle and high school students' participation in "nonromantic sexual activity," see Manning et al. (2005).

2. The fact that one's environment greatly affects sexual behavior has been highlighted by other scholars (e.g., see Laumann et al. 2004).

3. This process of defining what behavior is appropriate under certain circumstances has been described by sociologist W. I. Thomas (1923) as determining the "definition of the situation."

4. The effects of drinking on the student body, even those who do not drink, have been documented by the Harvard School of Public Health's College Alcohol Study research team. See Wechsler et al. (1994) for more on "secondhand binge effects."

5. See also Glenn and Marquardt (2001) regarding college women's marital aspirations.

6. Students' plan to marry later is consistent with national data on the age at first marriage, which has increased to a median age of 25 for women and 27 for men. This represents a significant increase since the mid-twentieth century, when the age at first marriage was 20 for women and 23 for men (Bianchi and Casper 2000).

7. See also Arnett (2004) for a discussion of women's "deadline" for marrying.

8. A national study revealed that 63 percent of college women were interested in finding a potential future spouse during their college years (Glenn and Marquardt 2001).

9. Arnett 2001, 2000, 1998.

10. Arnett 2000, 1994.

11. A similar sentiment was echoed by female students at Duke University who were interviewed by a journalist from *Rolling Stone* magazine (Reitman 2006).

12. The majority of students on both campuses live on campus or in nearby apartments or houses; very few commute from their parents' homes.

13. There are numerous other reasons why men and women have different goals for the types of relationships they seek. I will discuss these further in chapter 6.

14. Michael, Gagnon, Laumann, and Kolata 1995.

15. The experience may be somewhat different for commuter students who do not have 24-hour access to campus facilities. However, the overwhelming majority of students at both campuses I studied live on campus or in nearby student apartments or houses. Examining how commuters are affected by the hookup culture on campus is beyond the scope of this study.

16. The fact that fraternity men are among the most sexually active on campus can be explained by Martin and Hummer (1989). They found that the selection process for gaining entry into a fraternity ensures that the most macho, athletic, and "womanizing" men will be admitted to brotherhood, while those who do not live up to these standards are more likely to drop out during the pledge process or never attempt to pledge in the first place.

17. See Martin and Hummer (1989) for more on how fraternity members use alcohol in sexual situations.

18. See Boswell and Spade (1996) for a discussion of how the characteristics of certain fraternities make them more conducive to the sexual exploitation of women.

19. See Williams (1998) for a discussion of how college women use alcohol to navigate sex and relationships.

20. Bergen 1998. Also see Sanday (2007).

21. See Glenn and Marqurardt (2001) and Williams (1998).

22. In terms of racial diversity, I conducted interviews with two African American students (one male, one female) and two Asian American students (one male, one female). Although the number of interviews with students from diverse backgrounds was too small to state anything conclusively, my findings do confirm what others have found. That is, how men and women meet, interact, and form sexual or romantic relationships varies by race. See Glenn and Marqurardt (2001) and Williams (1998).

23. Minority students are also significantly less likely to binge drink (Wechsler 1994). This fact may also decrease the likelihood that they are involved in hooking up.

24. I interviewed two gay men and one bisexual woman in a focus group at Faith University.

25. For more on the experience of gay men on campus, see *Queer Man on Campus* (Dilley 2002).

26. See also Glenn and Marquardt (2001) for a discussion of how college women believe they bear the burden of initiating "the talk." This expression refers to a woman asking a hookup partner: "What are we?" or "Where is this going?" Furthermore, Glenn and Marquardt found that although women often initiate this conversation, it is generally men who decide if a series of hookups will evolve into a relationship.

NOTES TO CHAPTER 5

1. See Ericksen (1999) for a discussion of how the general public finds out what is "normal" in the realm of sexual behavior. Specifically, Ericksen found that surveys on sexual behavior do more than merely tell the public about patterns of human behavior; rather, they actually *shape* subsequent sexual behavior by telling the public what is "normal." Thus, Ericksen suggests that perception of what is normal affects what becomes the norm. While Ericksen focuses on how perception is affected by cultural messages (in the form of academics, journalists, activists, and the like touting the results of sex surveys), she acknowledges that there are many places where one can receive messages about sexual norms.

2. This finding is consistent with what Moffatt (1989) found in his ethnographic study of campus life at Rutgers University in the late 1970s and 1980s. That is, gossiping about sexual activity among one's peers is a central activity among college students. See also Holland and Eisenhart (1990) on how peer influence affected college women in the late 1970s and early 1980s.

3. This is consistent with Glenn and Marquardt's (2001) finding that many women are looking for "Mr. Right" during their college years.

4. Coontz 2005.

5. The discrepancy between the number of sexual partners for men and women has been found in quantitative studies. For instance, Laumann et al. (1994) found that the median number of sex partners since age 18 for adult men in the United States is six, while the corresponding number for women is two. This discrepancy may be partially due to reporting bias (see Schwartz and Rutter 1998).

6. See Martin and Hummer (1989) for a more detailed discussion of how fraternity men "use" women.

7. See Schwartz and DeKeseredy (1997) for a discussion of the role fraternities play on the college campus in fostering an environment conducive to both a sexual conquest mentality and sexual abuse of college women.

8. See Thorne (1993) for a discussion on how childhood socialization contributes to the sexual scripts that men and women play out as adults.

9. See Scholly et al. (2005) for a discussion of how college students' misperceptions of their peers' sexual behavior can encourage engaging in "risky" sexual behavior to conform to what they mistakenly believe is the norm.

10. Recall from chapter 3 that college students believe that one must have sexual intercourse in order to "lose" their virginity. Oral sex is considered a less serious form of sexual interaction. Therefore, engaging in oral sex does not preclude one from being considered a virgin. See Carpenter (2005) for a detailed discussion of how men and women perceive virginity loss.

11. At State University, a few students mentioned the legend that the statue of their mascot would fly away if a virgin graduated from their school. A colleague pointed out that there are similar legends at many institutions of higher education (see Bronner 1990).

12. The students that made positive comments about virginity seemed to fit what Carpenter (2005) refers to as the "gifters" (i.e., people that perceive virginity loss as giving a gift of oneself). See Sprecher and Regan (1996) for more on how college students perceive virginity.

13. This is consistent with Carpenter's (2005) analysis of the meaning many men assign to virginity loss (i.e., that virginity is a stigma they wanted to "get rid of").

14. Glenn and Marquardt 2001.

15. See the American College Health Association's National College Health Assessment (ACHA-NCHA) sexual health data from spring 2003 to fall 2005.

16. Carpenter 2005.

17. Paul, McManus, and Hayes 2000.

18. Although the college men I spoke with also believed that their classmates were more sexually active than they themselves were, women were more likely to quantify the difference between themselves and their female counterparts in terms of a different average number of partners.

19. See Scholly et al. (2005) for a full discussion of the comparison between misperceptions of alcohol use and misperceptions of sexual behavior on the college campus.

20. See Lambert et al. (2003) for a discussion of how the concept of "pluralistic ignorance" can shed light on how college students feel pressure to conform to their perceived norms of the hookup culture.

21. This finding is consistent with what Moffatt (1989) found among undergraduates at Rutgers University in the 1970s and 1980s. See Carpenter (2005) for a detailed discussion on how virginity loss is viewed by some as a stigma.

22. The encounter Stephen discusses could be interpreted as rape given that the woman was too intoxicated to give "meaningful consent." Unfortunately, most of such cases are not reported or prosecuted (Bergen 1998). See Sanday (2007) for a discussion of the connection between fraternities and rape on the college campus.

23. Moffatt also found in his ethnographic study that undergraduate students at Rutgers University were unclear on what other students were doing sexually. "They had their guesses, but they only knew for certain about themselves and perhaps about their closest friends" (1989, 186).

24. Similarly, Holland and Eisenhart found in their study of college women in the late 1970s and early 1980s that "women appeared not to agree on the amount and kind of sexual intimacy appropriate for different stages of a romantic relationship" (1990, 244).

25. Very few students in my sample suggested that one should have to wait for marriage or engagement to have sexual intercourse.

26. Glenn and Marquardt (2001) also found that many college women say that what others do sexually is none of their concern. In the quantitative portion of their study, 87 percent of their respondents agreed with the statement that "I should not judge anyone's sexual conduct except my own."

27. See Modell (1989) for the historical antecedents of the ethic of individual choice among youth in the United States. See Arnett (1998) for how independent decision making factors into the transition to adulthood among contemporary youth.

NOTES TO CHAPTER 6

1. Cultural expectations for sexual behavior began to change in the 1960s as other changes swept the nation. Among these changes were the second wave of feminism, the advent of the birth control pill, and the growth of the youth culture (D'Emilio and Freedman 1988). See Risman and Schwartz (2002) for a discussion of how the sexual revolution has affected teen sexual behavior and relationships.

2. A Web site even sold "Team Aniston" T-shirts so that American women could show their support for the jilted, good-girl wife.

3. The sexual double standard refers to the idea that society has different guidelines for men and women when it comes to what is permissible sexual behavior (D'Emilio and Freedman 1988; Reiss 1997; Rubin 1990). The rules for men's sexual behavior have remained the same throughout the twentieth and the beginning of the twenty-first century. That is, men are free to have "sexual relations," including sexual intercourse, prior to marriage. Moreover, single men are more or less entitled to engage in heterosexual activity whenever they have the opportunity to do so. For women, the rules are different. Historically, women were expected to remain "chaste" until they married. Only married women were supposed to engage in sexual intercourse. Single women who flouted this rule were considered promiscuous (Rubin 1990; Willis 1992). The societal standard for female sexual behavior meant that women were believed to be either "good" girls or "bad" girls. Thus, in theory men were permitted to have sexual intercourse prior to marriage with "bad" girls while "good" or "respectable" girls waited until they were married to have sex (Rubin 1990). See Hynie et al. (1997) for a summary of some of the contemporary debates among scholars regarding the sexual double standard.

4. The students I spoke with did not appear to go on traditional dates in high school; however, many of them did have an exclusive relationship for part of their high school years. See Schneider and Stevenson (1999) for a complete description of the lives of America's teenagers.

5. Recall from chapter 3 that a "random" hookup refers to a sexual encounter between two partners who do not know each other well (or at all) prior to the evening of the hookup.

6. One male interviewee did indicate that he was interested in a relationship but was having difficulty finding one. However, this interviewee mentioned that he is very shy and does not feel comfortable meeting new people. Thus, his struggles in finding a relationship seemed to have more to do with his personality traits than the overall situation of men on campus.

7. Komter 1989.

8. The interest some women had in finding a potential marriage partner during college is consistent with Glenn and Marquardt's (2001) finding that

while many women are "hooking up and hanging out," they are simultaneously "hoping to find Mr. Right." Specifically, Glenn and Marquardt found that 63 percent of college women would like to meet their future spouse in college.

9. Rubin 1990; Willis 1992.

10. Teachman 2003. See Earle and Perricone (1986) for a discussion of how men and women's attitudes toward premarital sex can differ more than their actual behavior.

11. This finding is consistent with what others have found. For instance, only 23 percent of Americans approved of premarital sexual intercourse under certain conditions in 1963 compared to a 76 percent approval rate by 1996 (Reiss 1997). This raises the question: What conditions must be present for premarital intercourse to be accepted? Sherwin and Corbett addressed this question by examining "changes in sexual norms reported by students at the same university on three occasions over a 15-year time period: 1963, 1971, and 1978" (1985, 258). They found that there was a significant increase in approval for sexual intimacy; however, this increase was "most noticeable for those male-female relationships where affection and commitment was present and least noticeable for casual male-female relationships" (1985, 258). See Harding and Jencks (2003) for more on changing attitudes toward premarital sex from the 1960s through the end of the twentieth century.

12. See also Glenn and Marquardt (2001) regarding the labeling of college men as "players."

13. It seems that the terms "whore" and "slut" are so strongly associated with women that the modifier "man" or "male" has to be put before these words to indicate an exception.

14. The reader should note that in the sections that follow on the unwritten rules for the hookup scene, the majority of quotes are from men. Female interviewees were aware that there is a sexual double standard as well as what behaviors might lead to labeling a woman a "slut." However, male interviewees were more vocal on this subject and thereby provided the most useful data (or quotes) to illustrate each unwritten rule.

15. Glenn and Marquardt 2001; Laumann et al. 1994.

16. In Carpenter's (2005) book on virginity loss she discusses a 1924 novel, *The Plastic Age*, on the changing customs of white college youth. In this novel, author Percy Marks refers to "dirty" men who "chase around with rats" (i.e., cheap women). Thus, terms such as "houserat," which appear to apply to the contemporary college campus, may prove to have historical antecedents.

17. Lemert 1967.

18. Lemert (1967) referred to this type of behavior as "secondary deviation."

19. College women's attempt to avoid stigmatization is something that has been found in different eras as well. Holland and Eisenhart (1990) found

that college women on the two campuses they examined, in the late 1970s and early 1980s, actively sought steady boyfriends in order to avoid the potential problems managing their reputation if they were single. See Holland and Eisenhart (1990) also for more examples of college women's strategies to manage their reputation and other problematic aspects of "romantic relations" on campus.

20. See Cassell (1984) for a discussion of how many women feel they must be "swept away" by their romantic feelings in order to justify engaging in sexual intercourse.

21. See also Glenn and Marquardt (2001) on "the talk."

22. The odds may be against women who hope to turn a hookup into a relationship. In a representative study of undergraduates at a large college in the northeastern United States, only 12 percent of hookup encounters segued into a relationship (Paul, McManus, and Hayes 2000).

23. According to a couple of interviewees, the term "friends with benefits" is something they originally heard on television. A cruder version of "friends with benefits" was referred to by one interviewee as a "fuck buddy." This term has been used on the HBO sitcom *Sex & the City*.

24. See Afifi and Faulkner (2000) for more discussion on sexual activity in cross-sex friendships.

25. In a few cases, students said women also initiate "booty calls."

26. A few women I spoke with seemed to indulge in hooking up for its own sake (i.e., they were not looking for a relationship at the time) even after freshman year. For instance, one woman I interviewed wanted to be free for a while because she had had two consecutive serious relationships stemming from high school. Another woman had a "bad experience" with a hookup partner and wanted to stay single as a result. However, even these women admitted they wanted relationships in the past or hoped to have them in the near future. None of the women I spoke with wanted to "just hook up" indefinitely.

NOTES TO CHAPTER 7

1. Although there are other places where they meet people to date, such as work, the gym, or church, bars and parties remained among the primary meeting places for the heterosexual singles in my sample.

2. In a sense, it is not surprising that women would be fearful or cautious around strange men. In general, survey research indicates that women are fearful of crime, particularly sexual victimization (U.S. Department of Justice, Bureau of Justice Statistics 1998). Therefore, strange men could be feared as potential perpetrators.

3. Thomas 1923.

4. See Rose and Frieze (1989) for a discussion of how the advice literature has shaped young singles' scripts for a first date. Importantly, the authors note that "cultural norms for the first date are explicit, formal, and have changed little over the past 30 years" (1989, 259).

5. Since the inception of dating in the early part of the twentieth century, it has been the man's responsibility to initiate the date, pick the woman up in his car, and pay for any costs incurred during the course of the date (Bailey 1988).

6. There may be other times at which men and women choose to engage in hookup encounters when the opportunity (i.e., "campus circumstance") presents itself. For instance, many young alumni go to reunion events where alcohol is served and many familiar faces are present. This atmosphere might also be conducive to hooking up, although none of the men and women I spoke with mentioned it.

7. I am thankful to Rob Palkovitz, a member of the Individual and Family Studies Department at the University of Delaware, for reviewing my manuscript and suggesting the concept of "script-switching." This concept is analogous to what Elijah Anderson has dubbed "code switching." This refers to inner-city youth living by the "code of the street" to survive when interacting with their peers in public, while switching to a more polite form of interaction around teachers, close friends, and family members (Anderson 1999).

8. The fact that men want different qualities in potential partners after college illustrates Blumer's (1986) idea of the changing meaning of social objects. During college, many men view women as "sex objects." After college, when more men are looking for serious romantic relationships, they view women as potential marriage partners.

9. Although I did not ask alumni direct questions about the use of dating Web sites, a couple of people mentioned using them or having friends who did.

NOTES TO CHAPTER 8

1. Coontz 1992.

2. For example, see Glenn and Marquardt (2001).

3. Although Whyte (1990), in his quantitative study of women in Detroit, examined changes and continuities in dating throughout most of the twentieth century, he did not consider the contemporary hookup scene on the college campus.

4. Skipper and Nass 1966.

5. Bailey 1988.

6. Gagnon and Simon 1987.

7. This finding confirms what previous researchers have found (see Glenn and Marquardt 2001; Paul, McManus, and Hayes 2000; Williams 1998).

8. Whyte 1990. See also Kinsey 1953.

9. In fact, Paul, McManus, and Hayes (2000) found that 30.4 percent of the college students in their study had engaged in at least one hookup that culminated in sexual intercourse. This finding is particularly interesting when one considers that the definition of hooking up employed by Paul, McManus, and Hayes referred to encounters with a stranger or brief acquaintance (or what interviewees in my sample referred to as "random" hookups).

10. Rubin 1990.

11. Carpenter 2005.

12. Reiss 1997; Harding and Jencks 2003.

13. Laumann et al. 1994.

14. Those born between 1933 and 1942 had their first experience of intercourse at approximately 18, while the age for those born 20 to 30 years later decreased by six months (Laumann et al. 1994).

15. Laumann et al. 1994.

16. See Hollander (1997) for a discussion of how different religious affiliations (i.e., Catholics and "mainstream" Protestants versus conservative or fundamentalist Christians) affect attitudes on premarital sex.

17. Rubin 1990, 46.

18. See Carpenter (2005) for more on how many people view virginity as a stigma.

19. See Martin and Hummer 1989; Boswell and Spade 1996; Sanday 1992.

20. Bailey 1988; Whyte 1990. See also Thornton (1990).

21. See King and Christensen (1983) for a discussion of the stages in dating relationships.

22. Women were advised to avoid kissing on the first date (Duvall 1958).

23. Bailey 1988.

24. Goffman 1977.

25. Despite the fact that sexual intercourse is expected in exclusive relationships, some research indicates that a sizable percentage of college couples are not having intercourse. Specifically, Glenn and Marquardt (2001) found that 24 percent of the college women they surveyed had a boyfriend but had never had sexual intercourse.

26. Horowitz 1987; Moffatt 1989; Strouse 1987.

27. Duvall 1958.

28. The expectation that the man is responsible for paying for the date is tied, in part, to the relative economic positions of men and women during the 1920s, when dating became the dominant script for young heterosexual interactions throughout the United States.

29. There is no doubt that some college students feel more welcome than others at campus parties and nearby bars. Recall from chapter 4 that minority

students as well as gay and lesbian students were far less involved with the alcohol-centered hookup scene on campus.

30. In Waller's (1937) classic study of the dating script at Penn State University, he found that fraternity men dominated the dating scene, while freshman men were generally blocked from dating co-eds. This restriction was not placed on freshman males by the administration; rather, upperclassmen attempted to combat their institution's unfavorable sex ratio (six men for every woman) by excluding some of the "competition" from participating at all. Although women, at least those at Penn State, had a much more favorable sex ratio on their side, there were other issues that might prevent them from participating in the dating scene. For instance, a woman who did not meet the standard of feminine beauty might find herself "waiting for the phone to ring" while her more attractive classmates were being treated to an evening of socializing.

31. Waller 1937; Bailey 1988.

32. See Wechsler 2003.

33. Cooper 2002; Dermen, Cooper, and Agocha 1998.

34. See Peralta (2001) for a discussion of the effects of drinking on the college culture.

35. See MacAndrew and Edgerton (1969) for a discussion of cross-cultural variation in how alcohol affects members of a society. Interestingly, there are some cultures that use alcohol but do not connect it to sexual activity.

36. See Williams (1998) for more on the connection between alcohol and sexual behavior among college women.

37. A couple of male students from State University told me that if a man hooks up with a woman his peers deem "fat," he can neutralize any teasing he might receive the morning after by proclaiming that he "went hoggin'." However, when I asked students directly during interviews if they knew what this term meant, most did not.

38. See also Williams 1998.

39. Bailey 1988.

40. Waller 1937.

41. Bailey 1988.

42. Waller 1937.

43. Bailey 1988.

44. Bailey 1988, 70.

45. U.S. Bureau of the Census, Current Population Reports, 1998.

46. See Arnett (2004) for a thorough discussion of "emerging adults" and what factors they believe are most important in making the transition to adulthood. See Arnett (1994) for a discussion of the transition to adulthood specifically among college students.

47. Bailey 1988

48. Bailey 1988.

49. See Sarch for a discussion of how contemporary single women use the telephone to "exert control and power" in their relationships with men, while being "confined by the cultural belief that a woman ought to have a man without pursuing one aggressively" (1993, 128).

50. Virtually any sociology textbook defines power as the ability to impose one's will on others (e.g., see Andersen 2003).

51. This is consistent with Glenn and Marquardt's (2001) finding that the burden is on college women to initiate "the talk" in order to see if a series of hookups with the same partner can evolve into a relationship. Women ask, men decide.

52. Goffman 1977.

53. Waller 1937.

54. Behrendt and Tuccillo 2004.

55. Waller 1937.

56. Although none of the college men in my sample were afraid that women might exploit them financially, many feared women "clinging onto them" by trying to form an unwanted serious relationship.

57. Rubin 1990.

58. Rubin 1990; Skipper and Nass 1966.

59. Skipper and Nass 1966, 417.

60. Reitman 2006.

61. Rubin 1990.

62. See Duvall 1958.

63. See Holland and Eisenhart (1990) for a discussion of gender roles, sexual intimacy, and the cultural model of romance.

64. Duvall 1958, 205.

65. Skipper and Nass 1966, 417.

66. Laumann et al. 1994.

67. Laumann et al. 1994.

68. Rubin 1990.

69. Paul et al. (2000) found in their quantitative study of a large university in the northeastern United States that approximately 22 percent of undergraduate students had never engaged in a hookup.

NOTES TO THE METHODOLOGICAL APPENDIX

1. It is interesting to note that there were more female volunteers for the undergraduate portion of the study and more male volunteers for the alumni portion. Perhaps this difference reflects women's difficulty coping with the hookup culture on campus and men's difficulty coping with the switch to a more traditional dating script after college.

2. In rare instances, I conducted interviews at public places, such as a restaurant or coffee shop, per the request of the participant.

3. Straus and Corbin 1998.

4. As I indicated in chapter 1, my sample also lacked diversity in terms of sexual orientation (96 percent of the students and young alumni I interviewed were heterosexual).

Bibliography

Adair, Richard. 1996. *Courtship, Illegitimacy, and Marriage in Early Modern England*. Manchester: Manchester University Press.

Afifi, Walid A. and Sandra L. Faulkner. 2000. On Being "Just Friends": The Frequency and Impact of Sexual Activity in Cross-Sex Friendships. *Journal of Social and Personal Relationships* 17: 205–222.

American College Health Association. American College Health Association—National College Health Assessment (ACHA-NCHA) Web Summary. Updated April 2006.

Amott, Teresa L., and Julie A. Matthaei. 1996. *Race, Gender, and Work: A Multicultural History of Women in the United States*. Boston: South End Press.

Andersen, Margaret L. 2003. *Thinking about Women: Sociological Perspectives on Sex and Gender*. Boston: Allyn & Bacon.

Anderson, Elijah. 1999. *Code of the Street: Decency, Violence, and the Moral Life of the Inner City*. New York: W. W. Norton.

Armstrong, Elizabeth A., Laura Hamilton, and Brian Sweeney. 2005. Hooking Up and Party Rape: The Social Organization of Gender and Sexuality at a Large Research University. Paper given at American Sociological Association, Philadelphia, PA.

Arnett, Jeffrey Jensen. 2004. *Emerging Adulthood: The Winding Road from the Late Teens through the Twenties*. Oxford: Oxford University Press.

Arnett, Jeffrey Jensen. 2001. Conceptions of the Transition to Adulthood: Perspectives from Adolescence through Midlife. *Journal of Adult Development* 8: 133–143.

Arnett, Jeffrey Jensen. 2000. Emerging Adulthood. *American Psychologist* 55: 469–480.

Arnett, Jeffrey Jensen. 1998. Learning to Stand Alone: The Contemporary American Transition to Adulthood in Cultural and Historical Context. *Human Development* 41: 295–315.

Arnett, Jeffrey Jensen. 1994. Are College Students Adults? Their Conceptions of the Transition to Adulthood. *Journal of Adult Development* 1: 213–224.

Arnett, Jeffrey Jensen. 1994. Adolescence Terminable and Interminable: When Does Adolescence End? *Journal of Youth and Adolescence* 23: 517–537.

Bailey, Beth L. 1988. *From Front Porch to Back Seat: Courtship in Twentieth-Century America.* Baltimore: Johns Hopkins University Press.

Baldwin, John, and Janice Baldwin. 1988. Factors Affecting AIDS-Related Sexual Risk-Taking Behavior among College Students. *Journal of Sex Research* 25: 181–197.

Baruch, Elaine H. 1980. The Politics of Courtship. *Dissent* 27: 56–63.

Behrendt, Greg, and Liz Tuccillo. 2004. *He's Just Not That Into You: The No-Excuses Truth to Understanding Guys.* New York: Simon Spotlight Entertainment.

Bell, Robert A., and Nancy L. Buerkel-Rothfuss. 1990. S(he) loves me, S(he) Loves Me Not: Predictors of Relational Information-Seeking in Courtship and Beyond. *Communication Quarterly* 38: 64–82.

Bergen, Raquel K. 1998. *Issues in Intimate Violence.* Thousand Oaks, CA: Sage Publications.

Bettor, Laura, Susan S. Hendrick, and Clyde Hendrick. 1995. Gender and Sexual Standards in Dating Relationships. *Personal Relationships* 2: 359–369.

Bianchi, Suzanne M., and Lynne M. Casper. 2000. American Families. *Population Bulletin* 55 (December).

Blumer, Herbert. 1969. *Symbolic Interactionism: Perspective and Method.* Berkeley: University of California Press.

Bogart, Laura M., Heather Cecil, David A. Wagstaff, Steven D. Pinkerton, and Paul R. Abramson. 2000. Is It "Sex"? College Students' Interpretations of Sexual Behavior Terminology. *Journal of Sex Research* 37: 108–116.

Bogle, Kathleen A. 2005. The Shift from Dating to Hooking Up: What Scholars Have Missed. Paper given at American Sociological Association, Philadelphia, PA.

Boswell, A. Ayres, and Joan Z. Spade. 1996. Fraternities and Collegiate Rape Culture: Why Are Some Fraternities More Dangerous Places for Women? *Gender & Society* 10: 133–147.

Bromley, Dorothy D., and Florence Britten. 1938. *Youth and Sex: A Study of 1300 College Students.* New York: Harper & Brothers.

Bronner, Simon J. 1990. *Piled Higher and Deeper: The Folklore of Campus Life.* Little Rock: August House.

Bruce, John A. 1976. Intergenerational Solidarity versus Progress for Women? *Journal of Marriage and the Family* 38: 519–524.

Carpenter, Laura M. 2005. *Virginity Lost: An Intimate Portrait of First Sexual Experiences.* New York: New York University Press.

Carpenter, Laura M. 1998. From Girls into Women: Scripts for Sexuality and Romance in *Seventeen* Magazine, 1974–1994. *Journal of Sex Research* 35: 158–168.

Carroll, James L., and Lynnly M. Carroll. 1995. Alcohol Use and Risky Sex among College Students. *Psychological Reports* 76: 723–727.

Cassell, Carol. 1984. *Swept Away: Why Women Fear Their Own Sexuality.* New York: Simon and Schuster.

Cate, Rodney M., and Sally A. Lloyd. 1992. *Courtship.* Newbury Park, CA: Sage Publications.

Cohen, Lindsey L., and R. Lance Shotland. 1996. Timing of First Sexual Intercourse in a Relationship: Expectations, Experiences, and Perceptions of Others. *Journal of Sex Research* 33: 291–299.

Coontz, Stephanie. 2005. *Marriage, a History: From Obedience to Intimacy or How Love Conquered Marriage.* New York: Viking.

Coontz, Stephanie. 1992. *The Way We Never Were: American Families and the Nostalgia Trap.* New York: Basic Books.

Coontz, Stephanie. 1988. *The Social Origins of Private Life: A History of American Families.* New York: Verso.

Cooper, M. Lynne. 2002. Alcohol Use and Risky Sexual Behavior among College Students and Youth: Evaluating the Evidence. *Journal of Studies on Alcohol* 63: 101–117.

Cupach, William R., and Sandra Metts. 1995. The Role of Sexual Attitude Similarity in Romantic Heterosexual Relationships. *Personal Relationships* 2: 287–300.

D'Emilio, John, and Estelle B. Freedman. 1988. *Intimate Matters: A History of Sexuality in America.* New York: Harper & Row.

Dermen, Kurt H., M. Lynne Cooper, and V. Bede Agocha. 1998. Sex-Related Expectancies as Moderators between Alcohol Use and Risky Sex in Adolescents. *Journal of Studies on Alcohol* 59: 71–77.

Desiderato, Laurie J., and Helen J. Crawford. 1995. Risky Sexual Behavior in College Students: Relationships between Number of Sexual Partners. *Journal of Youth & Adolescence* 24: 55–69.

Dilley, Patrick. 2002. *Queer Man on Campus: A History of Non-Heterosexual College Men, 1945–2000.* New York: Routledge Falmer.

Duvall, Evelyn R. M. 1958. *The Art of Dating.* New York: Association Press.

Earle, John R., and Philip J. Perricone. 1986. Premarital Sexuality: A Ten-Year Study of Attitudes and Behavior on a Small University Campus. *Journal of Sex Research* 22: 304–310.

Eble, Connie. 1996. *Slang and Sociability: In-Group Language among College Students.* Chapel Hill: University of North Carolina Press.

Ericksen, Julia A. 1999. *Kiss and Tell: Surveying Sex in the Twentieth Century.* Cambridge, MA: Harvard University Press.

Fass, Paula S. 1977. *The Damned and the Beautiful: American Youth in the 1920s.* New York: Oxford University Press.

Felmlee, Diane, Susan Sprecher, and Edward Bassin. 1990. The Dissolution of Intimate Relationships: A Hazard Model. *Social Psychology Quarterly* 53: 13–30.

Gagnon, John H., and William Simon. 1987. The Sexual Scripting of Oral Genital Contacts. *Archives of Sexual Behavior* 16: 1–25.

Gagnon, John H., and William Simon. 1973. *Sexual Conduct: The Social Sources of Human Sexuality.* Chicago: Aldine.

Gilbert, Lucia A., Sarah J. Walker, Sherry McKinney, and Jessica L. Snell. 1999. Challenging Discourse Themes Reproducing Gender in Heterosexual Dating: An Analog Study. *Sex Roles* 41: 753–774.

Glaser, B. G., and A. L. Strauss. 1967. *The Discovery of Grounded Theory: Strategies for Qualitative Research.* Chicago: Aldine.

Glenn, Norval, and Elizabeth Marquardt. 2001. *Hooking Up, Hanging Out and Hoping for Mr. Right: College Women on Dating and Mating Today.* An Institute for American Values Report to the Independent Women's Forum.

Glick, Peter C. 1975. Some Recent Changes in American Families. *Current Population Reports* 52: 23.

Goffman, Erving. 1977. The Arrangement between the Sexes. *Theory and Society* 4: 301–331.

Gordon, Michael. 1973. *The American Family in Social-Historical Perspective.* New York: St. Martin's Press.

Gordon, Michael. 1981. Was Waller Ever Right? The Rating and Dating Complex Reconsidered. *Journal of Marriage and the Family* 43: 67–76.

Grauerholz, Elizabeth. 1987. Balancing the Power in Dating Relationships. *Sex Roles* 17: 563–571.

Grazian, David. 2007. *Confidence Games: The Experience of Urban Nightlife.* Chicago: University of Chicago Press.

Greer, Arlette E., and David M. Buss. 1994. Tactics for Promoting Sexual Encounters. *Journal of Sex Research* 31: 185–201.

Hammer, Jill C., Jeffery D. Fisher, Patricia Fitzgerald, and William A. Fisher. 1996. When Two Heads Aren't Better than One: AIDS Risk Behavior in College Age Couples. *Journal of Applied Social Psychology* 26: 375–398.

Hansen, Sally L. 1977. Dating Choices of High School Students. *Family Coordinator* 26: 133–138.

Harding, David J., and Christopher Jencks. 2003. Changing Attitudes toward Premarital Sex. *Public Opinion Quarterly* 67: 211–226.

Hogben, Matthew, Donn Byrne, and Merle E. Hamburger. 1996. Coercive Heterosexuality in Dating Relationships of College Students: Implications of Differential Male-Female Experiences. *Journal of Psychology and Human Sexuality* 8: 69–78.

Holland, Dorothy C., and Margaret A. Eisenhart. 1990. *Educated in Romance: Women, Achievement, and College Culture.* Chicago: University of Chicago Press.

Hollander, Dore. 1997. Times They Are A-Changin', Mostly. *Family Planning Perspectives* 29: 151.

Horowitz, Helen L. 1987. *Campus Life: Undergraduate Cultures from the End of the Eighteenth Century to the Present.* New York: Alfred A. Knopf.

Hynie, Michaela, John E. London, and Ali Taradash. 1997. Commitment, Intimacy, and Women's Perceptions of Premarital Sex and Contraceptive Readiness. *Psychology of Women Quarterly* 21: 447–464.

Kalbfleisch, Pamela J. 1993. Interpersonal Communication: Evolving Interpersonal Relationships. Hillsdale, NJ: Lawrence Erlbaum Associates.

Kass, Amy A., and Leon R. Kass. 2000. *Wing to Wing, Oar to Oar: Readings on Courting and Marrying.* Notre Dame, IN: University of Notre Dame Press.

King, Charles E., and Andrew Christensen. 1983. The Relationship Event Scale: A Guttman Scaling of Progress in Courtship. *Journal of Marriage and the Family* 45: 671–678.

Kinsey, Alfred C., Wardell B. Pomeroy, Clyde E. Martin, and Paul Gebhard. 1953. *Sexual Behavior in the Human Female.* Philadelphia: W. B. Saunders.

Kirn, Walter. 1998. When Sex Is Not Really Having Sex. *Time,* February 2, 30–31.

Koeppel, Liana B., Yvette Montagne-Miller, Dan O'Hair, and Michael J. Cody. 1993. Friendly? Flirting? Wrong? In Paula Kalbfleisch, ed., *Interpersonal Communication: Evolving Interpersonal Relationships.* Hillsdale, NJ: Lawrence Erlbaum Associates.

Komter, Aafke. 1989. Hidden Power in Marriage. *Gender and Society* 3: 187–216.

Lambert, Tracey A., Arnold S. Kahn, and Kevin J. Apple. 2003. Pluralistic Ignorance and Hooking Up. *Journal of Sex Research* 40: 129–133.

Lance, Larry M. 1976. Sex-Integrated and Sex-Segregated University Dormitory Living: A Trend Analysis of College Student Sexual Permissiveness. *Human Relations* 29: 115–123.

Laner, Mary R., and Nicole A. Ventrone. 2000. Dating Scripts Revisited. *Journal of Family Issues* 21: 488–500.

Laumann, Edward, Stephen Ellingson, Jenna Mahay, and Anthony Paik. 2004. *The Sexual Organization of the City.* Chicago: University of Chicago Press.

Laumann, Edward, John H. Gagnon, Robert T. Michael, and Stuart Michaels. 1994. *The Social Organization of Sexuality: Sexual Practices in the United States.* Chicago: University of Chicago Press.

Laws, Judith Long, and Pepper Schwartz. 1977. *Sexual Scripts: The Social Construction of Female Sexuality.* Washington, DC: University Press of America.

Lemert, Edwin M. 1967. *Human Deviance, Social Problems, and Social Control.* Englewood Cliffs, NJ: Prentice Hall.

Leslie, Leigh A., Ted L. Huston, and Michael P. Johnson. 1986. Parental Reactions to Dating Relationships: Do They Make a Difference? *Journal of Marriage and the Family* 48: 57–66.

Lipson, D. Herbert. 2002. Off the Cuff. *Philadelphia Magazine.*

Lystra, Karen. 1989. *Searching the Heart: Women, Men, and Romantic Love in Nineteenth-Century America.* New York: Oxford University Press.

MacAndrew, Craig, and Robert B. Edgerton. 1969. *Drunken Comportment: A Social Explanation.* Chicago: Aldine.

Manning, Wendy D., Monica A. Longmore, and Peggy C. Giordano. 2005. Adolescents' Involvement in Non-romantic Sexual Activity. *Social Science Research* 34: 384–407.

Martin, Patricia Y., and Robert Hummer. 1989. "Fraternities and Rape on Campus." *Gender & Society* 3(4): 457–473.

McComb, Mary C. 1998. Rate Your Date: Young Women and the Commodification of Depression Era Courtship. In S. Inness, ed., *Delinquents and Debutantes: Twentieth-Century American Girls' Cultures,* 40–60. New York: New York University Press.

McPhee, Phoebe. *The Alphabetical Hook Up List: A–J.* New York: MTV Pocket Books.

Michael, Robert T., John H. Gagnon, Edward O. Laumann, and Gina Kolata. 1994. *Sex in America: A Definitive Survey.* Boston: Little, Brown.

Miller, Randi L., and Michael Gordon. 1986. The Decline in Formal Dating: A Study in Six Connecticut High Schools. *Marriage and Family Review* 10: 139–154.

Mills, C. Wright. 1959. *The Sociological Imagination.* New York: Oxford University Press.

Moffatt, Michael. 1989. *Coming of Age in New Jersey: College and American Culture.* New Brunswick, NJ: Rutgers University Press.

Mongeau, Paul A., and Kristen L. Johnson. 1995. Predicting Cross-Sex First-Date Sexual Expectations and Involvement: Contextual and Individual Difference Factors. *Personal Relationships* 2: 301–312.

Mongeau, Paul A., Mary Clair M. Serewicz, and Lona F. Therrien. 2004. Goals for Cross-Sex First Dates: Identification, Measurement, and the Influence of Contextual Factors. *Communication Monographs* 71: 121–147.

Moore, Monica M. 1995. Courtship Signaling and Adolescents: Girls Just Wanna Have Fun? *Journal of Sex Research* 32: 319–328.

Morr, Mary C., and Paul A. Mongeau. 2004. First-Date Expectations: The Impact of Sex of Initiator, Alcohol Consumption, and Relationship Type. *Communication Research* 31: 3–35.

Murray, Thomas E. 1991. How College Slang Is Like the Forty-Eight-Hour Dork Effect. *American Speech* 66: 220–223.

Murstein, Bernard I. 1974. *Love, Sex, and Marriage.* New York: Springer.

Murstein, Bernard I. 1980. Mate Selection in the 1970s. *Journal of Marriage and the Family* 42: 777–778.

Paul, Elizabeth L., and Kristen A. Hayes. 2002. The Casualties of Casual Sex: A Qualitative Exploration of the Phenomenology of College Students' Hookups. *Journal of Social and Personal Relationships* 19: 639–661.

Paul, Elizabeth L., Brian McManus, and Allison Hayes. 2000. Hookups: Characteristics and Correlates of College Students' Spontaneous and Anonymous Sexual Experiences. *Journal of Sex Research* 37: 76–88.

Peralta, Robert. 2001. Getting Trashed in College: Doing Alcohol, Doing Gender, Doing Violence. Unpublished dissertation, University of Delaware.

Poulson, Susan L., and Loretta P. Higgins. 2003. Gender, Coeducation, and the Transformation of Catholic Identity in American Catholic Higher Education. *Catholic Historical Review* 89: 489–510.

Reiss, Ira. 1997. *Solving America's Sexual Crises.* Amherst, NY: Prometheus Books.

Reitman, Janet. 2006. Sex and Scandal at Duke. *Rolling Stone,* June 1.

Risman, Barbara, and Pepper Schwartz. 2002. After the Sexual Revolution: Gender Politics in Teen Dating. *Contexts* 1: 16–24.

Rose, Suzanna, and Irene H. Frieze. 1989. Young Singles' Scripts for a First Date. *Gender & Society* 3: 258–268.

Rosenblatt, Roger. 1998. What's Sex Got to Do with It? *Time,* February 9.

Rothman, Ellen K. 1984. *Hands and Hearts: A History of Courtship in America.* New York: Basic Books.

Rubin, Lillian. 1990. *Erotic Wars: What Happened to the Sexual Revolution?* New York: Farrar, Straus, Giroux.

Sanday, Peggy Reeves. 2007. *Fraternity Gang Rape.* 2d ed. New York: New York University Press.

Sanders, Stephanie, and June Machover Reinisch. 1999. Would You Say You "Had Sex" If . . . ? *Journal of the American Medical Association* 281: 275–277.

Sarch, Amy. 1993. Making the Connection: Single Women's Use of the Telephone in Dating Relationships with Men. *Journal of Communication* 43: 128–144.

Schneider, Barbara, and David Stevenson. 1999. *The Ambitious Generation: America's Teenagers, Motivated but Directionless.* New Haven, CT: Yale University Press.

Scholly, Kristen, Alan R. Katz, Jan Gascoigne, and Peter S. Holck. 2005. Using Social Norms Theory to Explain Perceptions and Sexual Health Behaviors of Undergraduate College Students: An Exploratory Study. *Journal of American College Health* 53: 159–166.

Schwartz, Martin D., and Walter S. DeKeseredy. 1997. *Sexual Assault on the College Campus: The Role of Male Peer Support.* Thousand Oaks, CA: Sage Publications.

Schwartz, Pepper, and Janet Lever. 1976. Fear and Loathing at a College Mixer. *Urban Life* 4: 413–431.

Schwartz, Pepper, and Virginia Rutter. 1998. *The Gender of Sexuality.* Thousand Oaks, CA: Pine Forge Press.

Seal, David W., and Gina Agostinelli. 1994. Extradydadic Involvement: Moderating Effects of Sociosexuality and Gender. *Sex Roles* 31: 1–22.

Sherman, Alexa Joy, and Nicole Tocantins. 2004. *The Happy Hook-Up: A Single Girl's Guide to Casual Sex.* Berkeley, CA: Ten Speed Press.

Sherwin, Robert, and Sherry Corbett. 1985. Campus Sexual Norms and Dating Relationships: A Trend Analysis. *Journal of Sex Research* 21: 258–274.

Shorter, Edward. 1975. *The Making of the Modern Family.* New York: Basic Books.

Simon, William, and John H. Gagnon. 1986. Sexual Scripts: Permanence and Change. *Archives of Sexual Behavior* 15: 97–120.

Simon, William, and John H. Gagnon. 1984. Sexual Scripts. *Society* 22: 53–60.

Simon, William, and John H. Gagnon. 1987. A Sexual Scripts Approach. In J. Geer and W. O'Donahue, eds., *Theories of Human Sexuality,* 363–383. New York: Plenum.

Skipper, James K., and Gilbert Nass. 1966. Dating Behavior: A Framework for Analysis and an Illustration. *Journal of Marriage and the Family* 28: 412–420.

Smith, Eleanor R., Donn Byrne, and Paul J. Fielding. 1995. Interpersonal Attraction as a Function of Extreme Gender Role Adherence. *Personal Relationships* 2: 161–172.

Sprecher, Susan. 1990. The Impact of AIDS on Heterosexual Dating Relationships. *Journal of Psychology and Human Sexuality* 3: 3–23.

Sprecher, Susan, and Pamela C. Regan. 1996. College Virgins: How Men and Women Perceive Their Sexual Status. *Journal of Sex Research* 33: 3–15.

Sprecher, Susan, and Constantine Sedikides. 1993. Gender Differences in Perceptions of Emotionality: The Case of Close Heterosexual Relationships. *Sex Roles* 28: 511–530.

Stepp, Laura S. 2003. The Buddy System: Sex in High School and College: What's Love Got to Do with It. *Washington Post,* January 19.

Strauss, Anselm, and Juliet M. Corbin. 1998. *Basics of Qualitative Research: Techniques and Procedures for Developing Grounded Theory.* Thousand Oaks, CA: Sage Publications.

Strouse, Jeremiah S. 1987. College Bars as Social Settings for Heterosexual Contacts. *Journal of Sex Research* 23: 374–382.

Surra, Catherine A. 1990. Research and Theory on Mate Selection and Premarital Relationships in the 1980's. *Journal of Marriage and the Family* 52: 844–865.

Teachman, Jay. 2003. Premarital Sex, Premarital Cohabitation, and the Risk of Subsequent Marital Dissolution among Women. *Journal of Marriage and Family* 65: 444–455.

Thomas, William I. 1923. *The Unadjusted Girl.* Boston: Little, Brown.

Thorne, Barrie. 1993. *Gender Play: Girls and Boys in School.* New Brunswick, NJ: Rutgers University Press.

Thornton, Arland. 1990. The Courtship Process and Adolescent Sexuality. *Journal of Family Issues* 11: 239–273.

Townsend, John M., and Gary D. Levy. 1990. Effects of Potential Partners' Physical Attractiveness and Socioeconomic Status on Sexuality and Partner Selection. *Archives of Sexual Behavior* 19: 149–164.

U.S. Bureau of the Census, Current Population Reports. *Marital Status and Living Arrangements,* 1998.

U.S. Department of Education, National Center for Education Statistics. *Digest of Education Statistics,* 2002.

U.S. Department of Education, National Center for Education Statistics. *Digest of Education Statistics,* 2000, Table 248.

U.S. Department of Health and Human Services, National Center for Health Statistics, 2001.

U.S. Department of Justice, Bureau of Justice Statistics. 1998. *Sourcebook of Criminal Justice Statistics.* Washington, DC: U.S. Government Printing Office.

Vaughan, Diane. 1986. *Uncoupling: Turning Points in Intimate Relationships.* New York: Vintage Books.

Waller, Willard W. 1938. *The Family.* New York: Cordon Company.

Waller, Willard W. 1937. The Rating and Dating Complex. *American Sociological Review* 2: 727–734.

Wechsler, Henry, and Bernice Wuethrich. 2003. *Dying to Drink: Confronting Binge Drinking on College Campuses.* New York: St. Martin's Press.

Wechsler, H., A. Davenport, G. Dowdall, B. Moeykens, and S. Castillo. 1994. Health and Behavioral Consequences of Binge Drinking in College: A National Survey of Students at 140 Colleges. *Journal of the American Medical Association* 272: 1672–1677.

Wetzstein, Cheryl. 2005. Sexual Chaos at College. *Washington Times,* August 9.

Whyte, Martin K. 1990. *Dating, Mating, and Marriage.* New York: Aldine de Gruyter.

Williams, Kimberly M. 1998. *Learning Limits: College Women, Drugs, and Relationships.* Westport, CT: Bergin & Garvey.

Willis, Ellen. 1992. *No More Nice Girls: Countercultural Essays.* Hanover, NH: Wesleyan University Press.

Wolfe, Tom. 2000. *Hooking Up.* New York: Farrar, Straus, Giroux.

Index

About the Author

Kathleen A. Bogle is Assistant Professor of Sociology and Criminal Justice at LaSalle University in Philadelphia. She received her Ph.D. in sociology from the University of Delaware.